Yugoslavia and Political Assassinations

Yugoslavia and Political Assassinations

The History and Legacy of Tito's Campaign against the Émigrés

Christian Axboe Nielsen

BLOOMSBURY ACADEMIC
LONDON • NEW YORK • OXFORD • NEW DELHI • SYDNEY

BLOOMSBURY ACADEMIC
Bloomsbury Publishing Plc
50 Bedford Square, London, WC1B 3DP, UK
1385 Broadway, New York, NY 10018, USA
29 Earlsfort Terrace, Dublin 2, Ireland

BLOOMSBURY, BLOOMSBURY ACADEMIC and the Diana logo
are trademarks of Bloomsbury Publishing Plc

First published in Great Britain 2021
This paperback edition published in 2022

Cover design by Adriana Brioso
Cover background © Maxim Gertsen / Alamy Stock Vector

A catalogue record for this book is available from the British Library.

A catalog record for this book is available from the Library of Congress.

ISBN: HB: 9781-7883-1524-1
         PB: 9780-7556-3490-3
       ePDF: 9781-7883-1687-3
      eBook: 9781-7883-1686-6

Typeset by Integra Software Services Pvt. Ltd.

To find out more about our authors and books visit www.bloomsbury.com
and sign up for our newsletters.

Contents

Preface

The primary focus of my research since my return to academia in 2008 has been the police in socialist Yugoslavia – both the ordinary police and the 'secret' police. I have visited numerous archives, read many books and still hope to produce one day a history of the police in socialist Yugoslavia. This, however, is not that book. Indeed, the present book is one I did not intend to write. While doing extended archival research from 2012 to 2014, I actually tended to skip over the many documents pertaining to the Yugoslav State Security Service's engagement with hostile émigrés. After all, I was much more interested in policing *in* Yugoslavia than in any intelligence operations aimed at émigrés outside the country.

And then, as has happened before, the reality of the world outside academia intervened. In early 2014, the German authorities contacted me and asked me whether I would be willing to prepare an expert report for a criminal court case at the Provincial High Court (*Oberlandesgericht*) in Munich. The two accused in the case were high-ranking former officials of the Yugoslav State Security Service, alleged to have acted as accessories to the murder of the Croat émigré Stjepan Đureković in Munich in the summer of 1983.

I accepted the offer to act as an expert witness for the court, and though I kept teaching a full load at the university, I temporarily pulled the handbrake on most of my other academic research. For the next two years until the conclusion of the case in the summer of 2016, I plunged into an intriguing but fiendishly complicated world of foreign intelligence operations, detailed dossiers, subterfuge and émigré intrigue. In addition to the relevant archival material I had previously collected, the court in Munich very frequently sent me DVDs, so that I in the end had received many thousand additional pages of documentation from various archives. In the end, I produced one report and a lengthy addendum and testified on the witness stand in the case. Like my previous experiences as an expert witness at the United Nations' International Criminal Tribunal for the Former Yugoslavia and elsewhere, it proved to be a challenging and fascinating experience.

After the conclusion of the case, I asked for and received the enthusiastic permission of the court to convert my report into a book and to use the materials I had obtained from the court. For this, I am very grateful to Judge Manfred

Dauster and the Seventh Criminal Court Division of the Provincial High Court. Since I had written the report and the addendum in German, translating it into English as I produced this book gave me the opportunity to carefully consider every sentence and document once again, while also adding the kind of contextual and academic material that does not necessarily appear in an expert report prepared for trial.

Since so little has been written in English about the Yugoslav State Security Service and its operations against émigrés, I very much hope that readers will find this book to be an important contribution to Yugoslav (and in particular Croatian) historiography, as well as to the study of intelligence and security services more generally. That having been said, I am acutely aware that there are so many aspects – and in particular so many assassinations – that I can only barely mention even in a book at this length. And I am quite certain that my pronounced reticence in willing to engage in "whodunnit" type speculation will frustrate some readers. While returning to the more general field of policing in my next publications, I therefore hope that I might also in the future have time to write some more detailed articles on matters that can only be alluded to here.

While writing this book, I have kept my cards relatively close to my chest, and while many colleagues knew that another book was on its way, only a few people knew precisely what I was writing. I particularly want to thank two very knowledgeable and generous colleagues, Mark Biondich and Mate Nikola Tokić, for reading the entire first draft of the manuscript and for taking time to offer constructively critical and very useful comments. Mate Nikola Tokić has written a ground-breaking book, *Croatian Radical Separatism and Diaspora Terrorism during the Cold War* (Purdue University Press, 2020), which I strongly encourage readers to read as a companion to my own book.

The colleagues at the office of the German Federal Attorney General (*Generalbundesanwalt*) and the Bavarian State Office of Criminal Investigation (*Bayerisches Landeskriminalamt*) also deserve thanks and appreciation for their professionalism and courtesy towards me and for their questions regarding my conclusions. For assistance, advice and rewarding conversations and e-mails about this topic and relevant documentation during the past few years, in addition to Mark Biondich and Mate Nikola Tokić, I would like to thank Hrvoje Klasić, Igor Omerza, Siniša Pavlović, Isabel Ströhle, Vjeran Pavlaković and Nikolina Židek. All of them left their mark in some way, shape or form on the final manuscript, some of them more than they can know. Thank you also to Hannes Grandits and to his colleagues and students who provided me with useful feedback at a colloquium in Berlin in June 2019. As always, I alone bear responsibility for the contents of this book, and the opinions and conclusions expressed herein are mine alone.

At I.B. Tauris and Bloomsbury, my thanks go out to Thomas Stottor, who first helped to secure the contract for this book (and the next one, stay tuned!), as well as to Tomasz Hoskins, Nayiri Kendir and Giles Herman. Thank you to Viswasirasini Govindarajan for prompt responses to queries about editing.

Finally, I would like to thank my wife, Dorotea Smešnjak, who is in turn presumably grateful that the statute of limitations has probably passed regarding certain ethical violations (note to future historians: search for *Operativna Akcija 'Sačekuša'*) she committed many years ago when she worked in the Croatian State Archives. She put up with my very frequent absences during the long Munich trial and has given me much support in more ways than I can count.

It is May 2020, and the world has become an even stranger place than it usually is. In a few days, on 13 May, it will be the 76th anniversary of the establishment of the Yugoslav State Security Service. So on that note, I close with a quote from the irrepressible Ilija Čvorović, the protagonist in my favourite Yugoslav film, *Balkanski špijun* (Balkan Spy), whose perpetual expression of paranoid annoyance and astonishment was never far from my mind while writing this book: '*Mene, ako se sete na Dan bezbednosti – sete se, ako se ne sete, nikom ništa. To je bila moja dužnost da radim. Najveće zadovoljstvo biće mi misao da sam jednog čoveka izveo na pravi put.*'

Aarhus
May 2020

Introduction

In a Munich courtroom packed with onlookers and members of the German, Croatian and international press, the excitement and anticipation were palpable on 14 October 2014 as Bavarian police officers opened a door and calmly led in two elderly men clad in suits and ties. Were it not for the setting or the handcuffs that they were also wearing, the appearance of these two gentlemen would not have raised an eyebrow. Had they walked down the streets of Munich or Zagreb, anyone who bothered to glance at them would have thought that they were either businessmen on their way to a meeting or perhaps retired friends going for a beer or a coffee.

Yet as the setting and the presence of numerous journalists and tight security measures suggested, these two men in the courtroom of the Munich High Court were no ordinary accused. Innocuous though they might have seemed, Zdravko Mustač and Josip Perković had in fact for decades worked for the Yugoslav State Security Service, both having advanced to high-ranking posts. Indeed, on the eve of the collapse of Yugoslavia, Mustač had served as the head of the entire service. Now, decades later, they both stood accused of having planned and organized the brutal murder of a Croat émigré.

The murder occurred on 29 July 1983 in the Munich suburb of Wolfratshausen. On that day, a mixed group of Yugoslav agents and career criminals shot and then bludgeoned to death the Croat émigré Stjepan Đureković. A manager in a major state-owned company, it later emerged that Đureković had been spying for West Germany. After he absconded from Yugoslavia in April 1982, Đureković published a number of highly incendiary books criticizing the regime in Yugoslavia. The perpetrators murdered Đureković in a garage which he had rented and used as an informal printing press. Photos from the crime scene vividly illustrate the brutality of the killing, with spattered blood surrounding Đureković's prostrate body. In the tightknit Croat émigré community in Munich, few doubted that the Yugoslav State Security Service – known colloquially as the 'Udba' – stood behind the assassination. But in socialist Yugoslavia, no state official stood forth and publicly claimed responsibility for the murder.

The killing of Đureković was no isolated occurrence. In the late 1970s and early 1980s, it seemed that an émigré Croat was assassinated every few months in Western Europe, and particularly in West Germany, where the largest number of Croat émigrés resided. Occasionally, suspicious killings of vociferous opponents of the Yugoslav state transpired even further afield, in North America or Australia. The majority of the victims were Croats, but others fell victim as well – some émigré Serbs and ethnic Albanians from Kosovo died in mysterious circumstances that appeared linked to their alleged anti-Yugoslav activities.

Most of those involved in the planning and execution of targeted assassinations have never been prosecuted, and many of them have long since passed away, including socialist Yugoslavia's long-time leader Josip Broz Tito (1892–1980). In the case of Đureković, two of the alleged organizers of the murder were eventually put on trial in Munich, but this court case marked an exception. Almost two years after the trial of Zdravko Mustač and Josip Perković commenced in Munich, the High Court on 3 August 2016 convicted both of them of aiding and abetting the murder of Stjepan Đureković and sentenced both of them to life in prison.[1] In May 2018, the German Constitutional Court confirmed their sentences. Mustač is currently his sentence in a German prison, while Perković has been extradited to Croatia to serve the rest of his sentence there.[2] Together with Krunoslav Prates, a Croat émigré and informant for the Yugoslav State Security Service, who was convicted and sentenced to life imprisonment in 2008, they are the only persons who have to date been convicted (with all appeals exhausted) of participating in the assassinations of Yugoslav émigrés.

This record of relative impunity is particularly stark when set against the extent of the assassinations. In the forty-six years of the existence of socialist Yugoslavia (1945–1991), the country's leadership oversaw a campaign of targeted assassinations that dwarfed that of any other communist state. Although Bulgaria achieved lasting international notoriety through the killing of the dissident Bulgarian author Georgi Markov with a ricin-tipped umbrella in 1978, it was non-aligned but still communist Yugoslavia, and not any of the Eastern Bloc countries, that most aggressively pursued assassination as a means of protecting the party-state and its ideology of 'brotherhood and unity' among the diverse Yugoslav peoples. The confirmed list of victims numbers in the dozens, and the true tally may extend into triple digits. This book will provide a detailed analysis of how and why the Yugoslav State Security Service carried out assassinations – and also many kidnappings – of émigrés. None of those killed had been convicted in a court of law, but the death penalty meted out was no less fatal for being unofficial.

The Yugoslav case raises important questions about state-sanctioned extrajudicial killings, campaigns against real and alleged enemies of the state and terrorism. Recent events around the world, from drone strikes on suspected terrorists in the Middle East, North Africa and Asia to the assassinations and assassination attempts against former Russian spies Alexander Litvinenko and Sergei Skripal in the UK, serve as powerful reminders that these questions remain as pertinent as ever long after the demise of Yugoslavia. As Adam Entous and Evan Osnos wrote in the wake of the US assassination of Major General Qassem Suleimani, the head of the Iranian Quds Force, 'the question of legality betrayed a grim truth: a state's decision to kill hinges less on definitive matters of law than on a set of highly malleable political, moral, and visceral considerations'.[3]

Murder, targeted killing, extrajudicial killings or assassinations?

At the simplest level, not all killings are murders, and only a tiny percentage of murders are assassinations. For example, in most legal systems, the killing of someone in self-defence or unintentionally can be an act punishable by law but is not legally classified as murder. In all societies, people are murdered, but barring periods of extreme political conflict, most murders have non-political motives. The *Oxford English Dictionary* defines assassination as 'the murder of a person (esp. a prominent public figure) in a planned attack, typically with a political or ideological motive, sometimes carried out by a hired or professional killer; a murderous attack of this kind'.[4] Assassinations are by their very nature also extrajudicial killings. The victim of an assassination has not been afforded due legal process, even though those ordering or organizing the assassination may make grandiloquent claims that the victim has been 'condemned to die'.

Here it is important to distinguish further between assassinations carried out by assailants acting based on individual political motives or based on the motives of a political group, on the one hand, and assassinations perpetrated by agents of a state, on the other hand. The use of assassinations as a component of state policy can be traced far back into history and across regime types. The fact that the present book focuses on socialist Yugoslavia's campaign of assassinations should not blind us to the use of assassinations by many non-communist regimes, including contemporary democracies.[5] As long as states have existed, assassinations have been part of their arsenal, though state leaders have often gone to great lengths to conceal their involvement and create plausible deniability.[6] Particularly since 9/11, countries such as the United States and the UK have aggressively pursued campaigns of killing alleged terrorists around the world, and Israel has since 2000 'openly acknowledged its policy of assassinating Palestinian insurgents'.[7]

To the general public, political assassinations typically connote the killing of prominent political leaders or heads of state such as presidents, kings and queens, prime ministers and charismatic political actors such as Gandhi or Martin Luther King, Jr. Yet as seen above in the *OED* definition, no minimum criterion of political gravitas obtains. Ultimately, the actors who plan and carry out the assassination have themselves decided according to their own subjective methods and criteria that the person whom they assassinate deserves to die.

Are assassinations and targeted killings two terms for the same thing? Focusing on the Israeli case, Steven R. David argues based on three points that they are not. First, David finds 'assassination' to have a 'pejorative connotation'.[8] Second, targeted killings can target individuals at any level, whereas assassinations as noted tend to be linked to leadership figures. Third, Israel uses the terms 'targeted thwarting' or 'interceptions', not 'assassinations'. However, David's arguments are all subjective and seem largely to rest on his own – and the Israeli state's – dislike for and need to distance themselves from the term 'assassination'. It seems more accurate to regard 'targeted killings' and 'assassinations' as synonyms, but whereas a tendency exists for state actors to employ the former term to describe their actions, non-state actors are regarded as perpetrating killings more commonly described as 'assassinations'.

A brief overview of available literature

In socialist Yugoslavia, it was not possible to write freely about political émigrés, who were generally regarded as suspect or anti-Yugoslav elements by the country's leadership and the press. Besides occasional coverage in newspapers, actual books about the political émigrés were confined to officially sanctioned publications which repeated and disseminated the regime's views. In 1978, the Yugoslav authorities – more specifically the Federal Secretariat for Internal Affairs (*Savezni sekretarijat za unutrašnje poslove*, SSUP) – issued a white paper on the 'terrorism of the fascist emigration stemming from Yugoslavia'.[9] Sreten Kovačević's *Hronologija antijugoslovenskog terorizma, 1960–1980* (Chronology of Anti-Yugoslav Terrorism, 1960–1980) and Milenko Doder's *Jugoslavenska neprijateljska emigracija* (The Yugoslav Hostile Emigration) are good examples of semi-official publications on this topic.[10]

Outside of Yugoslavia, émigrés of course enjoyed much more freedom to speak and publish as they desired, which as we will see was one of the reasons they were persecuted by the Yugoslav State Security Service. Many émigrés were prolific if extremely polemical and biased writers, and thus no attempt will be made here to provide an exhaustive overview of their writings. Rather, it is more important to note that several Croat political émigrés who were later assassinated were among the more diligent publicists. For example, Bruno Bušić, who was killed in France in 1978, wrote frequently about the Croat national cause and among other things also accused the Yugoslav state of 'state terrorism'.[11] And as already noted Stjepan Đureković, though not a writer by profession, managed to publish numerous monographs deeply critical of Yugoslavia in the brief period between his elopement to West Germany in 1982 and his murder in 1983.[12] On occasion, Croat émigrés also received moral support from Western journalists who were captivated by their cause, such as the West German journalist Hans-Peter Rullmann.[13]

Both the official Yugoslav literature on the émigrés and the literature of the émigrés suffered from enormous subjectivity. Briefly put, authors writing in Yugoslavia often took a very dim and negative view of émigrés and their motives, with very little effort made to understand the context in which these émigrés were operating and little if no room afforded for criticism of the shortcomings of the Yugoslav political and economic system. Conversely, the political freedom afforded the émigrés did not engender more objectivity or self-criticism. Instead, the claustrophobia and atmosphere of self-pity and victimhood which often existed in émigré communities prevented the development of self-criticism and any acknowledgement or appreciation of even the most modest progress attained in socialist Yugoslavia. And, of course, most émigré publications remained in a state of deepest denial with regard to the crimes committed by themselves or their forefathers during the Second World War.[14]

Unfortunately, the lack of introspection and self-criticism on the part of Cold War Croat émigrés with respect to the crimes of the Ustaša regime has persisted and to a worrying extent become mainstream thinking in Croatia since 1991. It is particularly unfortunate that a number of prominent publicists in Slovenia and Croatia on émigré issues have also been key participants in the very troubling wave of right-wing revisionism of that regime in Croatia in recent years. Their rehabilitation of the Ustaša quisling state and their denial of its fascist and systematically criminal nature ultimately also reflect negatively on the ability of these authors to come to terms with the more problematic and malignant aspects of the activities of nationalist émigrés in the period from 1945 to 1991.[15]

With the introduction of political pluralism and the collapse of Yugoslavia in 1991, the doors stood wide open for the publication of both newspaper articles and books about – and often written by – political émigrés. Particularly in Croatia, many of the most politically significant émigrés repatriated to the newly independent successor states and became active in their 'recovered' homelands, often with very interesting consequences.[16] Most germanely, for the present topic, a number of émigrés who had for years been in the crosshairs of the Yugoslav State Security Service ended up working side by side in the newly established intelligence and state security services of the Yugoslav successor states with those agents who had for years observed and pursued them.[17]

The often uncritically positive tone adopted by post-Yugoslav publications about political émigrés showed that the subjectivity of the émigré publications was now the default mode at home as well. Probably the most prolific author on the topic has been Bože Vukušić.[18] His publications include *Tajni rat UDBE protiv hrvatskoga iseljeništva* (The Secret War of Udba against the Croat Emigration), *Tajni rat UDBE protiv hrvatskih iseljenika iz Bosne i Hercegovine* (The Secret War of the Udba against Croat Émigrés from Bosnia and Herzegovina), *Likvidacija Bušića: opstruirana istraga i sudska farsa u Hrvatskoj* (The Liquidation of Bruno Bušić: The Obstructed Investigation and Judicial Farce in Croatia), *Tajne iz Udbinih arhiva – Egzekucije bez suđenja* (Secrets from Udba's Archives: Extrajudicial Executions), *Miro Barešić – sve za Hrvatsku* (Miro Barešić – Everything for Croatia) and *Zločini komunističke mafije: od slučaja Đurekovića do 'lex Perković'* (Crimes of the Communist Mafia: From the Đureković Case to 'Lex Perković').

Vukušić is himself a former émigré who served several years of a life sentence in West Germany for the 1983 revenge killing of another émigré, Jusuf Tatar, whom Vukušić believed to be responsible for the assassination of Đureković.[19] Vukušić was released from prison in 1990, and quickly put himself at the disposal of those working to create an independent Croatian state. In one of his books, Vukušić reproduces a photo where he stands proudly next to Anđelko Brajković, who was convicted of killing the Yugoslav ambassador to Sweden. Brajković was later released after other Croat extremists hijacked a Swedish airplane. Besides the obvious subjectivity that this lends to Vukušić's writings, an assessment of the reliability of his many claims is seriously crippled by the lack of verifiable sources or proper citation methodology in a number of his publications. In Serbia, the prolific writings of the Serb publicist Marko Lopušina on security issues including émigrés are completely unsourced and therefore of highly questionable value, though some claims made in his works can be corroborated.[20] The historian Petar Dragišić observes that the history of the emigration is a 'historical phenomenon which is to a great extent contaminated by journalistic banalization, but also by political motives'.[21]

The non-Yugoslav scholarly historiography of the relationship between the Yugoslav State Security Service and the émigrés is still modest, particularly in English, but a few works should be mentioned here. Exploiting many archival sources, Mate Nikola Tokić has written a detailed account history of Croat émigré terrorism which also provides us with a nuanced portrait of the evolution of their political ideology.[22] Alexander Clarkson and Christopher Molnar have examined the Yugoslav and in particular Croat émigré experience in West Germany after the Second World War.[23] Srđan Cvetković has summarized the activities of the Yugoslav State Security regarding Yugoslav émigrés of all ethnicities.[24]

In addition to publications about political émigrés, the Council for the Confirmation of Postwar Victims of the Communist System Killed Abroad, which was part of the larger Commission for the Confirmation of Wartime and Postwar Victims, produced a report in 1999 about political killings of Croats after the Second World War.[25] The Croatian Parliament (*Sabor*) created the commission and appointed as its chair Vice Vukojević, a lawyer and Croatian Constitutional Court judge who had also been a Croat nationalist dissident and émigré.[26] Bože Vukušić was hired as a researcher. The council listed sixty-eight Croat assassination victims and five Croat victims of 'kidnappings with fatal consequences'. The first registered assassination was that of Ivo Protulipac in 1946 in Italy, and the last one was that of Ante Đapić in 1989 in West Germany. 'The council also registered thirty attempted killings, as well as three successful and two unsuccessful kidnappings of Croat political émigrés in the period from 1946 to 1990'.[27] For many of the names on the Sabor's list of Croat victims, it is difficult to find any precise details regarding their deaths, such as the date and place of death, the manner of killing, suspected perpetrators, etc. Although there is no doubt that some of the persons listed in the report were assassinated by the Yugoslav State Security Service, the authors did not provide any supporting documentation for many of the cases included on the list. The credibility of the list is therefore highly questionable. Moreover, although the report includes a bibliography of sorts, there are no specific source references to substantiate the many claims made in the report.

Although some of the publications about political émigrés have indeed made significant contributions to the historiography of the former Yugoslavia and its successor states, the publications since 1991 have also been notable for assuming a dichotomy in which émigrés were by definition pure, morally innocent and positive actors struggling valiantly against a corrupt, repressive, 'totalitarian' and even evil Yugoslav communist regime. The aforementioned report's use of phrases such as 'state terror' is indicative. The benevolence and nobility of the émigrés' intentions are taken for granted, while the very act of protecting the Yugoslav state and its population against émigré threats is by contrast portrayed as illegitimate and dastardly. Most problematically, the acts of the Yugoslav regime appear to have been taken in a vacuum from which the hostile and often violent acts contemplated or carried out by the Croat émigrés are strangely absent. As this book will illustrate, the intertwined history of the Yugoslav State Security Service and the political emigration is rather more complicated than such a dichotomy would suggest. Finally, the more recent historiography, like much of the former Yugoslav and other Eastern European historiography of communist rule, suffers from a lack of methodological sophistication and, in particular, a pronounced and rather ironic willingness to read many of the documents of the Yugoslav State Security Service at face value.[28]

Forget the smoking gun

In criminal investigations, the colloquial term 'smoking gun' refers to evidence that obviously and in a clear-cut manner proves that criminal conduct has occurred and unequivocally identifies the perpetrators. Looking back nearly two decades to when I began my own career analysing leadership structures in complex international criminal cases at the United Nations' International Criminal Tribunal for the former Yugoslavia (ICTY), I remember learning very early on that smoking guns rarely ever exist in such cases.

It is therefore important for me to dispel at the outset any expectations that this book will furnish such a smoking gun, or that it will ever prove possible to ascertain the exact number of assassinations of émigrés perpetrated by the Yugoslav state. This book is based on a very large quantity of primary source documents, the vast majority of them produced by the Yugoslav State Security Service itself. I believe that the quantity and quality of sources which I have examined to date as a whole point incontrovertibly to the conclusion that the Yugoslav State Security Service at the direction of Josip Broz Tito and the League of Communists of Yugoslavia carried out a considerable number of assassinations of Yugoslav émigrés. Most of the documentary evidence is circumstantial, some of it expressly admits the existence of the practice of assassinations, though without specifically taking responsibility for any specific assassination. Many of the available oral sources are for various reasons inherently unreliable. I personally doubt that written sources still exist – if indeed they ever did – in which the Yugoslav State Security Service or its political superiors take explicit and direct responsibility for assassinations. I also believe that a number of the deaths of émigrés which other émigrés attributed to the Yugoslav State Security Service were in all likelihood accidents or natural deaths. Conversely, it is plausible that some deaths which were deemed unsuspicious were in fact assassinations. Yet the bottom line remains clear. When examined in its totality, the available information in my opinion incontrovertibly supports the conclusion that the Yugoslav State Security Service utilized assassinations as part of its arsenal in fighting 'the hostile emigration.'

Focus and structure

Although I will provide an account of the Yugoslav State Security Service's struggle against the political emigration as a whole, the vast majority of this book will focus on the protracted contest with the Croat political emigration. Even a cursory glance in the archives of the Yugoslav State Security Service reveals that the Yugoslav party-state leadership from the outset until the very end of the state's existence regarded Croat political émigrés as by far the largest émigré threat. The tables of contents of analytical documents compiled by the Federal Yugoslav State Security Service regularly showed that many more pages were devoted to Croats than to any other nationality of émigrés, with a clear preponderance also visible in the number and activity of Croat émigré organizations.[29] Moreover, the aforementioned court case in Munich has facilitated access to a bonanza of sources on this subject.

Having identified the primary objective of this book, I find it equally important to note what this book does *not* aspire to do. This book will not recount or analyse all of the numerous assassinations of émigrés which have over the years been ascribed to the Yugoslav State Security Service. To do so would result in a much too long book and would almost inevitably lead to conjecture of precisely the type which I wish to avoid. Rather, this book takes a structural analytical approach to the issue of assassinations and the work of the Yugoslav State Security Service abroad and will therefore focus mostly on a few select cases for which extensive documentation exists, first and foremost the case of the assassination of Stjepan Đureković.

This book is also not a legal analysis or commentary on the trial of Mustač and Perković. Although I have testified as an expert witness in that case and in eight other criminal cases in The Hague and in other jurisdictions and have cooperated closely with investigators, lawyers and judges in those jurisdictions over the years, I am not myself a lawyer. Hence, though this book necessarily takes the Munich trial of Mustač and Perković as its point of departure and devotes an entire chapter to the killing of Stjepan Đureković of which the accused were convicted, this is not a book about that trial or about the accused. I have no intention of commenting on any issues related to the guilt of the accused, the verdict reached by the judges or the legal questions regarding the extradition of the accused from Croatia to Germany. As is the case with many major criminal trials, there are controversial legal aspects of the trial of Mustač and Perković and some very strong opinions about the legitimacy of the trial. For example, Anto Nobilo, the lead Croat defence lawyer for Josip Perković, in late 2018 published a book in which he strongly impugned not only the extradition of his client, but also the trial chamber and key elements of the trial itself.[30] Nobilo, one of the most prominent defence lawyers in Croatia, has announced his intention to sue for miscarriage of justice at the European Court of Human Rights.

As has been the guiding motive of all of the analysis I have over the years performed for various courts and tribunals, I approach this topic from the perspective of a historian and an analyst. In other words, whereas the parties in a criminal case are primarily focused on the innocence or guilt of the accused, I by contrast am entirely absorbed and motivated by the structural analysis of one or more of the organizations for which the accused worked – in this case the Yugoslav State Security Service. Such a focus is in fact the primary trait of leadership analysis, a topic which I have written about elsewhere.[31] As such, in writing this book, let me repeat that I take no position on the legal culpability of the accused or about any other facet of the trial in Munich. Nor do I in this book generally try to ascertain the identities of the Udba's assassins in the various assassinations presented here.

As my main mission in this book is to explore the workings of the Yugoslav State Security Service outside Yugoslavia's borders, I also do not intend to explore the various motives that have been aired over the years and during the

Munich trial for the assassination of Stjepan Đureković. For me, both as an expert witness and as the author of this book, the deeper motives and the various political intrigues and controversies surrounding Đureković and his employer, the Croatian oil company INA (*Industrija nafte*) fall outside my ambit. I will of course necessarily allude to these matters and fully understand the lively interest in them, but I will not direct my attention to them in this book.[32] Indeed, I for the most part in this book do not attempt to identify the perpetrators of the Udba's many assassinations, nor do I systematically discuss or analyse these. As an analyst, I am first and foremost interested in understanding and describing the leadership structures and methods utilized by the Udba.

Furthermore, as a historian and as an analyst, I accept that, particularly given the still very restricted access that obtains for many of the key archives of the Yugoslav State Security Service, our state of knowledge is imperfect and will evolve as more documents become available. However, I firmly believe that a sufficient amount of documentation exists to warrant the writing of this book, and that it is possible with a very high degree of certitude to describe the key operations of the Yugoslav State Security Service with respect to the 'hostile emigration'. As I hope will become readily apparent to the reader, this book rests on the analysis of a very large number of archival sources, many of which were until recently unavailable.

Finally, while many of the most prominent (or notorious) Croat émigrés play a crucial role in this book, this book does not intend to – and indeed cannot – provide a comprehensive history of the Croat emigration. I would reiterate, however, that this book can be profitably read in conjunction with Mate Nikola Tokić's new book on Croat diaspora terrorism.

After this introduction, Chapter 1 will present an overview of the establishment and structure of the Yugoslav State Security Service, as well as its relationship with other Yugoslav intelligence and security services. Based on internal documents from the Service, the ambit of the Service's work is sketched, with an emphasis on the Service's crucial role in maintaining the hegemony of the League of Communists of Yugoslavia against real and perceived enemies both internal and external.

Chapter 2 focuses more specifically on the 'fascist', 'extreme' or simply 'hostile' emigration as an important subset of the perceived external threats to Yugoslav state security. As the Second World War came to an end, tens of thousands of fascists and collaborators, particularly Croats, fled the coming communist takeover of power in Yugoslavia. They settled in many countries, from Argentina and Australia to Canada, West Germany and Sweden. Embittered and extremely hostile to socialist Yugoslavia, these émigrés refused to reconcile themselves to the new reality and dreamt of and planned for an eventual return to a 'free Croatia'. The most extreme and proactive among them began to engage in political demonstrations and violent attacks on Yugoslav consulates, embassies and companies around the world. While the Yugoslav State Security Service had already previously targeted émigrés who were alleged notorious war criminals in Yugoslavia, the increase in violent attacks of a terrorist nature inspired the Yugoslav authorities to consider reprisal operations, or even operations of a preventative nature against extreme émigrés.

Chapter 3 starts by moving away from the historical narrative and back to the technical level. This chapter explains the rules, regulations and directives that allowed the Yugoslav State Security Service to infiltrate émigré organizations, identify the most extreme émigrés and neutralize their plans and members before they could undertake violent acts against Yugoslavia – or carry out reprisal attacks.

By the end of the 1960s, a more restive and dynamic generation of émigré Croats embarked upon an accelerated and more intensive campaign of attacks on Yugoslav targets both abroad and within the country. Croat extremists used hijackings, explosive devices and other violent methods to draw international attention to their cause. Chapter 4 details how in 1972 an entire group of young Croats infiltrated to Bosnia and started a failed armed uprising. Tito and the Yugoslav leadership were apoplectic and ordered the Yugoslav State Security Service to 'take the fight' to the émigrés. Although the Service had already carried out a small number of targeted killings abroad, the new doctrine unleashed a remarkably intensive new phase in its activities. The intensity and frequency of targeted killings in the late 1970s and early 1980s were designed to convey the indelible message that the extremists could not hide and would be heavily penalized for further attacks on Yugoslavia.

Chapter 5 brings to bear the context and information from previous chapters in an analysis of the assassination of Stjepan Đureković. The chapter starts by presenting Đureković and the circumstances of his illegal and covert emigration to West Germany in 1982. Closely hewing to the available sources, the chapter minutely reconstructs both his activities and the surveillance of the Yugoslav State Security Service culminating in his assassination in Munich in July 1983.

The book concludes with a short chapter summarizing the surprising and paradoxical reconciliation between segments of the Yugoslav State Security Service and the most extreme émigré Croats during the collapse of Yugoslavia. Even though Yugoslav functionaries and agents had spent decades investigating, combating and even killing extreme nationalist Croats, some Croat members of the Yugoslav State Security Service played a crucial role in enabling the return of these émigrés to Croatia on the eve of its independence. By declaring their loyalty to Croatia and its former dissident nationalist president Franjo Tuđman, and a willingness to combat Yugoslavia and the Serb minority in Croatia, prominent members of the service secured controversial *de facto* amnesties for themselves.

Sources and terminology

The bulk of the sources cited in this book are archival documents stemming from the archives of Slovenia, Croatia, Bosnia and Herzegovina and Serbia. I personally identified and collected many of these sources myself starting in 2012, when I went to the Archives of the Republic of Slovenia in order to access documents which were at the time largely inaccessible in the archives of the other Yugoslav successor states. In the meantime, access has improved considerably in the Croatian State Archives, though the question of access to the documents of the Yugoslav State Security Service remains quite politicized, including in Slovenia and Croatia. Access in Serbia to relevant documentation is very restricted, but luckily the nature of the Yugoslav security services meant that many copies of federal documentation were placed in archives outside Belgrade.

In addition to the primary sources which I was able to collect myself, I have benefitted tremendously from the large amount of documentation which the German authorities obtained through the course of their investigations and the trial of Josip Perković and Zdravko Mustač. These documents were made available to me as a court-appointed expert witness in that trial. In those cases where primary (archival) sources are cited without specific reference to a specific archive, then this is because I obtained the documents in question through the Provincial High Court.

In terms of the sources made available to me as a result of my participation as an expert witness in the Munich trial, I have chosen to rely predominantly on the archival documents disclosed to me. With very rare exceptions, I do not quote witness testimony from the trial, not least because of doubts that I harbour about the credibility of many of the witnesses called. In doing so, I follow the methodology that I used in both my expert report at the Munich trial and in the reports I wrote as a research officer for the Leadership Research Team in the Office of the Prosecutor at the ICTY.[33]

As all researchers working on the history of security and intelligence services know, the information contained in the sources of these services needs to be treated with considerable caution and scepticism, particularly when the information concerns those persons whom these services regarded as their adversaries. At some level, it would be preferable to add the word 'allegedly' to almost any sentence in this book in which the Yugoslav State Security Service makes any assertions about émigrés. Doing so would however quickly prove awkward and tiresome. I have tried to make the unverified and in many cases unsubstantiated nature of the Service's claims explicit where such claims participate to allegations of criminal acts by émigrés. At the same time, it must be stated that there can be no doubt that many of these allegations were accurate, and that Croat émigré extremists in particular had a demonstrable track record of translating their violent anti-Yugoslav thoughts into violent acts. But the reader of this book should most certainly approach all claims of the Yugoslav State Security Service with caution and scepticism. To a considerable extent, this book shows the world of the émigrés through the biased lenses of the Service, but in doing so also highlights the methodologies, operations and results of the Service's protracted battle with 'the hostile emigration'.

Dealing with the language(s) and terminology of a defunct state poses certain challenges, beginning with the key term 'security', which existed in several different variants in socialist Yugoslavia. Like many scholars of Yugoslav history, I refer to the language formerly known as Serbo-Croatian as Bosnian/Croatian/Serbian, or BCS, and when referring to terms in BCS, Macedonian, or Slovenian, I will use the term used by the originator of the document in question.[34] Already the word 'security' – known variously in the official languages of socialist Yugoslavia as *bezbednost, bezbjednost, sigurnost* and *varnost* – illustrates the challenge at hand. Further complicating matters, the Yugoslav State Security Service, like many state bureaucracies, rather incessantly persisted in revising its own internal terminology. I have tried to be as consistent as possible in translating terms to English. Unless otherwise noted, all translations from other languages to English are my own.

The Yugoslav State Security Service of course relied heavily on acronyms, and was colloquially known in Yugoslavia – and even until the present day – under these acronyms. Technically speaking, the three main names of the Yugoslav State Security Service were the Department for the Protection of the People (*Odelenje za zaštitu naroda*), from 1944 until 1946, the State Security Administration (*Uprava državne bezbednosti*) from 1946 until 1966, and then finally the State Security Service (*Služba državne bezbednosti*), officially abbreviated as OZN-a

UDB-a and SDB, respectively.[35] In everyday speech, however, these were usually spoken simply as 'Ozna' and 'Udba', such as in the famous popular sayings attributing omnipotence and omniscience to the 'secret police': '*Ozna sve dozna*' (Ozna finds out everything) and '*Udba nam je sudba*' (Udba is our fate). 'The Udba' proved the most long-lived moniker for the Yugoslav State Security Service, and is still frequently used – and abused – today by journalists, political commentators and others in the former Yugoslavia. I have therefore with some trepidation decided to use 'the Udba' in this book as a synonym for the much more unwieldy term 'Yugoslav State Security Service'.

The Establishment and Structure of the Yugoslav State Security Service

The Yugoslav State Security Service or 'Udba' was a complex, multi-layered and deliberately byzantine state apparatus that for obvious reasons abhorred transparency and had no desire to make its inner workings understandable to the general public. Much of the same can be said for the Yugoslav party-state as a whole, and this hence presents enormous challenges to researchers wishing to understand and analyse how the Service operated as a pillar of the system. Therefore, this chapter provides the reader with a succinct summary of the establishment and structure of the Yugoslav State Security Service. Based on internal documents from the Service, the ambit of its work is sketched, with an emphasis on its crucial role in maintaining the hegemony of the party-state against real and perceived enemies both internal and external. Special emphasis is placed on explaining why the Yugoslav regime continued to see itself as being under a permanent existential threat.

Yugoslavia's leader Josip Broz Tito and his colleagues in the communist-dominated partisan movement idolized the Soviet Union and were also heavily influenced by its security services. In establishing socialist Yugoslavia, the Yugoslav communists initially slavishly imitated their idols, and the 1946 Yugoslav federal constitution was a slightly reworked version of the 1936 Soviet constitution. Like the Soviet Union and the 'people's republics' in Eastern Europe, Yugoslavia was conceived of as a party-state, where all matters would be decided by the ruling communist party, initially called the Communist Party of Yugoslavia (*Komunistička partija Jugoslavije*, KPJ) and since November 1952 the League of Communists of Yugoslavia (*Savez komunista Jugoslavije*, SKJ). Until 1990, no free multi-party elections were held in Yugoslavia, and all posts of importance in the government and in the state apparatus were thus reserved for party members. The leading role of the SKJ was emphasized in the four constitutions promulgated in Yugoslavia in 1946, 1953, 1963 and 1974, with separate constitutions for the six republics (Slovenia, Croatia, Bosnia and Herzegovina, Serbia, Montenegro and Macedonia) and the two autonomous provinces (Vojvodina and Kosovo).

As is the case with virtually all institutions in socialist Yugoslavia, the origins of the Yugoslav State Security Service are to be found in the Second World War, known in Yugoslavia as the People's Liberation Struggle (*Narodnooslobodilačka borba*, or NOB).[1] On 29 November 1943, the Anti-Fascist Council of the People's Liberation of Yugoslavia (*Antifašističko veće/ vijeće narodnog oslobođenja Jugoslavije*, or AVNOJ), which had convened for the first time precisely one year earlier, agreed on the outlines of the structure of postwar Yugoslavia. The AVNOJ in turn elected a National Committee for the Liberation of Yugoslavia (*Nacionalni komitet oslobođenja Jugoslavije*, or NKOJ). Approximately six months later, with the partisans increasingly confident of victory and needing to consolidate control over those areas liberated from Axis and collaborationist control, the NKOJ decided to establish a unified intelligence agency to replace the disparate partisan-controlled intelligence agencies operating from Slovenia to Macedonia. Significantly, a Soviet military mission arrived in Bosnia in February 1944. Led by Lieutenant General Nikolaj Kornjejev, its members, particularly Colonel Nikolaj Timofejev, seem to have advised the Yugoslavs on how to establish and structure the new intelligence service.[2] Subsequently a number of leading officers of the service also received formal training in the Soviet Union.

On 13 May 1944, Tito, in his capacity as supreme commander and commissioner for people's defence, established the Department of the Protection of the People (*Odjeljenje za zaštitu naroda*, OZN-a). Tito wrote that 'it is already now necessary to create a unified powerful organization which would direct a political intelligence service abroad and on occupied territory, and a counter-intelligence service in the NOVJ [People's Liberation Army of Yugoslavia], both on liberated and non-liberated territory'.[3]

The chief of the Ozna, Lieutenant General Aleksandar 'Marko' Ranković, was directly subordinate to Tito and reported on the work of the Ozna to the NKOJ.[4] Ozna representatives in the main staffs were responsible directly to the chief of Ozna, providing a direct line of command for their work and reporting. Significantly, the Ozna was explicitly introduced as an organization that would form the nucleus of the future system of state security.

Five days after Tito's decree, Ranković sent his first communication as chief of the Ozna. Neither a decree nor an order, Ranković's dispatch resembled a musing on the rationale for the existence of intelligence services, which 'had always been a strong tool in the hands of a country/state in the struggle against its internal and external enemies'.[5] Following the official rhetoric of the AVNOJ, Ranković further wrote that the state security service would be 'one of the guarantees for the preservation of the new democratic authority in a federal democratic Yugoslavia. ... The organs of Ozna must be the most consequential protectors and keepers of the legacies of the people's liberation struggle. Strict and implacable towards enemies, just toward every honest person. Ozna will become the most cherished organization among our people.' Ranković sounded the warning that the forces of the NOB must continuously be on guard against those enemies who sought to infiltrate and thwart it.

On 15 August 1944, Tito signed a decree establishing the Corps of the People's Defence of Yugoslavia (*Korpus narodne odbrane Jugoslavije*, KNOJ), an internal army which could be resubordinated under Ozna command and which had the task of 'liquidating' all remaining enemy activity on the liberated territory of Yugoslavia.[6] As the Partisans expanded their grip to control ever larger portions of Yugoslavia in the spring of 1945, the Ozna functioned as the extended arm of the Communist Party. In addition to maintaining discipline in the KPJ and the partisan movement, and uncovering any 'enemy' elements, the Ozna also sought to constrict and control the activities of those 'bourgeois' political parties that had joined the anti-fascist coalition. Both internally and externally, the Ozna was 'the auxiliary organ of the Party', as noted by Savo Zlatić at a July 1945 meeting of the Central Committee of the Communist Party of Croatia.[7]

The Ozna existed until March 1946, when it was split into separate civilian and military intelligence and state security services. From March 1946 until the middle of 1966, the state security service was known as the Administration of State Security (*Uprava državne bezbednosti*, UDB-a, or Udba), a change in name which also signified the shift from the revolutionary seizure of power to protector of the security of the existing state. Although the Udba retained a system of internal military-style ranks until the early 1950s, a gradual demilitarization of the service also took place.

Throughout the first two decades of socialist Yugoslavia, Ranković and the Udba functioned as the party-state's most formidable shield against 'internal enemies'. Widely feared and with a reputation for being omnipresent and omniscient, the Udba bore down hard on anyone suspected of the least opposition against the regime. In the Yugoslav case, after the historic split between Yugoslavia and the Soviet Union in 1948, the might of the state's repressive apparatus also came to be felt by pro-Stalin 'Cominformists'. No one living in Yugoslavia, including members of the League of Communists, could afford to doubt the Udba's might and reach.

In July 1966, the dismissal of Aleksandar Ranković, who had under Tito exercised command and control of the Udba and had in his capacity as vice president been generally perceived both at home and abroad as the likely successor to Tito, rocked Yugoslavia.[8] Although he had formally ceased to be the minister for internal affairs in 1953, Ranković was widely considered to have retained control over the police. Yet now he was removed from his post and later from the SKJ on charges of having organized the illegal surveillance of Tito and other senior SKJ leaders. After this date and until the dissolution of Yugoslavia, the state security service was known as the State Security Service (*Služba državne bezbednosti*, SDB), and in a linguistic foreshadowing of the impending decentralization, in Croatia as the SDS (*Služba državne sigurnosti*). Colloquially, however, the Service remained known as 'the Udba'. Ranković and those most closely associated with him were accused of 'bureaucratic statism', as they had resisted a liberalization of the Yugoslav state and economy.

The purge of Ranković initiated more of a decentralization than any real liberalization of the state security service, accelerating up to the 1974 constitution, which massively decentralized the structure of the Yugoslav state.[9] Briefly put, the League of Communists was determined to ensure that no one other than Tito could ever again amass the amount of power that Ranković had held, but not so interested in dismantling the party-state's grip on the population. Notwithstanding the new constitution in 1974, the federal authorities continued to have primary responsibility for all matters affecting the security of the country as a whole. The SSUP had a directing, coordinating and supervisory role with respect to all matters pertaining to internal affairs.[10] The federal secretary could still define the overall policy orientation of the work of the SDB, including its republican and provincial components. Most saliently for the present topic, the Federal State Security Service until the dissolution of Yugoslavia retained primary authority and responsibility for all activities of the civilian security services outside the country.

Nonetheless, given the extent of the decentralization effected by the new constitution, it is correct to speak from 1974 onwards of state security services in the plural form in Yugoslavia. In addition to the Federal State Security Service, all six republics and the two autonomous provinces Vojvodina and Kosovo operated state security services. Legally and operationally, these state security services were interlinked and hierarchically subordinated to the Federal State Security Service. Very specific rules and regulations existed for cooperation, exchange of information and joint operations, but particularly in the last decade of the Yugoslav state's existence, the Federal State Security Service gradually became less of a commanding instance and more of a clearinghouse and coordination mechanism. This meant that to the degree that a republican state security service was conducting operations which were limited to its own area, then it largely sufficed to provide general notice subsequently to the federal authorities that this operation had been carried out.

However, it should be noted that until the death of Tito in May 1980, he as the supreme leader of the country had the final say in all matters of state policy and operations. Likewise, it is necessary to emphasize that the decentralization did not translate into a weakening or disintegration of the principles of the party-state. As such, the state security services still primarily served the League of Communists of Yugoslavia, the hierarchy of which itself mimicked the structure of the Yugoslav state. In this manner, the party-state power nexus remained intact, albeit with its own concurrent process of increasing autonomy for the republican and provincial leagues.

The Yugoslav State Security Service and the Constitutional Structure of the SFRJ

In socialist Yugoslavia, matters of policing were coordinated and controlled by the Ministry for Internal Affairs, also known during much of this period as the Secretariat for Internal Affairs (*Ministarstvo za unutrašnje poslove*, MUP, or *Sekretarijat za unutrašnje poslove*, SUP, respectively). Mirroring the federal structure of the country, ministries/secretariats of internal affairs existed at the federal level, in the six republics, and in the two autonomous provinces. At the top of each ministry/secretariat stood the minister/secretary, who was a member of the respective federal, republican or provincial government, known in the official terminology as the executive council (*izvršno veće/vijeće*). The republican and provincial ministries of internal affairs existed alongside, but were subordinate to, the Federal Ministry of Internal Affairs. As noted above, particularly during the first two decades of Yugoslavia's existence, the organs of internal affairs functioned in a very centralized manner.

As in many other countries, policing in socialist Yugoslavia was primarily divided between public security (*javna bezbednost/bezbjednost/sigurnost*), which included the regular uniformed police (*milicija*), and the state security service, colloquially known as the secret police. While this book focuses primarily on the state security service, both the public security service and the hierarchy of the ministry as a whole will feature from time to time. Beneath the minister/secretary, each of the two services was headed by an assistant minister or undersecretary. Generally speaking, the minister/secretary was responsible for the political administration of internal affairs in accordance with the guidelines formulated by the federal presidency and the respective government(s). The assistant minister or undersecretary was in turn charged with the actual operational implementation and everyday management of policing. Of course, both the minister/secretary and the assistant minister or undersecretary were members of the League of Communists and were as such integral members of the Yugoslav party-state.

As in virtually all modern states, the Yugoslav constitution provided the legal foundation for the state and its functioning, and all four Yugoslav constitutions (1946, 1953, 1963 and 1974) emphasized the leading role of the SKJ. The SKJ was the sole legitimate representative of the 'working class' in whose hands all power theoretically rested, as noted in the preamble to the final constitution in 1974.[11]

> The League of Communists of Yugoslavia, the initiator and organizer of the people's liberation struggle and the socialist revolution and the conscious bearer of the longings and interests of the working class, through the legitimacy of historical development, became the organized leading ideological and political force of the working class and all working people in the construction of socialism and in the realization of the solidarity of working people and the brotherhood and unity of the nations and nationalities of Yugoslavia. With its commanding ideological and political work in conditions of socialist democracy and social self-management, the League of Communists is the initiator and bearer of political activity as regards the protection and further development of the socialist revolution and relations of social self-management, and especially as regards the strengthening of socialist social and democratic consciousness, and is responsible for this.[12]

The centrality of the SKJ and the interwoven nature of the party-state is worth underlining because the primary task of the Yugoslav State Security Service was to protect the constitutional order of the state. Hence, by definition the Service also protected the interests of the SKJ.

The three most important executive organs in Yugoslavia were the federal presidency,[13] the federal assembly (parliament)[14] and the federal executive council (government).[15] The latter was known as the *Savezno izvršno veće/vijeće*, or SIV. The president of the presidency was the highest office in Yugoslavia, and the holder of that position was the head of state. Josip Broz Tito held this position until his death. Thereafter and until the country's collapse, the presidency rotated annually among representatives from the republics and the autonomous provinces. The work of the federal presidency was further described in a rulebook.[16] At the end of 1980, a series of 'services of the presidency' were also established in order to carry out 'expert matters and other affairs' for the presidency, including analytical tasks related to state security.[17]

Other intelligence and security agencies in Yugoslavia

Before proceeding to a detailed presentation of the Yugoslav State Security Service, a quick glance should be cast on other related agencies in Yugoslavia. A proliferation of intelligence and security agencies is a feature of many modern states, and Yugoslavia was in this respect no exception. In addition to the Yugoslav State Security Service, a number of other security and intelligence services existed. Indeed, at a session of the Executive Bureau of the SKJ Presidency held in March 1971, Stane Dolanc counted thirteen Yugoslav intelligence and counterintelligence services operating outside of Yugoslavia: the federal Yugoslav State Security Service, six republican, two provincial, two military and two services of the Federal Secretariat for Foreign Affairs.[18]

Unfortunately, even less is known about the structure and operations of these other services, because the relevant archives are even less accessible than those pertaining to the Yugoslav State Security Service. However, to the extent that these other services appear in the documents of the Yugoslav State Security Service, we are able to discern some aspects of their roles in the struggle against the political emigration.

On the civilian side, the Federal Secretariat for Foreign Affairs (*Savezni sekretarijat za inostrane poslove,* SSIP) operated its own intelligence agency. Originally called the Administration for Research and Documentation (*Uprava za istraživanje i dokumentaciju,* UID), it was later renamed the Service for Research and Documentation (*Služba za istraživanje i dokumentaciju,* SID). It was responsible for collecting intelligence outside Yugoslavia that might be of relevance for the 'political, security, economic and other interests of the SFRJ'.[19] This broad mandate included the monitoring of 'hostile émigrés'.[20] The existence of the SID was not known to the general public and was not elaborated in the federal law defining the ambit of the work of the SSIP because all matters pertaining to the SID were classified as a state secret.[21] Although the SID was in principle only one part of the SSIP, a report on the Service from May 1983 reveals that there were internal discussions regarding the extent to which all employees of the SSIP should to some extent be involved in intelligence work.[22]

On the military side, the relevant ministry was the Federal Secretariat for People's Defence (*Savezni sekretarijat za narodnu odbranu*, SSNO), which included the Security Administration (*Uprava bezbednosti*, UB).[23] Within the Yugoslav People's Army (*Jugoslovenska narodna armija*, JNA), the general staff had the Second Administration, which also acted as a sort of intelligence agency. The military security and intelligence services were responsible for all security matters which were directly related to the JNA and to military security. In terms of counterintelligence, the military security and intelligence services worked to protect military secrets, to monitor foreign military attaches, to prevent attacks on or the infiltration of military facilities in Yugoslavia and to prevent the recruitment of JNA personnel as agents of foreign intelligence services. The legal ambit of the military security and intelligence services encompassed all those citizens of Yugoslavia who were active members of the JNA as well as civilians who worked for the JNA. As will be seen subsequently, both the UB and the Second Administration took a very expansive view of this ambit, and interagency rivalry and disagreements with the civilian state security services were therefore common.

The military security and intelligence services had their own networks of agents and informants abroad. These could be military attaches in Yugoslav consulates and embassies or Yugoslav or foreign citizens, who had been recruited by these services. The Yugoslav military and civilian agencies could under certain circumstances agree to place their own agents or informants abroad at each other's disposal.[24] In addition, joint operations could be undertaken, and personnel could be seconded to other agencies.[25] However, there are only rare glimpses of such cooperation in the documentation of the Yugoslav party-state and organs of internal affairs. For instance, at a session of the Executive Bureau of the SKJ Presidency in March 1971, its head Stane Dolanc quoted from a dispatch of the military mission at the Yugoslav embassy in West Berlin.[26] Yet as mentioned in the introduction, the military archives remain closed, and we therefore possess only a primitive understanding of the role of these services vis-à-vis émigrés.

Many documents in the archives reveal that the state leadership as well as the respective leaderships of the Yugoslav security and intelligence services understood the need to coordinate their actions in order to achieve common goals and minimize rivalries.[27] For example, in February 1975, leading representatives of the SSUP, the SSNO and the SSIP agreed on unified principles for the execution of tasks related to state security.[28] The Yugoslav state presidency and the SIV devised and issued the overall policy guidelines for this coordination, and the relevant legislation was revised and amended on several occasions.[29] Particularly in the 1980s, there were long-term attempts at creating and maintaining a unified system of security for the whole country.[30]

Yugoslavia under continuous external threat

Socialist Yugoslavia emerged devastated and deeply traumatized from the ashes of the Second World War. Even by the appalling standards of that war, Yugoslavia and its population had suffered disproportionately, certainly when compared to Western Europe. It is often correctly stated that the Second World War in Yugoslavia can only be properly understood if it is recalled that the war was not just a war in which Nazi Germany, fascist Italy and several of their allies attacked and occupied Yugoslavia, but also a brutally atrocious, fratricidal war in which more Yugoslav citizens were killed by other Yugoslav citizens than were killed by the occupying Axis forces.[31]

In the immediate postwar period, Yugoslavia stood forth as the most loyal ally of Stalin's Soviet Union in Eastern Europe. Informed by the messianic and Manichean world view of Stalinism, the Yugoslav State Security Service did its utmost to crush opposition to the establishment of communist rule. When Soviet-Yugoslav relations deteriorated to the point that Yugoslavia was expelled from the Cominform in June 1948, a Stalinist witch hunt against those Yugoslav communists loyal to Stalin ensued, engulfing also countless members of the Yugoslav security services.[32] The result was that, by the autumn of 1948, Yugoslavia stood completely isolated, a member of neither of the two ideological camps which the Soviet ideologist Andrei Zhdanov prophesied would destroy each other. Moreover, the Tito-Stalin split meant that, in addition to the anti-Yugoslav fascist émigrés, a considerable number of pro-Cominform émigrés now also resided outside Yugoslavia, conspiring against the country.[33]

The Cold War and the Tito-Stalin split, along with crises such as the Soviet-led invasions of Hungary in 1956 and Czechoslovakia in 1968, combined with Yugoslavia's membership from the 1960s in the Non-Aligned Movement to shape a dramatic world view for the Udba.[34] Seen from their perspective, they resided in a hostile international environment in which the Yugoslav state was in perpetual danger of attack from a vengeful Soviet Union and also from the capitalist West.[35]

The structure of the Yugoslav State Security Service

This section presents a relatively brief overview of the Yugoslav State Security Service. As has already been mentioned, the overall structure of the state and its guiding ideological and political principles remained quite consistent over the course of the state's existence and several revisions of the constitution, as did the overall ambit and focus of the Service. Nevertheless, within the Service, changes of terminology and the organization of working units changed relatively frequently, with constant discussions about revisions of the Service's structure. It would tax the reader's patience, and add little analytical value, to examine these proposals and changes in detail, so the structure presented here instead reflects the outlines of the Yugoslav State Security Service from the second half of the 1960s until the end of Yugoslavia. This is the period in which most assassinations were planned and committed.

When presenting the Yugoslav State Security Service, it is necessary to note at the outset that there was nothing inherently criminal or sinister about the existence of this service. While the security services of communist states have earned a deservedly negative reputation – East Germany's *Stasi*, Albania's *Sigurimi*, Romania's *Securitate* and of course the Soviet KGB come to mind – because of their record of systematic human rights abuses and their persecution of large segments of their populations, a state security service is a rather important if not essential feature of all modern states. Regardless of their political ideology and structure, contemporary states in the nineteenth and twentieth centuries established security services in order to protect the established order of the state. Indeed, the Yugoslav constitution itself and all salient documents dealing with the organization and functioning of the Yugoslav State Security Service frequently emphasize that the primary role of the Service was to protect the constitutionally established state order.[36] No clearer illustration can be given than Article 313 of the 1974 Constitution, which charged the federal presidency of the state with monitoring both the domestic and international situation in order to protect 'the constitutionally established order (state security)'.[37] Likewise, Article 281 of the constitution regulated the tasks of the federal state and its organs, and charged these with the responsibility for the protection of state security and the coordination of all related matters.[38] Yet, in contrast to state security services in democracies, the Yugoslav State Security Service existed to protect a one-party state, and it was this role as a guardian of dictatorship which ensured its highly repressive role.

It should therefore come as no surprise that the main state body supervising the work of the State Security Service after 1974 was called the Council for the Protection of the Constitutional Order. Councils with this name and function existed at the federal, republican and provincial levels within the respective presidencies at each level. The federal council was established on 26 December 1974 pursuant to Articles 331 and 337 of the constitution.[39] The council's primary task was to direct and supervise the work of all state organs involved in protecting state security.[40] The council was constituted from members of the Federal Executive Council (government), and the chair of this council, the federal secretaries for internal affairs, people's defence and foreign affairs were *ex officio* members. Other members could be appointed by the presidency. The federal presidency and the presidencies of the republics, as well as the Federal Executive Council, could charge the council with specific tasks in order to coordinate the work of state agencies dealing with state security.[41]

In January 1975, the following members of the Council for the Protection of the Constitutional Order were elected:

President:

- Vladimir Bakarić, member of the federal presidency

Appointed members:

- Lazar Koliševski, member of the federal presidency
- Vidoje Žarković, member of the federal presidency
- Stane Dolanc, secretary of the Executive Committee of the presidency of the Central Committee of the Presidency of the SKJ

Ex officio members:

- Džemal Bijedić, president of the Federal Executive Council
- Franjo Herljević, federal secretary for internal affairs
- Nikola Ljubičić, federal secretary for people's defence
- Miloš Minić, federal secretary for foreign affairs[42]

In September 1982, new appointments were made to the Council:

President:

- Lazar Koliševski, member of the federal presidency

Appointed members:

- Petar Stambolić, member of the federal presidency
- Vidoje Žarković, member of the federal presidency
- Franjo Herljević, member of the Presidency of the Central Committee of the SKJ

Ex officio members:

- Milka Planinc, president of the Federal Executive Council
- Stane Dolanc, federal secretary for internal affairs
- Branko Mamula, federal secretary for people's defence
- Lazar Mojsov, federal secretary for foreign affairs[43]

Particularly noteworthy in the above two compositions of the Federal Council for the Protection of the Constitutional Order is the roleplay reversal of Franjo Herljević and Stane Dolanc, who switched between being federal secretary for internal affairs and being members of the Presidency of the Central Committee of the SKJ. These shifts highlight the interwoven nature of the party-state as pertains to the most important organs of state security and internal affairs.

The Federal Secretariat for Internal Affairs and the State Security Service

The SIV consisted of secretariats (ministries), which functioned as executive organs of the federal state.[44] The Federal Secretariat for Internal Affairs (*Savezni sekretarijat za unutrašnje poslove*, SSUP), which was the highest organ of the police in Yugoslavia, was one of these secretariats, whose functions were outlined in Articles 363–368 of the 1974 Constitution.[45] The federal secretaries were nominated for four-year terms by the Federal Assembly, although in practice their terms differed greatly in length. The competencies and jurisdictions of the federal secretariats were further defined by the Law on the Organization and Jurisdiction of Federal Executive Organs and Federal Organizations.[46] Together with the federal presidency, the SIV could direct the work of the SSUP, and the federal secretary had to report to the SIV about the SSUP's work.[47] Underlining again the nature of the party-state, the secretary also had responsibilities vis-à-vis the presidency of the Central Committee of the League of Communists of Yugoslavia, of which the secretary was, of course, a member.[48] Hence the leadership of the SKJ also received information on the state security service's operations.[49]

The following persons served as federal secretaries (or ministers) for internal affairs in Yugoslavia:

- Aleksandar Ranković, 1945–1953
- Svetislav Stefanović, 14 January 1953–18 April 1963
- Vojin Lukić, 18 April 1963–12 March 1965
- Milan Mišković, 12 March 1965–18 May 1967
- Radovan Stijačić, 18 May 1967–30 July 1971
- Džemal Bijedić, 30 July 1971–3 December 1971
- Luka Banović, 3 December 1971–17 July 1974
- Franjo Herljević, 17 May 1974–16 May 1982
- Stane Dolanc, 16 May 1982–15 May 1984
- Dobroslav Ćulafić, 15 May 1984–16 March 1989
- Petar Gračanin 16 March 1989–14 July 1992[50]

It should be noted that the period from 1971 until 1984 was exceptional, in that none of the federal secretaries during this period were Serbs. This was very likely a reaction to the early Yugoslav period, where Ranković and other Serbs had been perceived as dominating the Service.

The SSUP could issue orders to the subordinate republican and provincial secretariats of internal affairs, including their state security services. The SSUP could also in principle carry out inspections or audits of subordinate secretariats in order to ensure that these were complying with the relevant federal instructions and regulations.[51] However, it appears that the inspection carried out in 1986–1987 was the first since 1966.[52]

The subordinate secretariats for internal affairs had to keep the SSUP notified in a timely manner about all 'events, manifestations and findings relevant to the security of the SFRJ'.[53] In the course of the 1980s in particular, the republican and provincial state security services began to operate more independently, and it appears that they also began to withhold relevant information from the SSUP. The Croatian SDS and the Slovenian SDV also opposed the proposed establishment of a comprehensive centralized database for the SSUP.[54] In their reconstruction of the work of the SDS in the period from 1980 to 1990, Josip Perković and Jan Gabriš concluded that the SDS had 'to a great extent' become a republican state security service, i.e. one that operated primarily to serve the interests of the Socialist Republic of Croatia instead of Yugoslavia's as a whole.[55] According to Perković and Gabriš, 'the greater independence of Croatia and Slovenia with respect to the SDS SSUP [the Federal State Security Service], in contrast to other republican services, was common knowledge'.[56]

Besides the constitution, the main laws governing the operation of the Yugoslav State Security Service were:

- the Basic Law of Internal Affairs;[57]
- the Law on the Implementation of Internal Affairs in the Jurisdiction of Federal Administrative Organs;[58]
- the Law on the Foundations of the System of State Security.[59]

According to Article 7 of the Law on the Foundations of the System of State Security, the six republics and two autonomous provinces were, in cooperation and coordination with the SSUP SDB, primarily responsible for protecting state security on their respective territories.[60] If operations were restricted to the territory of one republic or province, very little coordination with the SSUP SDB was necessary, but as soon as operations affected more than one republic or province, coordination with the SSUP SDB was mandatory. As will be seen, this was also the case for all operations containing international elements.

The actual operational and technical details of the work of the state security service were not prescribed in these laws. Rather, in addition to the laws, most of which were published in the official gazettes of Yugoslavia, there was also a large number of internal rulebooks, instructions, directives, etc. Without exception, these internal documents were classified as official or state secrets. Unless otherwise noted, all federal rulebooks and similar prescriptive documents were binding for the state security services in the republics and in the autonomous provinces. These more detailed documents and their implementation will be dealt with extensively in Chapter 3.

Like all other secretariats, the work of the Secretariat for Internal Affairs and hence that of the Yugoslav State Security Service was financed from the federal budget. There are, however, indications that the federal SDB possessed so-called black registers (*crne kase*) or slush funds containing hard currency, and it is likely that these were used at least in part for covert operations outside Yugoslavia. Some of these funds might well have come from legal or illicit foreign trade. Already at the end of the 1940s, the US Central Intelligence Agency (CIA) asserted that the federal Udba was directly involved in smuggling, which it should be noted was not at all unusual for intelligence and state security services, including of course the CIA itself.[61]

The principal internal structural feature of the Yugoslav State Security Service was its division into administrations (*uprave*). Although the number and purpose of these administrations varied over time, their function was to delineate the major areas of the work of the service. For the purposes of this book, the predominant thematic structure of the administrations from 1966 until 1991 was as follows:

First Administration: counterintelligence with respect to foreign intelligence services

Second Administration: enemy émigrés

Third Administration: internal enemies

Fourth Administration: translation services

Fifth Administration: analysis and reporting

Seventh Administration: counterintelligence protection of federal organs and organizations, close protection of designated state and foreign officials

Eighth Administration: documentation and data processing

Ninth Administration: technical operations

Tenth Administration: surveillance of embassies and consulates

Eleventh Administration: covert surveillance and observation

Twelfth Administration: cooperation with foreign intelligence services

Thirteenth Administration: general affairs[62]

There was no sixth administration, as it was at some point disbanded and not reconstituted.

Work was organized internally within each administration of the Yugoslav State Security Service, and reporting was also separate. The structure of the administrations in the republican and provincial state security services mirrored that of the federal SDB. Hence, the Second Administration of the federal SDB would communicate predominantly with the second departments or sections of the subordinate state security services. Of course, at any given time, several administrations could and did conduct joint operations and exchange information pursuant to the orders issued by the leadership of the SDB.

However, the governing principle of work in the service was 'linear work' (*linijski rad*). Specifically, this meant that orders and exchange of information related to, for example, hostile émigré activity, would be sent hierarchically from the Second Administration in the federal SDB to the second administration in the Croatian SDS, which would in turn further distribute to the second sections in the regional centres of the SDS. Conversely, a report prepared by an SDS officer working in the second section of the SDS centre in Rijeka would be sent to the second administration of the Croatian SDS in Zagreb and would then be forwarded, in whole or in part, to the Second Administration in the federal SDB. The SDS centres were not permitted to communicate directly with their colleagues in the SSUP SDB (and vice versa), as all communications had to run through the republican headquarters of the SDS. Linear interrepublican teams (*linijski timovi*) combining, for example, the second administration of the SDS in Croatia with the second administration of the SDB in Montenegro under the supervision of the Second Administration of the federal SDB could also be formed.[63] This would occur if an operation required the involvement of several administrations of the SDB or geographically spanned several republics, with the federal SDB acting as a coordinator.[64] Other intelligence or security services could also be involved in joint operations where necessary.

The Secretariat for Internal Affairs and the State Security Service of the Socialist Republic of Croatia

Just as the SSUP constituted one of the component secretariats of the Federal Executive Council (SIV), so the Croatian Republican Secretariat for Internal Affairs (RSUP SRH) constituted one of the component secretariats of the Republican Executive Council of the Socialist Republic of Croatia. The secretaries were elected by the SRH parliament (*Sabor*) for four-year terms.[65] The secretary had to report to the parliament about the work of the secretariat.[66] Together with the Yugoslav and SRH constitutions and relevant federal legislation, the SRH Law on Internal Affairs provided the framework for the work of the republican secretariat.[67]

Also, just as in federal legislation, the relevant laws in Croatia equated state security with the protection of the established constitutional order. Article 1 of the 1979 SRH Law on Internal Affairs defined internal affairs as '1. the protection of the constitutional order (hereafter, state security)'.[68] This protection was provided by the SDS through 'the identification and prevention of activities, which aim at the undermining or destruction of the constitutional order'.[69]

Further mirroring the structure of the SSUP, the SRH RSUP, as well as all other republican secretariats for internal affairs, had two principal branches: the Public Security Service (*Služba javne sigurnosti*, SJS) and the State Security Service (*Služba državne sigurnosti*, SDS). Internally, the work of the SDS was further regulated by relevant directives, rulebooks and other regulatory documentation, all of which had to be compatible with federal legislation and regulations. Some of the more significant of these included:

- SRH RSUP, Rulebook of 31 July 1975 on the Internal Organization and the Systematization of Posts in the SDS RSUP SRH;
- SRH RSUP, Rulebook of 20 December 1978 on the Internal Organization and Manner of Work of the State Security Service;
- SRH RSUP, Rulebook (Consolidated Text) of 2 June 1981 on the Internal Organization and Manner of Work of the State Security Service;
- SRH RSUP, Rulebook of 22 October 1985 on the Internal Organization and Manner of Work of the State Security Service.

Article 16 of the Rulebook of 2 June 1981 confirmed that the SDS performed its work on the basis and within the framework of the constitution, relevant legislation and the established policies of the *Sabor* and the directions pronounced by the Executive Council of the *Sabor*.[70] The republican secretary offered additional direction in coordination with the Executive Council and the council of the republican secretariat. The republican secretary developed and approved the annual work plan of the SDS based on the political orientation and the recommendations of the SDS's internal units.

The SDS was led by an undersecretary who was nominated by the republican government, and his position was defined as a 'leading function' (*rukovodeća funkcija*).[71] The undersecretary assisted the republican secretary with the administration of certain areas of work, and carried out various tasks which were defined by the regulations and which were entrusted to him by the secretary.[72] During the period from 1980 until 1989, the undersecretary for the SDS of the SRH RSUP also served as the deputy head of the republican secretariat.[73] As a matter of practice, the republican secretary was responsible for the political leadership of the secretariat while the undersecretary for the SDS managed all operational aspects.

In the period from 1980 until 1990, there were three republican secretaries for internal affairs in Croatia:[74]

- Zlatko Uzelac, 1979–1982
- Pavle Gaži, 1982–1983
- Vilim Mulc, 1983–1990

The deputy secretaries, who as noted simultaneously served as undersecretaries and leaders of the SDS, were:[75]

- Vinko Bilić, 1979–1982
- Zdravko Mustač, 1982–1986
- Đuro Pešut, 1986–1990

The assistant secretaries for the SDS were:

- Srećko Šimurina, 1979–1985
- Josip Perković, 1985–1990
- Franjo Vugrinec, 1987–1990

The SRH secretary for internal affairs determined the internal organizational structure of the SDS in compatibility with the federal structure.[76] This structure was confirmed by the parliament and the government.[77] As noted, the undersecretary ran the SDS on a day-to-day basis.[78] A steering council consisting of senior officials existed within the SRH RSUP. This council was in charge of drafting and evaluating suggestions regarding the work of the secretariat.

Mirroring the internal administrations in the SSUP SDB, an array of sections existed in the SDS. In principle, the structure at the level of the republican secretariats was identical to that of the SSUP SDB, but some deviations did on occasion occur. According to the 1977 Regulations on the Internal Organization and Systematization of the SDS, eight sections existed:

1. Section for the Processing of Internal Enemies
2. Section for the Processing of Enemy Émigrés
3. Section for the Processing of Foreign Intelligence Services
4. Section for Operational Technical Matters
5. Section for Matters of Statistics and Documentation
6. Section for Matters of the Protection of People and Buildings
7. Section for Analysis[79]
8. Independent Section for Defence Preparation[80]

A comparison with the contemporary structure of the Slovenian SDV clearly shows that the structures of the SDS could be quite different. In 1975, the SDV exhibited the following structure:

1. Section for the Internal Territory
2. Section for External (Foreign) Territories

3. Section for Counterintelligence
4. No fourth section
5. Section for Information, Documentation and Archives
6. Section for Operational Technical Matters
7. No seventh section
8. Section for Investigative Documentation and Technical Means[81]

Within the SDS there was a further regional hierarchy ensuring that the SDS could cover the entire territory of the Socialist Republic of Croatia. This territory was divided into four groups covered by SDS centres, as follows:

1. SDS Centre Zagreb
2. SDS Osijek, Split and Rijeka
3. SDS Centres Pula, Karlovac, Bjelovar and Varaždin
4. SDS Centres Sisak and Gospić[82]

The internal structures of these centres to a significant extent mirrored that of the SDS, which again highlights the 'linear' nature of the SDS's work (*linijski rad*). There were both horizontal and vertical lines of reporting. For example, documentation related to hostile émigrés (the second line) was sent back and forth from the Second Administration of the SSUP SDB and the Second Section of the SDS centres in Croatia. However, all communications between the SDS centres and the SSUP SDB had to run through the SDS of the SRH RSUP.

Planning and reporting constituted an important function of the SDS. The SDS had to compile an annual plan for its work that was compatible with the guidelines given to it by the SSUP SDB and by those SRH government organs – the presidency, government and parliament – which were responsible for the SDS's work. In addition to regular reporting, the SDS was also obliged to compile and disseminate reports to appropriate republican and federal authorities on the work completed over the course of the year.

The republican Council for the Protection of the Constitutional Order (*Savjet za zaštitu ustavnog poretka*), a body of the SRH Presidency established in 1975, played a particularly significant role in directing and overseeing the work of the SDS.[83] Like its federal counterpart, the Council had the authority to direct the SDS to pay attention to particular matters and to require that the SDS report on its progress in working on these matters. In addition to meeting several times a year, the Council at least once annually submitted a report to the SRH Presidency.[84] At its very first meeting, held on 10 July 1975, the members of the Council were told that the term 'security' was to be understood in a very broad sense. As such, the Council would 'also deal with questions from the realms of the economy and a whole array of questions of socioeconomic, political, cultural and other areas of life, particularly from the aspect of the order confirmed by the SFRJ Constitution and the SRH Constitution'.[85] Yet the council was not supposed to evolve into an operational body, but rather instead a coordinating and directing body. The council would receive periodic updates 'on hostile activity, not only from the SDS, but also from the SJS [Public Security Service], the public prosecutors the courts and other organs'.[86] Furthermore, the council would examine the relationship of the SDS to other security services and to other state security services in Yugoslavia. The degree to which the council could supervise and control the work of the SDS was discussed.

The council therefore functioned as a political control mechanism.[87] The members of the SRH Council for the Protection of the Constitutional Order were elected by the SRH Presidency, and were to be drawn from 'the ranks of the membership of the Presidency, other functionaries in the Republic, as well as from the ranks of socio-political, scholarly and specialist as well as public employees'.[88] The first president of the council was Zvonimir Jurišić.[89] Already at the very first meeting of the council, the activities of 'the extreme terrorist emigration' were discussed, with specific mention of the arrest of a person who had brought explosives into Yugoslavia with the intention of disrupting the tourist industry.[90]

In July 1980, the following members were elected:

As president:

- Kazimir Jelovica, member of the SRH Presidency

As members:

- Milutin Baltić, Secretary of the Presidency of the Central Committee of the SKH
- Petar Fleković, President of the Executive Council of the SRH Sabor
- Augustin Jukić, Commander of the Territorial Defence Staff
- Jelica Radojčević, member of the SRH Presidency
- Nikola Šegota, President of the Sociopolitical Council of the SRH Sabor
- Zlatko Uzelac, Secretary for Internal Affairs in the SRH RSUP

The secretary of the Council was Veljko Mihovilović, an advisor in the SRH Presidency. The president of the Council was responsible for proposing the agenda for its meetings.[91]

In May 1982, the composition of the Council changed as follows:

As president:

• Tode Ćuruvija, member of the SRH Presidency

As members:

• Marijan Cvetković, Secretary of the Presidency of the Central Committee of the SKH
• Marijan Kalanj, Secretary of the Central Committee of the SKH
• Martin Špegelj, Commander of the Territorial Defence Staff
• Ante Marković, President of the Executive Council of the Sabor of the SRH
• Vlado Mihaljević, President of the Sociopolitical Council of the SRH Sabor
• Pavle Gaži, Secretary for Internal Affairs in the SRH RSUP

Mihovilović remained secretary of the Council.[92]

Members of the Council could invite other relevant officials to attend the Council's meetings; the undersecretary for the SDS was a frequent participant. By way of example, in the period between 9 July 1982 and the end of 1983, there were thirteen meetings of the SRH Council for the Protection of the Constitutional Order, which was somewhat less frequent than the monthly meetings which the members in principle wanted to have.[93] During this period, top officials of the SDS were regularly invited to participate in order that they might report to the Council and engage in discussions of relevant topics.[94] Zdravko Mustač often participated in his capacity as acting republican Secretary for Internal Affairs.[95]

The available documentation on the work of the Council makes it clear that the Council engaged intensively with issues pertaining to the structure, manner of work and operational priorities of the SDS. For example, in its meeting on 4 March 1981, the Council decided to accept the annual report on the work of the SDS in 1980, noting that the report encompassed the viewpoints expressed by the members of the Council. Likewise, the Council approved the work plan for the SDS for 1981, though not without directing the SDS's attention to the Council's own views on priorities and problems in the work of the SDS. In other words, a dialogue regarding the work of the SDS was visible between it and the Council.

Furthermore, the Council regularly received 'special information' bulletins or reports from the SDS. The purpose of these reports was to acquaint the political leadership of the republic with pressing current security challenges so that these could be adequately discussed in the Council.[96] At every session of the Council, the republican Secretary for Internal Affairs or his designated representative gave an oral presentation summarizing the newest and most pressing issues related to state security. According to Perković and Gabriš, the SDS also had to brief both the SRH Presidency and the Council daily.[97] In addition, the Secretary for Internal Affairs on occasion provided oral briefings to the Presidency of the SKH Central Committee, designated deputies in the Sabor and members of the parliamentary Committee for People's Defence and Social Self-Protection.[98] Under certain circumstances, regional, municipal and local government officials might also receive relevant information from the SDS.[99]

As can be seen with the reference to the SKH Central Committee, the party-state nexus of course informed all of the SDS's work. In April 1980, Vinko Bilić, then the SRH Deputy Secretary for Internal Affairs, observed that the constitutionally mandated leadership role of the League of Communists was 'extraordinarily welcome, both with respect to the direction of the Service as well as the identification of problems … of difficulties, yes also in certain organs in the identification of deviations of individuals in the organs of internal affairs'.[100] Bilić also recalled that a certain restructuring or 'correction' of the SDS had been undertaken in 1979. This restructuring led to the establishment of three new SDS centres in Sisak, Gospić and Varaždin. The restructuring was approved by the SRH Council for the Protection of the Constitutional Order, which also permitted itself to issue further recommendations for the work of the SDS.[101]

As regards specifically investigations, operations and analysis pertaining to the hostile emigration, the Second Section of the SDS was responsible and cooperated most closely with the Second Administration of the SSUP SDB.[102] All relevant information had to be shared with the SSUP SDB in a timely manner.[103] From 1979 until 1985, Josip Perković served as the chief of the SDS's Second Section; he was succeeded by Branko Traživuk.[104] Yet it should be noted that the Second Section of the SDS was primarily responsible for those émigrés who either stemmed from Croatia (predominantly Croats, but also some Serbs) or had resided there for longer periods before emigrating. This is an important distinction given the fact that Croats from Bosnia and Herzegovina – and particularly from Herzegovina – seem to be disproportionately represented among 'extreme' or 'fascist' émigrés. If a Bosnian Croat emigrated to Western Europe and engaged there in extremist activities, then the Bosnian SDB would be primarily responsible for monitoring him. If, however, he had previously spent years residing and working in Croatia, and thereafter emigrated to Western Europe, then the Croatian SDS would take the lead. Of course, given that in practice both 'kinds' of Bosnian Croats frequently associated abroad with Croats from Croatia (and other republics and provinces, including the Croat minority from Kosovo known as the Janjevci), interrepublican agency cooperation was required – always with mandatory supervision by the SSUP SDB. All of the work and operations of the republican state security services had to be performed 'in full cooperation with the Second Administration of the Federal State Security Service' and 'all applied means and methods were approved or initiated by the Second Administration of the Federal State Security Service'.[105]

It is important to emphasize that the general division of labour in the Yugoslav state security services was such that each nation primarily bore responsibility for operations pertaining to 'its own', not just with respect to hostile émigrés but also to all 'enemies of the state'. This unwritten rule helped to reinforce the important ideological slogan of 'brotherhood and unity', both by recognizing that each nation had its bad apples and by avoiding potential accusations that Serbs were unduly concerned with Croat extremists (or vice versa). In other words, the SDS would generally speaking deal with émigré Croats, particularly those stemming from Croatia, while the SDV would deal with émigré Slovenes. In practice, the lines were blurry and could be affected by a variety of factors. For example, while Herzegovinian Croats – seemingly always disproportionately represented in fervent Croat nationalist circles – primarily fell within the ambit of the SDB of Bosnia and Herzegovina, many of them had spent considerable time living in Croatia prior to emigrating. Hence the SDS also became involved in monitoring them. Conversely, although almost no Croat émigrés stemmed from Slovenia, the SDV became not infrequently involved in operations involving Croats in Italy, Austria and West Germany due to the geographic proximity of Slovenia to these countries.

In their summary of the ambit of the Second Section of the SDS, Josip Perković and Jan Gabriš stated that the Section primarily had to focus on the uncovering and prevention of:

- intentions, drafts, preparations and attempts to carry out terrorist attacks in Yugoslavia and abroad;
- intentions, drafts, preparations and attempts to infiltrate armed persons and groups into Yugoslavia;
- any kind of contact between the hostile emigration and the internal enemy;
- publications and propaganda of the hostile emigration which constitute libel or destroy or undermine the constitutionally protected order, endanger the country's security or disparage its international reputation.[106]

Seminal documents of the SSUP SDB for its work abroad

Having looked at the structure of both the Yugoslav State Security Service and the Croatian State Security Service and their relationship to the party-state, we next turn to an examination of the operations and documentation of the service. As might be imagined, the Yugoslav State Security Service produced gigantic amounts of paperwork. In addition to legal and regulatory documentation and quotidian bureaucratic paperwork, the intelligence cycle required a constant repetition of strategic planning, direction, operational intelligence gathering, processing, analysis and dissemination to relevant state organs and other intelligence services. Information had to be sorted constantly in order to be made available on a 'need-to-know' basis at a moment's notice. One of the most (in)famous ways of organizing information was the establishment of dossiers for persons held to be of interest (*bezbednosna zanimljiva lica*). Such persons would henceforth be permanently registered – excepting the occasional mass purge of files – in the operational record (*operativna evidencija*, OE). To quote a member of the Serbian State Security Service,

> the first operational rule is that before you begin to do anything, you check whether someone before you has done something or written something about that person. Therefore you go downstairs to the analysis section and 'pull' the person through the OE or ask the responsible analyst whether there have been carried out any earlier operations connected with the matter that now interests you.[107]

It is exceedingly difficult to say with precision how many persons received the attention of the Yugoslav State Security Service. It is known for certain that the Yugoslav authorities on several occasions ordered the destruction of large portions of the Service's archives, particularly personal dossiers.[108] In some cases, the decision to purge the archives was taken in connection with external threats to the country's security, particularly after the Tito-Stalin split. In other cases, the shredding and burning of documentation appear to have followed the purge of Ranković and also the temporary improvement of Soviet-Yugoslav relations.[109] In addition, the wars of Yugoslav succession in the 1990s had very negative consequences for archival documentation, and that and subsequent decades also witnessed the illegal misappropriation of sensitive archival documentation by various governments and politicians.[110]

Qualitatively speaking, what is clear about the dossiers is that once persons reached a level where they were sufficiently interesting to justify the establishment of a dossier, it often took years or even decades before their dossiers were terminated. Of course, in some cases, the end of the dossier came about only when the subject of the dossier was physically eliminated.

In order to concentrate on the foreign operations of the SDB and provide a relatively succinct analysis of the regulatory and administrative framework within which such operations occurred, the remainder of this chapter will devote itself to the presentation and analysis of several seminal SDB documents. In order of presentation, these are:

- The SSUP SDB instruction manual 'Operational Processing – Part II' (1974)
- The Instructions on the Counterintelligence Work of the SDB Abroad (date uncertain, probably 1967–1971)
- The Instructions on the Work of the Special Surveillance Unit (1968)
- The SDB Rulebook (1975)
- The Rulebook on the Work of the SDB Abroad (1979)

Together, these documents represent the most important SDB documents which have hitherto emerged from the archives pertaining to operations outside Yugoslavia. All of them stem from the period in which the Yugoslav state leadership in cooperation with the SDB adopted, for reasons which will be seen later, a significantly more offensive stance with respect to the struggle against the 'hostile emigration'. As such, these documents describe, in language ranging from mind-numbingly dry and bureaucratic articles to titillating euphemisms, the rationale, requirements and analysis related to operations abroad, including assassinations.

'Operational Processing – Part II'

In 1974, the SSUP produced an instruction manual entitled 'Operational Processing' (*operativna obrada*).[111] To date only the second part of the manual is available, but it provides an extensive portrait of the operational work of the SDB. The manual included a host of considerations of both a practical and historical nature regarding the use of operational measures and the advantages and disadvantages of utilizing such measures. The handbook also made it clear that the SDB operated outside of Yugoslavia in order to combat hostile émigré organizations. Overall, the handbook emphasized that the SDB always had to ensure that its work was politically approved by the SKJ leadership.

The handbook primarily focused on how to carry out the proper operational processing (*operativna obrada*, OO) of a person, organization or other object of interest to the SDB. Such processing could last for months and often even years, and the aim was obviously to gather as much relevant information about the target as possible. In order to do this, the agents of the SDB could avail themselves of broad palette of 'operational means and measures'.[112]

Once a person reached a certain level of notoriety or significance from the perspective of the SDB, that person would be nominated for operational processing. Activities which were likely to cause someone to appear on the SDB's radar included work for or association with foreign intelligence agencies, terrorism, sabotage, founding or participating in illegal organizations and the dissemination of propaganda against the Yugoslav party-state.[113] The nomination could occur at a regional SDS centre, or at the republican or federal level. This person could be a Yugoslav citizen in Yugoslavia, a foreign citizen in Yugoslavia or a Yugoslav citizen or person of Yugoslav descent living abroad. In the case of foreign diplomats, their status and the (supposed) intelligence activities in which they were engaging made their eligibility for operational processing almost an *ex officio* matter. Both for foreign diplomats in country and for émigrés abroad, the approval of the SSUP SDB was necessary in order to commence operational processing.

Before actual operational processing began, the relevant person was subjected to initial operational processing (*prethodna operativna obrada*, POO). If the person graduated to full-blown operational processing, the acronym 'OO' would henceforth appear at the first mention of this person's name in all SDB documentation. There are also documents in which operational control (*operativna kontrola*, OK) is mentioned as a precursor to OO.[114]

With respect to organizations in the emigration, they were to be studied 'comprehensively', with the following items prioritized: their programme, objectives, intentions, location, leadership and membership composition, and the structure of their meetings and organizational work. Special attention was to be given to extremists in their midst.[115] Once specific individuals had been identified for operational processing, the SDB aimed to learn as much as possible about the target, including personal, educational and professional background, character traits, physical appearance, familial relations and friendships, virtues, weaknesses or vices. From this information, the appropriate operational means and measures could be chosen, with special care taken to how to approach the target and exploit his or her overall situation. 'Almost every person has some weaknesses which he seeks to conceal from his surroundings, and by skilfully using these weaknesses, the Service is able to achieve better success in its processing'.[116] The best way of obtaining accurate information was of course to send an agent who would personally but covertly get to know the target. If that was not possible, informants would be recruited from among the family, colleagues or other acquaintances of the target. In addition to this, the interception of postal and telephone communications was employed. Obviously, the application and availability of measures depended to quite some degree on whether the target was located in Yugoslavia or abroad. Recruitment would typically proceed in a manner that the 'candidate' would be confronted with a situation or information that would force him or her to engage with the SDB: 'secret detention and interrogation, catching the candidate with compromising material or in the act of committing a crime or something similar'.[117] As in many countries, the strategic use of imprisonment and the shortening of prison sentences or the use of intimidation or threats against immediate relatives were other well-known methods for the (in)voluntary recruitment of informants. However, it should also be noted that there were numerous instances in which potential informants voluntarily approached the SDB. Motives for doing so ranged from patriotism to more base factors such as jealousy or hatred of others. Conversely, the Udba was also capable of inventing a criminal record for Yugoslav citizens who had been handpicked to infiltrate émigré organizations, thereby lending them a cover story that would help to ingratiate them with anti-Yugoslav émigrés.

No operational processing could proceed without the existence of a plan. Planning was identified as a 'basic principle in the work of the Service', which helped to ensure the systematic nature of the SDB's work.[118] Moreover, planning also helped the Service to maintain the initiative vis-à-vis the target. The operational officer who proposed that a person be subjected to operational processing was charged with putting together the necessary plan and obtaining approval for this plan from his appropriate superior officers. Once the plan was approved, it was ready for implementation.

As a matter of course, the plan would also have to include the infiltration of SDB agents or, more usually, informants into the groups or organizations that were allegedly engaged in anti-Yugoslav activities.[119] Both the initial infiltration and the maintenance of a productive relationship with the infiltrated informant required dexterous handling on the part of the agent who was running the informant. Infiltration was regarded as a very complex manner and as possibly dangerous for the person being infiltrated. Communications with the informant after infiltration had to be managed discretely through the use of classic espionage methods such as dead drops and encrypted communications. Confidentiality, efficiency and reliability were essential for communications with informants and agents abroad, and all communications had to be agreed upon in advance. Those agents working abroad had to undergo special training.[120]

Once infiltrated, the informant had to maintain the trust of those in the hostile surroundings in which he or she was located. 'Above all, the informant must find a common language and interest with the object of processing, without compromising himself too much in hostile activities, but not making it possible for the object to doubt him.'[121] As with persons infiltrated by law enforcement into organized criminal networks, it at times proved exceedingly difficult for the informants of the SDB and their handlers to toe the line between observing and actually participating in hostile or even terrorist activities. Indeed, as we shall see, an important element in post-Yugoslav nationalist narratives about the SDB and the émigrés is the accusation on the part of present-day nationalists that *all* terrorist activities attributed to the émigrés were in fact initiated and carried out at the behest of the SDB. The handbook made it clear that the informant

- must not be an initiator or organizer of enemy activity;
- must not on his own initiative undertake illegal activities or convince others to carry them out, because as such he becomes an accomplice and bearer of criminal responsibility, and cannot avoid the consequences;
- cannot avail himself of provocations or carry out any kind of instigation to enemy activity;
- cannot supply the enemy with material or other means, especially if that activity is expressed in broad strokes [*u grubim formama*];
- must not be intrusive in his manner, because he would then provoke suspicion;
- must follow instructions, must be disciplined, and his autonomy is very limited until such time as he is assessed to have attained the confidence of the target of the operational processing;
- must realistically observe things and events such that he faithfully reports them to the operational officer with critical observations, must not give his opinion about facts with which he is unfamiliar. Depending on personal ability, the informant must tell the operational officer only what he has heard and seen – without his own analysis. If he presents his opinion, this must be separate from what he reports.[122]

Clearly situations might arise in which the persons in organizations into which informants had been infiltrated might be asked to engage in hostile and/or illegal activities. Doing so might well be a way for the principal organizers of such activities to test the loyalties of persons in the organization.

> In this case, the informant can carry out some smaller tasks, and this exclusively with the permission of the operational officer. The informant must have a way of avoiding more complicated and or serious tasks which constitute criminal acts. He can be counseled to tell the target that he did not carry out the task because of security measures or because he was afraid, etc. If more serious criminal acts are in question, the informant should be advised to report this to the prosecutor or the court, so as in this manner to avoid responsibility and simultaneously prevent the harmful consequences of enemy activity.[123]

If there were indications that émigrés were planning an imminent attack on a Yugoslav target, or even merely preparing to disseminate illegal propaganda, it was deemed necessary to intensify operational processing. Such activities had to be prevented before they occurred, even if doing so meant undertaking measures that would blow the cover of the operation.[124] However, the informant should in such cases approach the appropriate authorities in which he was located and report such imminent activities as a concerned citizen or patriot, not revealing his relationship with the SDB. Deciding to undertake necessary actions that might reveal agents or otherwise cause the termination of a covert operation was a particularly difficult decision.

In the case of foreign operations, the element of foreign relations with other countries also had to be taken into account. The state of Yugoslavia's relations with a country in which operations were being carried out could affect the length and nature of the operation.[125] The length of the operation could also be affected by whether the SDB was working at home or abroad, whether there was a well-developed network of agents, whether adequate technical means (e.g. surveillance devices) existed for the implementation of the operation, etc.

The reliability of the SDB's informants had to be evaluated on a running basis in order to ensure the confidentiality and success of the operations in which informants were being used. The informant was not himself or herself to feel that he or she was being subjected to such scrutiny. Reports of informants could be compared for accuracy. The SDB could use standard operational measures such as physical or electronic or postal surveillance in order to check its informants. More trusted informants could also be used to test the loyalty of newer and less practised informants, ideally without either informant realizing that a loyalty test was being conducted. It was deemed particularly necessary to probe the loyalty of informants who had been infiltrated into hostile organizations, even more so if they were being used as double agents.[126] Yet if the informant was located abroad, both communications with him or her and the performance of loyalty checks became much more difficult.[127]

If it was concluded that an informant was unreliable or if the informant had revealed his or her engagement with the SDB to third parties, measures would be taken to cut ties with him or her.[128] This would not be done immediately, however. The possibility would be considered of passing disinformation through the unreliable informant in order to confuse the enemy.

By contrast, reliable and useful informants could expect to be rewarded for their efforts. In addition to being reimbursed for expenses (travel, fuel, meals, housing, etc.) incurred for approved operational purposes, the informant could be nominated for monetary awards. The remuneration and rewarding of the informant had to be proportional so as not to encourage avarice.[129] On the other hand, if the informant was truly motivated by patriotism, gifts or money might be misconstrued as insulting. Therefore, the handler could present the informant with presents around the holidays or the informant's birthday.[130]

At some point, all operations had to come to an end. One obvious reason why this might occur was the death of the target or the cessation of allegedly hostile activity by the target. In practice, the records of the SDB give the impression that once a person had become sufficiently interesting to warrant being placed under 'operational processing', it was very difficult for the person to lose this questionable status. In the eyes of the SDB, the handbook made it clear that absent a decision from the SDB to terminate an operation, an operation could be completed successfully through what was termed its 'realization' (*realizacija*).

There were five possibilities for operational realization:

1. The prosecution of the target pursuant to an indictment;
2. The 'physical destruction' of the target;
3. Engaging the target;
4. Warning or intimidating the target;
5. The deportation of the target (applied to hostile foreigners in Yugoslavia).[131]

In a later overview of the work of the Croatian SDS, Jan Gabriš and Josip Perković, who had both worked for years in the service, also mentioned the following: the kindling and exacerbation of mutual disputes in émigré organizations, blackmail, intimidation 'or the complete deactivation [*potpuno onemogućavanje*] of inspirers and organisers of the most extreme forms of hostile activity'.[132]

The end of an operation or a potential involuntary termination of an operation might also make the exfiltration of an informant necessary. Regardless of how or why the informant was recruited, the SDB had to protect the cover of the informant and ensure that the informant's physical safety was not endangered. The protection of the informant also extended to potential prosecution. An informant should not be prosecuted, particularly not with the target of the operation. If this occurred, the enemy would 'try to put all the responsibility for the entire hostile activity' on the informant in order to escape responsibility himself.[133]

In the course of the operation, the principal operational officer was responsible for devising a written proposal for the appropriate realization of the operation.[134] Permission was granted by the appropriate superior SDB officer. However, as will be seen later, in the case of the second mode of 'realization' – assassination – the permission of the highest levels of the Yugoslav party-state was needed.

All five modes of realization were regarded as possibilities, and often in the course of operations, several would be considered. Although the rulebook does not itself present any implicit or explicit hierarchy of desired solutions, the available documentation of the SDB tends to suggest that the killing of a targeted individual was the last resort. It should also be noted that in the rulebook the physical destruction of the target was mentioned in the historical context of postwar operations against terrorists, 'bandits' (*odmetnici*) and saboteurs conducted at the end of the Second World War and in the years thereafter.[135]

Furthermore, in a relevant rulebook from 1975, assassinations were not explicitly mentioned as a means for combatting the hostile emigration. Rather, the following means were listed:

- Arrest and prosecution;
- The banning and dispersal of émigré meetings;
- The disposal and confiscation of émigré propaganda and other materials with hostile intentions;
- The displacement (in the case of foreigners) to other countries or return to Yugoslavia (in the case of émigrés);
- The banning and dispersal of émigré organizations or groups;
- Interrogations and warnings;
- The searching of residences and other localities.[136]

That the author(s) of the handbook prioritized legal means including eventual prosecution could be seen from the amount of space devoted to these matters. By contrast, the sections regarding the 'physical destruction' of targets were very limited. It was emphasized that this most drastic form of operational realization required special planning and preparation. For this reason, it was also emphasized that every employee who participated in these most sensitive operations had to undergo special training but could count on the SDB's gratitude.

> When an agent is used for a liquidation, he must be specially trained, and he must be offered every assistance in the carrying out of the task. He must be given secure means [*sigurna sredstva*], he must be trained in the use of these means and receive personal protection, because the slightest mishap or deficiency can have great consequences for him.[137]

It is worth noting already here that the SDB, despite being the guardian of the constitutionally established order of the state, exhibited considerable ambivalence regarding the legality of operational means and measures. On the one hand, SDB agents were not to participate in or initiate any illegal activities.[138] On the other hand, the handbook made it clear that situations would arise in which the SDB would in fact undertake unconstitutional or otherwise illegal activities in the course of their operations. An example of this was the carrying out of secret searches, which were defined as 'the secret searching of persons, things and rooms presents an operational activity which is carried out when there is no other way to access materials and other evidence related to intelligence or enemy activity'.[139] In principle, the police or SDB were to obtain a search warrant from an investigative judge, but searches could be carried out 'without a warrant from an investigative judge or even without the presence of witnesses, if certain conditions and needs exist'. In practice, 'these certain conditions and needs' were interpreted very broadly as the need to keep the existence of surveillance or other operational activities hidden from the targets and others who might warn them. Clearly, in the case of searches of premises outside Yugoslavia, there was no chance of obtaining a search warrant unless the SDB wanted to reveal its interest in the targets to its foreign partners. However, the carrying out of illegal searches carried risks for the SDB both at home and abroad.

> A secret search is in fact a very complex and delicate action, and thus must be solidly planned and prepared. In the case of its discovery, it could come to criminal prosecution of those who carried it out, because it is a matter of the violation of constitutionally guaranteed rights, and when there is an international element, complications at the level of international relations are possible.[140]

Moreover, if the SDB at any later point wished to use the material obtained during such illegal searches as evidence in court cases, it had to find a way to 'legalize' the material. As will be seen later, the SDB did in fact use a process of 'legalization' (*legalizacija*) to regularize not just illegally obtained material but also even the kidnapping of Yugoslav citizens abroad.[141]

On agents and informants

One of the challenges when writing about the Yugoslav State Security Service concerns the sometimes ambiguous terminology used to describe the persons who worked officially or unofficially for it. The Serbo-Croatian term for 'employee' – *saradnik/suradnik* – is the same term used for one category of informants. One must therefore be careful when reading and translating documentation related to operations. The Udba made a distinction between, on the one hand, those informants who had been formally engaged and assigned a codename and, on the other hand, those persons who informally and occasionally provided information to the service. These persons were referred to as operational connections, contacts or positions (*operativne veze, operativne pozicije*).[142] In the case of the latter category, the persons often had no idea that they had engaged with the Udba in any manner. Writing about recruitment, the SSUP wrote in one document that 'it is not a simple matter to find and engage a person who fulfils the conditions to live and work in a hostile environment, and at the same time remain in touch with us and to carry out our tasks'.[143] It should also be noted that even top employees of the Udba expressed doubts or exasperation regarding terminology, and that we should not try to make sharp distinctions where these did not in practice exist.[144]

The informants of the Udba could be foreign or Yugoslav citizens. Particularly when the needs of the service dictated it, the informants were very often members of hostile émigré organizations. The leader of the responsible working unit of the Udba had to approve the engagement of informants. However, in the case of the recruitment of any informants outside of Yugoslavia, the head of the SSUP SDB personally had to grant approval.[145] The informants received codenames which were assiduously used in internal documentation so that their true identities would remain a closely guarded secret. Although the pseudonyms were sometimes mere alternative names, they could sometimes be quite colourful. Examples from the archives include Harlem, *Fajter* (fighter), *Kiklop* (cyclops), Happy (*Veseli*), Waterfall (*Vodopad*), Terminator, *Derviš* (dervish), Gremlin and *Varlok* (Warlock).

The engagement of informants among émigrés was a delicate matter. Often multiple informants would be recruited to work on the same target, and often they would be kept unaware that there were others than themselves working for the SDB. However, in some cases several informants and/or agents could create a *rezidentura* abroad, though again only with the permission of the head of the SSUP SDB. A *rezidentura* was defined as 'a group of secure and vetted informants/agents in Yugoslavia or abroad who are directed by an agent-resident'.[146]

Another important element of the work of the SDB was the use and dissemination of information and disinformation. As has perhaps become painfully obvious in our world today, not only is knowledge power, but so is the ability to create and disseminate false information. The SDB not only closely monitored émigré publications but also occasionally published their own forgeries of such publications. More usually, however, they sought to spread disinformation and fear through rumours carefully placed in émigré circles.

> Under the terms placement of information and disinformation is understood the deliberate offering of real and accurate, or half-true or false information, respectively as concerns information and disinformation, to foreign intelligence services and the Yugoslav emigration. ... However, in essence it is disinformation even if we place information which is precise, because we conceal the motive for placing it. ... we want to attain a certain objective, but we strive to keep the other side from discovering that objective.[147]

Because of the complexity of disseminating information and disinformation to foreign intelligence services and the emigration, not a single such act was to be undertaken without the permission of the chief of the federal SDB. Requests had to be made in written form with a detailed justification of what kind of information would be shared, with whom, and the goal of the placement.

> It is necessary, in a synchronized and centralized manner, to carry out the placement of information and disinformation, because a [regional] centre of the SDB cannot have an overview, but instead we achieve an overview in the SDB SSUP towards one certain service or towards the Yugoslav emigration. ... Related to this the recordkeeping was centralized in one place (in the SDB SSUP) regarding information and disinformation already provided to the opponent.[148]

One of the tactics contributing to the pursuit of the strategic objectives of the SDB's work was 'operational agitation' (*operativna agitacija*). This tactic was employed to achieve differentiation (*diferenciranje*) or demoralization (*demoralizacija*) or pacification (*pasivizacija*) of the target. Differentiation had as its goal distinguishing those members of a target organization who were genuinely of interest to the SDB – the initiators and organizers of concrete hostile and/or violent activities – from those whose role was more casual and inconsequential.

Demoralization was obviously intended to destabilize the workings of hostile organizations, as well as restrict their ability to attract new members, in the case of émigré organizations among Yugoslav migrant labourers. Pacification referred to the process of convincing currently active participants in hostile activities to desist. 'The considered application of our measures and steps will impress these persons into losing the will to engage in or continue already commenced enemy activity.'[149] Pacification should therefore not be read as a synonym for 'liquidation'.

Operational agitation was a particularly favoured tactic for targets in the emigration, 'because most often our operational tactics are limited to the dissolution, differentiation and demoralization of extreme groups and individuals. Given that the organizers and other participants are abroad, their criminal prosecution is not possible, as well as other measures which are at our disposal in Yugoslavia (summoning for discussions, warnings, etc.).'[150] Internal disputes or factionalism in émigré organizations provided ample opportunities for exploitation by the SDB.

> The worsening of such conflicts should be the permanent orientation of the SDB. The conflicts are often of such a nature that they lead to internal physical settlings of accounts and killings. For example, in 1969, several prominent émigrés from Ustaša groups were killed: Maks Luburić in Spain, [Mile] Rukavina and others in the Federal Republic of Germany. Because of this even more discord was created, mutual accusations arose, threats of revenge, individual fear, etc.[151]

As will be seen, this particular sentence in the training manual is particularly important because it relates to émigrés who were not just killed by unknown perpetrators, as the text might suggest, but were in fact assassinated by the SDB.

Although émigré issues often proved a fraught topic for Yugoslavia's bilateral relations with Western countries, it must be noted that cooperation with foreign authorities was not unusual. The manual highlighted this, noting that there existed 'a certain relationship of cooperation with the police' of countries such as West Germany and France which hosted many Yugoslav émigrés. The host countries were generally speaking keen on preventing terrorist attacks, including against Yugoslav embassies and consulates as well as other forms of Yugoslav representation. A considerable amount of intelligence related to the activities of hostile émigré organizations was therefore exchanged with the police and intelligence services of these countries.[152] Needless to say, the SDB on occasion also deliberately passed disinformation to their foreign partners and never trusted them completely.

Instructions on the counterintelligence work of the SDB abroad (date uncertain, probably 1967–1971)

In the world of intelligence and security services, intelligence and counterintelligence operations are two sides of the same coin. In his standard textbook on state security, Obren Ž. Đorđević wrote that a 'counterintelligence service is a specialized organization of a movement or a state which uncovers and prevents the activities of the opponent's intelligence services, and organizes and works on the protection of its own secrets and systems as well as on misinforming the enemy'.[153] In recognition of this fact, the SSUP SDB issued a directive regarding counterintelligence work abroad. The document bears no date but is signed by Federal Secretary for Internal Affairs Radovan Stijačić, who served in that capacity from 18 May 1967 until 30 July 1971.

The instructions started out by depicting the work of the SDB abroad as a logical and constituent element of the struggle of the SDB against the hostile activities of émigrés and foreign intelligence services. 'From abroad the organized activity of the hostile portion of the Yugoslav emigration evolves through certain organizations, groups and individuals who, besides politically propagandistic operations also organize and carry out terrorist operations aimed at the SFRJ, its representatives and citizens abroad.'[154]

The activities of the State Security Service abroad had to be planned, regulated and implemented through the SSUP SDB in order to ensure coordination and efficacy. For the success of operations, it was essential for the SDB to maintain and nurture a well-organized network of relevant informants abroad. The instructions listed the following categories of informants:

- Informants embedded in sources of hostile activity;
- Informants in 'double combinations' (i.e. double agents);
- Informants in contact with sources of hostile activity;
- Informants engaged in research, verification, surveillance and observation abroad;
- Informants-bases [*saradnici-baze*], who provide technical and other assistance in the performance of tasks abroad;

- Informants-liaisons [*saradnici-veznici*], who maintain direct or indirect contact between the SDB and informants abroad through the transmission of instructions, the transfer of intelligence materials and information or who perform similar services;
- Informants-residents [*saradnici-rezidenti*], who are reliable and specially trained citizens of the SFRJ who pursuant to instructions from the SDB manage a certain number of informants and contacts of the SDB abroad;
- Informants for the performance of especially sensitive operations [*posebno osjetljive operacije*] abroad.[155]

The last category of informants was the only one that was not more specifically explained in the instructions, hinting enticingly at the nature of such operations.

In the case of informants who resided in the countries in which operations were taking place, it was important to avoid blowing their cover. For this reason, it was strongly recommended that meetings between Udba agents and their informants take place in third countries, i.e. in a country other than the country of residence of the informant. Often, two Udba agents would travel to such meetings, with one of them charged with exercising countersurveillance measures before, during and after the other agent's meeting with the informant. This was done to ensure that foreign police and intelligence services – or in the case of émigrés, other émigrés – were not monitoring the informant or the agent in an attempt to identify informants and disrupt the operation. Although Udba personnel were embedded in Yugoslav consulates and embassies and could provide operational assistance if necessary, the goal was to avoid contact between informants and diplomatic personnel as much as possible. Needless to say, all contacts – whether between agents and informants, or between informants and their targets – were to be realized as innocuously as possible in order to avoid raising anyone's suspicion. The exploitation of family gatherings, cultural and sporting events, business meetings and other similar opportunities was therefore advised.

One section of the instructions dealt specifically with the financing of the work of the Udba abroad. It was emphasized that the expenditures had to be both rational and proportionally related to the desired goal of the operation. Insofar as possible, all reimbursements of expenses were to be made in dinars, a possible recognition of the constraints imposed by the Yugoslav economy. In case any economic gain was accrued by agents or informants during operations abroad, the SSUP SDB would decide on the disposal of these gains.

The instructions on the work of the special surveillance unit (1968)

In March 1968 the Third Sector of the SSUP SDB established a 'special working unit of the State Security Service for Surveillance Activities Abroad' and issued instructions regarding the work of this unit.[156] Of course, the SDB had been carrying out surveillance operations abroad for over two decades at that point, which had been carried out by 'especially verified employees from the border areas or by employees on temporary stays abroad'.[157] These employees predominantly hailed from Slovenia and Croatia. The SSUP SDB concluded that their work to date had not been bad, but that 'more complicated tasks with respect to [intelligence] centres and tasks' required better capacities for surveillance.[158]

The new surveillance unit was small, consisting of a mere thirteen members. It was to be deployed initially in Italy, Austria and in West Germany, as those areas were those 'where the State Security Service most actively monitors the activities of foreign intelligence services and the hostile portion of the emigration'.[159] For geographical reasons, the unit was to be placed in Ljubljana and would constitute an operational unit of the Slovenian State Security Service (SDV). The work of the special unit would be regulated by the SSUP SDB rulebook as well as a set of instructions regarding counterintelligence work abroad.[160]

According to the proposed regulations of the special unit for surveillance abroad, the group would officially be known as 'Group A'. It would perform tasks for both the SSUP SDB and for the republican state security services. The SSUP SDB emphasized that the work of the new special unit could only be successfully carried out if the republican state security services worked seamlessly together with the SSUP SDB. The ambit of the tasks which would be performed by the unit was as follows:

1. Surveillance of agents of foreign intelligence services and hostile émigrés;
2. Identification and observation of buildings of significance for counterintelligence;
3. Identification and verification of the location of points and centres used by foreign intelligence services and the identification of their agents;
4. Supplying of contacts of SDB operatives;
5. Verification through surveillance of SDB operatives, above all of those who are active as double agents;
6. Participation in the implementation of special operations.[161]

Only the chief of the SSUP SDB could issue permission for the use of Group A, and the permission was valid only for one specific task at a time. If there were competing, simultaneous proposals for the use of Group A, the chief of the SSUP SDB decided which operation would receive priority. Every proposal for the use of Group A had to include a plan describing how the proposed operation would be executed. The chief of the SDV in Slovenia had to approve this plan. If the plan did not pass muster, it could be postponed. The chief of the SSUP SDB and the Third Sector of the SSUP had to be updated constantly about all operations, both proposed and approved. After the completion of an operation, the leader of Group A had to submit a report about the operation in triplicate, with copies going to the SSUP SDP, the initiator of the operation and the SDV. Group A maintained an internal diary regarding its work.

The members of Group A stemmed from both the ranks of the SSUP SDB and those of the republican state security services. A successfully admitted member of Group A could serve for up to four years in the group. The members of the group were to maintain total confidentiality about their activities and about the existence of the group, even within their respective state security service.

It is worth emphasizing that a chronological coincidence exists between the establishment of Group A and the acceleration of assassinations of émigrés by the SDB.

According to the reconstruction of the Croatian SDS composed by Perković and Gabriš, within the Second Administration of the federal Udba in the 1980s, there existed

> a group for so-called special operations [*grupa za takozvano specijalno djelovanje*]. This group planned and carried out on its own various operations abroad and in doing so made use of their own group of agents [*agentura*]. They carried out psychological operations of intimidation, harassment and disinformation, fabricated various kinds of publicity material including the forgery of certain editions of some émigré newspapers, planned and organized burglaries of the headquarters of émigré headquarters in order to remove documents, and according to certain indications the group also organized the physical liquidation of individuals.[162]

Perković and Gabriš do not provide any name for this, but their description of it matches to a significant extent the official description of 'Group A.' It can therefore not be excluded that they are talking about this group. However, it should also be noted that certain activities described here correspond to those described by Božidar Spasić, who worked as an operative in the Second Administration of the federal Udba, and who will be mentioned later.[163]

A draft document on the functions of the SSUP SDB prepared at the end of 1971 specifically identified the extent to which the federal Udba played a role in operations targeting the emigration.[164] Among other things, the federal Udba held authority over decisions relating to:

- the use of technical equipment outside Yugoslavia;
- the use of surveillance outside Yugoslavia;
- the dissemination of information and disinformation;
- the dispatching of operatives or double agents abroad;
- the use of members of foreign intelligence services or political institutions;
- the planning and execution of 'special operations' (*specijalne akcije*) abroad;
- the use of a special encrypted communications system known as 'System 1100'.[165]

However, suggestions included in the draft document revealed that some republican or provincial SDBs wanted to limit the purview of the SSUP SDB to the more extreme or even to only the explicitly terrorist portion of the Yugoslav diaspora (*diverzantsko-teroristički element emigracije*).[166] A central register of intelligence related to the émigrés was maintained at the SSUP SDB with contributions from all subordinate services, the SID and the military services. This was done in accordance with criteria delineated by the SSUP SDB.[167]

> The point of departure is the assumption that republican and provincial SDBs analyse the activity of their own national groups of the hostile part of the emigration, the activity of the emigration on the territory of the respective republic or province (and the activity of the emigration in the press and other public publications), as well as operational undertakings and actions.[168]

In other words, the Croatian SDS was primarily responsible for those (ethnic Croat and Serb) émigrés who stemmed from Croatia, and had to monitor the activities and publications of émigrés towards Croatia. Bosnian Croat émigrés, by contrast, would be primarily the responsibility of the SDB in Bosnia and Herzegovina. (However, if they as in many cases had emigrated after spending considerable periods of time in Croatia, the SDS might be the main responsible agency.)

An additional document from 1975 confirms that the spirit of the 1971 document prevailed in the SDB.[169] On 1 August 1975, the SSUP adopted a new rulebook for the SDB. The legal and regulatory basis of the new rulebook was:

- Article 7, Paragraph 3 of the Law on the Implementation of Internal Affairs in the Jurisdiction of Federal Executive Organs (1971);
- Article 19, Paragraph 2 of the Law on the Foundations of the System of State Security (1974);
- the common Principles Regarding the Application of Means and Methods in the Implementation of Matters of State Security (1975);
- the Decision of the Federal Executive Council on the Matters of State Security, Which Are Implemented by Federal Organs (1975).

Article 2 of the rulebook made it clear that the work of the SDB in preventing anticonstitutional behaviour applied equally within and outside the borders of Yugoslavia. Article 9 confirmed that the federal SDB was responsible for approving operations outside of Yugoslavia, as well any operations affecting international actors or institutions in Yugoslavia. All hostile émigré activities were pursuant to Article 17 to be 'discovered, pursued, documented, analysed and prevented'. Article 19 offered a detailed description of relevant points in the SDB's work related to 'enemy and other subversive activity of the Yugoslav emigration against the SFRJ, its representations and citizens':

- enemy activity of émigré organizations, groups and individuals;
- preparations and the execution of sabotage or terrorist activities in the country or abroad;
- plans and attempts to infiltrate groups and individuals in the country for the purpose of provoking, organizing and carrying out guerrilla activities or armed revolts, respectively, and the taking of measures to destroy such groups and individuals infiltrated with such intentions;
- connections and strongholds (*veze i uporišta*) in the country and the joining by Yugoslav citizens of such hostile organizations and groups;
- oral and written propagandistic activity of the emigration directed at the undermining or destruction of the constitutional order and insulting the international reputation of the SFRJ;
- undertakes psychological and other measures and actions directed towards disorganizing, complicating and pacifying carriers of such activities, as well as the timely disabling of sabotage, terrorist or other activities against the SFRJ.

Article 19 further stated that 'the State Security Service monitors and studies the methods and means of [émigré] activities, organizational structure, the manner of work, sources of financing, the interrelations and connections of émigré organizations and groups and their connections to intelligence and police services and institutions as well as with foreign citizens and political organs and organizations'. The third section of the rulebook dealt with the methods and means of the SDB, including preventive work, operational investigation, preliminary operational processing, operational processing, operational actions and the evaluation of operations. Together these categories constituted a life cycle of all operations both inside Yugoslavia and abroad.

Preventive work → operational research → preliminary operational processing → operational processing → operational control→ operations (*operativne akcije*) → operational assessment and evaluation

Preventive work (Article 34) 'included a mixture of operational and other security measures, which the state security service undertakes domestically and abroad in order to identify and prevent hostile activities in a timely manner'.

Operational investigations (Article 35) strove for an 'all-encompassing overview' of all potential risks to state security. It was confirmed that the leader of the SSUP SDB was responsible for authorizing investigations abroad. The same applied to operations abroad (Article 39). Creativity and improvization were necessary to counter the enemy, and therefore the SDB prided itself on its ability to devise 'operational combinations' (*operativne kombinacije*) which combined the various methods and means of the SDB in order to best obtain intelligence and disrupt and prevent enemy activity.[170] Yet again, the head of the SSUP SDB had to approve all applications for the use of surveillance or searches abroad.[171]

The rulebook's description of the difference between preliminary operational processing and actual operational processing left something to be desired. Operational processing (Article 37) was undertaken if justified suspicion existed that a hostile activity was imminent. Preliminary operational processing (Article 36) designated measures which were utilized when the suspicion arose that a hostile activity might be planned. However, operational processing could be applied to émigrés and their organizations, as well as to other foreign actors, even when justifiable suspicion of their involvement in hostile activities did not yet exist.

During operations, the relevant case officer was responsible for maintaining an 'operational diary' (*operativni dnevnik*) as part of an operational dossier.[172] According to available templates of such diaries, all 'information about undertaken operational and operational-technical measures and about the results of these measures' was to be properly logged. The dossier for the operation contained an overview of all persons who were being processed in connection with the operation, relevant persons in contact with the aforementioned persons, a chronology of events and relevant supporting documentation.[173]

Operational control (Article 38) was directed towards those persons who had in the past attracted the interest of the SDB and been duly registered. Operational control could be applied permanently or temporarily and was designed to provide insight into the activities of these people.

The analysis and evaluation of concluded operations (Article 40) were an important constituent element of the work of the SDB. Such analyses permitted all those employees involved in an operation to take stock of the outcome of the operation, evaluate mistakes or missed opportunities, as well as other lessons learned. It was understood that if the SDB were to continue to improve the efficiency and success of its operations, this step was crucial.

The 1979 rulebook on the work of the State Security Service abroad

On 28 December 1979, Franjo Herljević, the federal Secretary for Internal Affairs, promulgated a rulebook regulating the work of the SDB outside of Yugoslavia.[174] This rulebook, which was classified as a state secret, represents the single most detailed document of its kind that has hitherto emerged from the archives of the former Yugoslavia. All SDS employees directly involved with operations abroad were obliged to read and abide by the rulebook, while other employees were to be acquainted with existence of the rulebook and its contents strictly on a 'need-to-know' basis. The contents of the rulebook had been agreed upon among all the secretariats for internal affairs in Yugoslavia, and it took effect on 1 January 1980.

In the first section of the rulebook, the foundation of the SDB's work was reiterated, including the direction of this work by the executive state organs and in particular the directives and strategic guidelines issued by the Federal Council for the Protection of the Constitutional Order. After emphasizing the significance of the legality of the work of the SDB and its links to the protection of the existing constitutional order, 'the basic principles of work' for operations were presented. The targets of the work of the SDB abroad were the 'countries, territories, groups, individuals and other places and areas' whence hostile activities emerged. The danger which such activities represented for Yugoslavia, its citizens and interests, was assessed to be a long-term and continuous security threat. All activities of the SDB abroad were to be planned on the basis of careful analysis and evaluation of the overall security situation.

Preparations for work abroad had to be 'comprehensive' and worked out in appropriate operational units or teams, always under the supervision and with the approval of the SSUP SDB. The list of preparations identified in the rulebook underlined the incredible complexity and risks posed by these most sensitive operations:

> the task which must be carried out; an evaluation of the justifiability and operational possibilities for implementation; the manner of implementation; the utility and efficacy of specific measures or actions, respectively; the phases of implementation; the forms of protection of the broader interests of the SFRJ and of the methods, means and capabilities of the State Security Service; the diversity of combinations and methods in the realization and variants of implementation; temporary security and political circumstances of the country in which the operation is carried out; the security of the participants; the manners, conditions and authorization of participants as regards the abandonment or modification of the implementation plan; the cover stories [*legende*] and their robustness; the system of communications between Yugoslavia and abroad; the use of written materials and technology; the level of risk; the economic feasibility and rationality; the types of measures which should be carried out in the course of certain operations; the consequences in the case of lapses and "blow-ups" [*padovi*], as well as the manner of extraction, concealment and camouflaging [*maskiranje i kamufliranje*] of our presence; the transfer across the border or "stealing" [*otudjivanje*] of materials and means when necessary; the role of informants and operational positions; the operational and broader exploitation of results and the number of participants and types of means which will be used (technology, etc.).[175]

The strict adherence to all of the above considerations and the approved plans was critical for the successful implementation of operations abroad. All levels of the SDB, from regional SDB centres within a republic or province up to the headquarters of the republican and provincial SDB centres, could be involved in planning, coordinating and executing operations abroad, always with the mandatory supervision and express permission of the SSUP SDB. In addition, the SSUP was specifically charged with carrying out special forms of analysis related to the particularly delicate nature of operations abroad. In the case of a crisis or war, the SDB could establish specific operational centres or points which would be exclusively responsible for dealing with work abroad. All data and information pertaining to all operations abroad were to be treated as a state secret. Even within the SDB, employees involved in such operations were permitted to discuss these operations only with their responsible superior officers and with those specific colleagues who were directly authorized to deal with these issues – the classic 'need-to-know basis'. The employees and informants involved also received the necessary technical equipment and financial assistance. The SDB obtained hard currency for operations abroad from the SSUP, and all expenditures had to be justified in advance and accounted for afterwards.

Needless to say, given the considerable risks that attached to operating outside of Yugoslavia, all operations had to be conducted covertly. The rulebook recommended exploiting all of the legal possibilities which the presence of Yugoslav citizens abroad afforded the SDB. Concretely, this meant that the SDB should avail itself not only of informants among Yugoslav workers and émigrés abroad, but also of Yugoslav diplomats, consular personnel, trade representatives, businessmen, tourists, short-term visitors, etc. Travel, meetings, international cooperation of all sorts – private, public, academic, scientific, cultural, business, even mixed marriages – could and should be exploited by the SDB.[176] The rulebook identified informants as the primary resource for the work of the SDB abroad. As has already been mentioned, all SDB employees involved in operations abroad received special training. Such training took place at various levels and locations within the SDB, and could also include supplementary training in conjunction with the military security and intelligence services and the SSIP SID.

The second section of the rulebook dealt with the basic tasks involved in operations abroad and with the types of information which were being collected. Here it was reemphasized that the overall goal was to establish, develop and exploit operational positions which should be located 'as deeply and directly as possible' in the 'hotspots [*žarišta*] of enemy activity'.[177] Hostile activities were defined as all acts aiming at the undermining or destruction of the 'self-managing socialist system, the independence, territorial integrity and non-aligned politics and security of the SFRJ'.[178]

The third section of the rulebook described the application of the means and measures at the disposal of the SDB when operating abroad. Essentially, these were the same means and measures which the SDB employed at home, with the main difference being the greatly increased risk of discovery and negative consequences for operations abroad. Employees were therefore reminded to be extra careful and responsible in executing such operations.

As noted in previous rulebooks and handbooks, the 1979 rulebook laid out various categories of informants that the SDB could use in its work. First, both foreign and Yugoslav informants could be used in the long term as informants embedded in target organizations and structures. In addition to them, there were double agents, residents, connections and, most intriguingly, 'informants (or operational connections or contacts) for special purposes', where 'special purposes' were defined as follows:

- the implementation of operations;
- the establishment of operational bases;
- covert surveillance;
- the recruitment of new informants;
- the creation of assault and special groups;
- the maintenance of dead drops and transmitters;
- the carrying out of courier services;
- the creation of illegal groups;
- the creation of illegal channels for the transfer of persons and materials across the border;
- the creation of joint pairs for various purposes;
- the carrying out of check and verification processes;
- investigation, observation, sketching and photography;
- the illegal embedding in an enemy environment or in a specific region, respectively, until the outbreak of a crisis or a war;
- the provision of different services related to the jurisdiction and activity of the SDB;
- the requisitioning of technical means and documentation, etc.

It is worth emphasizing that this list contained several vague and ambiguous terms. This was probably no coincidence, because such formulations gave operatives more flexibility in the field and afforded the SDB a broad ambit for the deployment of their operatives abroad. The use of euphemisms in the rulebook was also noteworthy. Terms such as 'special actions and other subtle operations' [*specijalne akcije i druge suptilne akcije*] or 'special tasks' [*specijalni zadaci*] left much to the imagination.[179]

A convincing cover story (*legenda*) had to be concocted to explain the informant's absence from work and travel. Recording or detailed note-taking during meetings with informants was discouraged, and informants were if at all possible not to carry any documentation or identification that might betray the purpose of their travel to such meetings. Needless to say, all informants were provided with pseudonyms, which would occasionally be changed. Every meeting with an informant had to be scrupulously organized and justified from an operational and financial point of view. If the informant travelled to Yugoslavia for personal or business reasons, such visits could be exploited in order to arrange convenient and inexpensive meetings.

SDB agents sent abroad had a duty to inform themselves as comprehensively as possible about the conditions (political, economic, cultural, etc.) in the country in which they would be operating. Agents typically travelled under false identities with officially produced fake passports provided to them by the SDB.[180] If their cover was blown the SDB obliged itself to organize their safe and expeditious extraction and return to Yugoslavia, including granting assistance to the agent and his family upon his return.

Communications with agents and informants abroad could take several different forms. If public communications systems such as telephones, telegrams and the post were used, all communications had to be encrypted. One-way transmitters, where the informant could only receive but not send messages to his or her handler in the SDB, were also employed. In some cases, communications were permitted to be passed through Yugoslav embassies and consulates or Yugoslav trade representations and companies abroad. However, such communications required the permission of the SSIP SID. Couriers were another option. In exceptional circumstances, 'chemical means for secret written communications,' e.g. invisible ink, could be employed. Indications also exist that the SDB developed proprietary systems of communications for their most trusted agents and informants.[181] As regards Yugoslav consulates and embassies, some information suggests that diplomatic personnel on occasion also furnished émigrés with weapons.[182]

Overall, it is worth emphasizing once again that as regarded SDB operations abroad every single deployment of agents or informants, every single communication with informants, and every single operational step and use of technical means and measures required the approval of the SSUP SDB. Notification regarding all operational changes, results and mishaps (such as the loss of cover by operatives or informants) had to be provided to the SSUP SDB immediately. Even after operations were terminated, the SDB was required to monitor still existing operational positions and analyse their reliability. And the location and activities of all former participants in 'special and other subtle operations' were to be verified from time to time.

The rulebook also dealt briefly with cooperation and coordination with the military security and intelligence services and with the SSIP SID. This section made it clear that interservice cooperation also covered operations abroad.

'Cooperation, coordination and synchronization of affairs are especially undertaken with the goal of avoiding irrationality in the creation, direction and placement of operational positions, as well as the duplication of work.' This cooperation, coordination and synchronization applied to all aspects of operations, and of course had to be coordinated through the SSUP SDB.

The final section of the rulebook treated the obligatory analysis of the work of the SDB abroad. The list of items to be analysed was exhaustive:

> the organization, leadership and personnel problems of the State Security Service; the possibilities, measures and solutions for work; the embeddedness, distribution, quality and possibilities of operational positions in relation to the organizers, sources and bearers of hostile activities towards the SFRJ in specific countries and regions; the work with operational positions; the system of communications with operational position; double agents; the cooperation and joint work with security services and security and intelligence organs of the armed forces of the SFRJ and the Federal Secretariat for Foreign Affairs; equipping and technical means; the training of personal and operational positions; material-financial problems; questions and problems of preparing and placing information and disinformation; special operations; residents and connections; 'blow-ups' [*padovi*], breakdowns and betrayals; the security-police apparatus and circumstances in foreign states from the perspective of possibilities for our work and the necessity of modifying methods.[183]

An appropriate unit within the SSUP SDB was charged with maintaining records related to operations abroad pursuant to a special set of instructions issued by the chief of the SSUP SDB.

The Institute of Security

Several of the seminal documents presented in this chapter make mention of the use of 'technical means and measures' by SDB agents and informants operating abroad. As with all other aspects of such operations, the use of these means and measures was tightly regulated and subject to the approval and continuous monitoring by the SSUP SDB. Codewords were used to refer to the use of the particular material or equipment utilized.[184] Upon the termination of operations, or when the technical equipment requisitioned for an operation was no longer needed, it had to be extracted, disposed of and/or returned to the SSUP SDB.

In order to better assist the SDB in the performance of its tasks both at home and abroad, the Institute of Security (*Institut bezbednosti*) was established in

1976 in Belgrade. This institute was responsible for all research, production, procurement and maintenance of technical equipment necessary for the work of both the regular police and the SDB.[185] Relatively little has been written about this institute, and not much documentation is available in the archives. The institute was without doubt also responsible for all equipment used by the SDB abroad, and the available documentation provides indications that the testing of weapons also could take place within the individual republics.[186]

Yugoslavia had its own producers of firearms, but the SSUP also ordered weapons from abroad. Some of this was done through companies such as Yuniversal Export, a shell company whose name seemed to have been borrowed from Ian Fleming's James Bond novels. In August 1982, a Walther PP pistol and a Walther PPK pistol were found at a rest stop on the highway between Stuttgart and Munich. It turned out that Walther PP pistol had been used in an assassination attempt against the Croat émigré Luka Kraljević. Given that Walther was a German company, the German authorities approached the company and were easily able to ascertain that the two guns had been sold to Yuniversal Export in October 1980. Yuniversal Export had purchased the weapons on behalf of the SSUP. The authorities then proceeded to ask their Yugoslav colleagues to trace the weapons. 'Pursuant to the query, the Yugoslav authorities stated that the weapons were stolen during the unrest in Kosovo during an attack on a police patrol.'[187]

2

Defining the Enemy: The Struggle against the 'Fascist Emigration' and the 'Enemy Emigration'

As the Second World War came to an end, tens of thousands of fascists and collaborators, particularly Croats from the territory of the Axis puppet Independent State of Croatia (*Nezavisna Država Hrvatska*, NDH), fled the coming communist takeover of power in Yugoslavia. They settled in many countries, from Argentina and Australia to Canada, Italy, Austria, West Germany and Sweden. Embittered and extremely hostile to socialist Yugoslavia, these émigrés refused to reconcile themselves to the new reality and dreamt of and planned for an eventual return to a 'free Croatia'. More than just their strong political opposition to the new order in Yugoslavia, many of the émigrés also carried the emotional trauma of having survived and in some case witnessed the mass executions of real and alleged collaborationists in the immediate postwar period, particularly at Bleiburg in Austria and multiple sites in Slovenia.[1] At the same time, many if not most of those who fled the collapsing so-called Independent State of Croatia either denied the massive and systematic crimes this state had perpetrated or saw nothing wrong with these crimes.[2] For the Croat political emigration, the dream of returning to an independent Croatian state functioned as the primary motivation for the four and a half decades of Yugoslavia's existence. Yet Tito already in May 1945 sternly proclaimed that those traitors and war criminals who had successfully fled abroad 'will never again see our beautiful mountains, our flowering fields. If this were to occur, then it would be for a very short time'.[3] Meanwhile, within early socialist Yugoslavia, Croat guerrillas calling themselves *križari* (crusaders) mounted an ultimately futile armed resistance against the imposition of communist rule.[4] The Yugoslav authorities took these threats to the new order extremely seriously, and by March 1946 at the latest had compiled a list of 'prominent figures of the Yugoslav political emigration'.[5]

As I have already stated in the introduction, it is not my intention to provide a detailed history of Yugoslav or even Croat political émigrés, as to do so would fill an entire separate book. Instead, this chapter will frame and summarize the lasting struggle between the socialist Yugoslav state and the political emigration, highlighting major events and watershed moments in this history. It deserves mentioning that both official Yugoslavia sources and émigré sources (and authors in Croatia after 1991) referred to a 'war' between the Yugoslav state and the émigrés. Thus, Josip Jurčević in his introduction to Bože Vukušić's book writes that the intensity and variety of means which the Yugoslav state applied against the Croat emigration is the reason why that activity can best be denoted with the term '*war against the Croat emigration*.'[6] Vukušić himself used the word 'war' in the titles of two of his books, referring to a 'secret war of the Udba' against the Croat emigration, and to the extreme emigration's 'war before the war,' depicting the 1991–1995 'Homeland War' as a sequel to the war that had occurred between 1945 and 1991. And in the sparse international historiography, Alexandar Clarkson writes of how 'militant Croatian nationalists and the Yugoslav state began to fight a proxy war on German territory'.[7] As we shall see, although the émigrés and their opponents in the Yugoslav State Security Service disagreed about virtually everything, they all shared a belief that they were engaged in a war for the future of Yugoslavia and Croatia.

Present from the outset, the antagonism between the émigrés and the Yugoslav State Security Service took many shapes. Their protracted duel was fought out not only in Yugoslavia but also in Yugoslav embassies and companies, and in the streets and buildings of far-flung cities and villages where émigrés had settled and plotted – or in the eyes of the Yugoslav authorities appeared to conspire – against the Yugoslav state. Eventually, the most extreme and proactive émigrés began to engage in political demonstrations and violent attacks on Yugoslav consulates, embassies and companies around the world. The Yugoslav state, in turn, unleashed the Yugoslav State Security Service on the émigrés with deadly results. It is the cyclical nature of this violence and the modalities of the Yugoslav State Security's operations that are the main focus of this book.

The hostile emigration

The key terms used by Yugoslav officials to label the emigration were '*neprijateljska emigracija*' (enemy or hostile emigration) and '*fašistička emigracija*' (fascist emigration). Indeed, the latter term remained in official use until the middle of the 1980s.[8] In his standard textbook used to instruct Yugoslav State Security Service employees, Obren Z. Đorđević described the two categories as follows:

> As the **fascist emigration** are understood members of émigré organizations whose goals are the creation of a fascist regime, or who engage in sabotage-terrorist activity as a means of political struggle. Émigré organizations which engage themselves against the existing constitutional order in our country, and who in doing so make use of non-violent means of political struggle, are designated as the **extreme emigration**. A **political émigré** is a person whose status as such is recognized, or who has the status of a refugee, and who does not belong to fascist or extreme émigré organizations. That means that the given émigré does not participate in any form of subversive activity against our country, and would not have to answer to our authorities if he were to come to Yugoslavia.[9]

As regarded the Croat emigration specifically, Đorđević believed that 'the common trait and goal of all Croat émigré organizations are the struggle against the socioeconomic and political system in the SFRJ, or the destruction of the Yugoslav state as a whole [*razbijanje jugoslovenske državne celine*], respectively'.[10]

While the fervent hopes of the Croat émigrés for, and the most paranoid fears of the Yugoslav leadership of, a full-fledged NATO attack on Yugoslavia with émigré support never materialized, the track record of the émigrés provided plenty of legitimate reason for concern. According to Mate Nikola Tokić, 'In total, anti-Yugoslav Croats committed on average one act of terror every five weeks world-wide between 1962 and 1983', and Western intelligence services would belatedly come to share the concerns of the Yugoslav party-state regarding the terrorist inclinations of the most extreme Croat émigrés.[11] Indeed, Tokić convincingly argues that the terrorism perpetrated by the second generation of Croat émigrés who left Yugoslavia only in the 1960s emerged from their frustration with the failure of the mostly Ustaša émigrés who had emigrated immediately after the Second World War. Disappointed that no major military East-West conflagration – and hence no invasion of communist Yugoslavia – had emerged, younger émigrés increasingly took matters into their own hands. The rapprochement between Yugoslavia and the West pursuant to the 1948 Tito-Stalin split only further served to frustrate the émigrés.

The history of the Yugoslav emigration after the Second World War is best understood in phases. As noted already, during the immediate postwar period a very large number of persons left Yugoslavia, primarily for ideological reasons and the fear of violent reprisals. The already very complicated and controversial historiographical discussions about the numbers and identities of victims in the Second World War in Yugoslavia, as well as the chaotic nature of the immediate postwar period and the expulsions of Italians, Germans and other minorities, make it difficult to state precisely how many people actually ended up emigrating from Yugoslavia. However, Ivo Goldstein cites estimates that approximately 200,000 people emigrated or were deported from Croatia.[12] Vladimir Žerjavić, the leading Yugoslav demographer, observed that the statistics on emigration from Croatia for the period from 1948 to 1991 were not reliable, and that therefore only estimates were possible, arriving at an estimation of 77,000 Croats emigrating from Yugoslavia for the period from 1948 to 1961.[13]

Without a doubt, the largest number of émigré Croats and what would become the most active émigré community were located in West Germany. Mate Nikola Tokić cites a West German estimate that up to one-fifth of the émigrés who fled from 'Croatian lands' immediately after the war had been members of the Ustaša.[14] The consensus among researchers seems to be that West German statistics regarding both Yugoslavs in general and Croats more specifically are spotty for the first postwar decades, but Alexander Clarkson cites a figure of 13,000 Croats who 'decided to stay in West Germany for personal or political reasons' immediately after the war.[15]

At least in the short-term, the Yugoslav communists were probably not sad to see large numbers of potential political opponents flee the country. After all, the (in)voluntary departure of fascists, other anti-communist forces and their sympathizers could only facilitate the consolidation of communist rule.[16] Yet the communists did regret that they were unable to apprehend Ante Pavelić and other leaders of the NDH, whom they regarded as particularly notorious war criminals.[17] For ideological reasons, Western governments of the era remained mostly resistant to the Yugoslav government's requests for the extradition of thousands of individuals suspected of war crimes.[18] For example, the Yugoslav authorities for decades tried to persuade the United States to extradite Andrija Artuković, a former NDH minister of justice and internal affairs. The original failure of the Artuković extradition – he was finally and belatedly extradited to Yugoslavia in 1986 – may only have fuelled Yugoslavia's suspicion that legal means were unlikely to succeed in high-profile cases.[19] Yet the perceived risk to former top NDH officials was substantial enough that most of them left Europe by the end of the 1940s for safer locations overseas. Therefore, the nascent Yugoslav State Security Service already at the outset targeted the most wanted fugitives, and the hunt for them influenced the later operations against the political emigration. Importantly, the first socialist Yugoslav code of criminal procedure enacted in August 1945 'specifically ordained that the commission of a crime [against the Yugoslav state] abroad could not confer impunity (the principle of universality)'.[20] And Article 92 of the 1966 Yugoslav federal criminal code specified that the penal provisions for political crimes in the criminal code also applied to persons who committed these crimes outside Yugoslavia.[21]

For obvious reasons, these first Yugoslav émigrés were defined by the regime as being 'counterrevolutionary' and 'fascist' with hostile intentions towards the Yugoslav state. The NDH had, of course, objectively been a fascist state, and one did not need to be a Yugoslav communist to conclude that those who viewed the NDH favourably were bitterly hostile to communist Yugoslavia.[22] Indeed, even as a large portion of the political and military leadership of the NDH made its way to long-term exile in countries like Argentina and Spain, a small number of NDH officials remained in Yugoslavia's neighbouring countries or returned to Yugoslavia in an attempt to foment armed uprisings.

Božidar Kavran was one of these officials. In 1948, he, with alleged approval from the former leader – *Poglavnik* – of the NDH Ante Pavelić, led an operation called 10 April (*Akcija 10. travnja*). 10 April had been the day of the proclamation of the NDH in 1941, and the new operation naively and prematurely attempted to topple communist rule in Yugoslavia. Informally called 'Kavran's operation', it ended as a fiasco with the arrest and execution of its leaders. The Yugoslav security forces mounted a successful counterinsurgency operation, Operation Guardian (*Operacija Gvardijan*).[23] Kavran's failure led the surviving NDH leaders to abandon further attempts at armed insurrection, as they instead placed their hopes and faith in a future Western invasion of Yugoslavia. While small groups of Crusaders continued to mount armed resistance well in the 1950s, their efforts were increasingly futile and sporadic, and many of the Crusaders were shot in armed skirmishes or upon capture.[24]

From this point onwards, most of those émigrés who had fled from Yugoslavia in the immediate aftermath of the war prioritized political solutions while still holding out hope for a general conflagration that would lead to the collapse of Yugoslavia. According to Mate Nikola Tokić, a 'general deradicalization of Croatian émigré separatism' took place, 'even if both the aims and rhetoric of the postwar movement remained as radical as ever'.[25] The actual use of violent means in the struggle for Croatian independence would reemerge only in the 1960s among a younger generation of émigrés.

In the meantime, once safely ensconced far away from Yugoslavia, the émigrés often proved very diligent in expressing and disseminating their political views. They wrote books and pamphlets, and they also quickly established their own journals. Given the total defeat of fascism and its thorough discrediting because of the Holocaust and other mass atrocities throughout Europe and the world, many of the émigrés realized that they needed to at least superficially distance themselves from the most explicit form of fascism. Instead, they emphasized their fervent anti-communist views, which made them much more palatable to countries in the West as the Cold War commenced. With the founding of the North Atlantic Treaty Organization (NATO) in 1949, the newfound ideological affinity between the émigrés and their host countries also sparked the fear in Yugoslavia that the alliance would organize and deploy the émigrés as special forces in future military attacks against Yugoslavia.

In addition to writing tirelessly in support of the creation of an independent Croatian state, the first generation of the political émigrés founded several political organizations in order to structure their work. Not surprisingly, given the geographical dispersion of the Croat diaspora and internal rivalries among leading émigrés, numerous organizations came to exist. In Argentina, Ante Pavelić established the Croatian State-Forming Party (*Hrvatska državotvorna stranka*, HDS) and also recreated the Croatian Armed Forces (*Hrvatske oružane snage*, HOS), which had originally been created in 1944. Although the HDS flopped, Pavelić remained a factor to be reckoned with in the emigration until his death in 1959.

Several other notable émigré leaders besides Pavelić emerged after the Second World War. The notorious Vjekoslav Luburić, who had overseen the concentration camps of the NDH and earned a reputation for particular brutality and fanaticism, obtained refuge in Franco's Spain. The defeat of the NDH had not lessened Luburić's extremism, and he styled himself as the 'General of the Drina' (*General Drinjanin*), playing an important role in the postwar operations of the *križari*. Luburić remained nominally allied with Pavelić, but tensions existed between the two, as Luburić suspected that Pavelić was straying from the Ustaša methodology and was no longer capable of being an effective leader.[26] The historic meeting in Buenos Aires in June 1954 between Pavelić and the former Yugoslav Prime Minister Milan Stojadinović – a Serb – confirmed Luburić's fears.[27] Among Pavelić's unforgivable sins in Luburić's eyes was negotiating a future division of Bosnia and Herzegovina between Croatia and Serbia. Luburić continued to maintain that Bosnia and Herzegovina belonged exclusively to Croatia. Towards the end of 1955, Luburić established the Croatian National Resistance (*Otpor – Hrvatski narodni otpor*, HNO) at the very time when Pavelić had been weakened by the fall of Juan Perón in Argentina. This organization had a specifically armed element known as 'Drina', after the river which forms part of the border between Serbia and Bosnia and Herzegovina.[28]

Luburić minced no words when describing his intentions regarding Yugoslavia. 'Our position is clear: Overthrow every Yugoslavia. Overthrow it together with Russians and Americans, with communists, with non-communists and with anti-communists. Overthrow it together with anyone who is trying to overthrow it. Overthrow it by means of verbal dialectic and dynamite, but overthrow it, for if there is one country without the right to exist, that can only be Yugoslavia.'[29]

The atrocious record of the NDH as well as widespread distaste for the manner in which Pavelić and his associates had absconded to far-flung hideouts after the war while expropriating the ill-begotten assets of the NDH created room for other political factions.[30] These supported Croatian independence but distanced themselves from the NDH leadership. Branko Jelić, who had represented the NDH in Germany but had been detained by the British during the war, emerged as 'the most serious contender' to replace Pavelić as the leader of the Croat political emigration.[31] Jelić had already become an important player among Croat political émigrés in the interwar period. Originally a supporter of Pavelić, Jelić was detained by the British in 1940 and spent the war in Gibraltar and on the Isle of Man. His internment allowed him to emerge with his reputation relatively unscathed. In October 1950, Jelić established the Croatian National Committee (*Hrvatski narodni odbor*, HNO), which would go on to become one of the major émigré organizations. 'The HNO was conceived of as an umbrella organization that would coordinate the efforts of all those working for Croatian independence, regardless of political affiliation.'[32] Yet Jelić, having learned the lessons of his wartime internment, disavowed those who openly advocated either fascism or communism, even as the HNO retained the goal of an independent Croatia 'within its complete ethnic and historical territory'.[33]

Finally, another important actor in the Croat emigration was Ivo Oršanić, who in 1951 established the Croatian Republican Party (*Hrvatska republikanska stranka*, HRS) in Argentina. Oršanić and the HRS supported Croatian independence and saw themselves as the legitimate political heirs of Ante Starčević, the nineteenth-century ideologue for Croatian statehood.[34] Unlike some other leading figures in the Croat emigration, Oršanić did not espouse violent means to attain his desired goals.

The *Gastarbeiter* and the Émigrés

In contrast to the first, primarily political phase, the driving factor for most members of the much larger and longer-lasting second phase of migration, which began in the 1950s and extended into the 1970s, was economics. Initially informally and even illegally, and later with official permission, tens of thousands of Yugoslavs sought better economic prospects abroad. Economic emigration from the South Slavic lands dated well back into the nineteenth century, but transportation and the increasingly intertwined nature of the global economy gave extra impetus to this process.

Like other communist countries, Yugoslavia had during its early Stalinist phase taken a very dim view of emigration. Travel outside of Yugoslavia had been very strictly restricted, and those attempting to across the border illegally risked being shot on sight. Nonetheless, thousands did flee, for both political and economic reasons. However, at the end of the 1950s and particularly starting in 1962, the Yugoslav authorities in cooperation with Western European governments facilitated the placement of Yugoslav workers in factories in countries like West Germany, France, Austria, Switzerland and Sweden. As the famous German word designating these workers – *Gastarbeiter*, or *Gastarbajteri* in Serbo-Croatian – suggested, these employees were initially viewed both by Yugoslavia and the host countries as temporary guest workers.[35] Croats were disproportionately represented among the *Gastarbeiter*.[36] The general assumption was that, having spent a few years working and accumulating savings in Western Europe, they would eventually return to Yugoslavia. Of course, events transpired quite differently, and many tens of thousands of Yugoslavs ended up staying permanently in Western Europe. In 1971, the SSIP counted approximately 551,000 Yugoslav *Gastarbeiter* abroad.[37] According to William Zimmerman, who calls the *Gastarbeiter* 'the seventh [Yugoslav] republic', the number of *Gastarbeiter* in 1977 was twice the population of the smallest republic, Montenegro.[38]

As mentioned previously, West Germany hosted the largest number of Yugoslavs and because of its postwar *Wirtschaftswunder* – the economic miracle – the country also attracted the largest number of *Gastarbeiter*. Their arrival caused an exponential increase in the number of Yugoslavs. Alexander Clarkson estimates that whereas there were approximately 30,000 Yugoslavs (of which perhaps 13,000 were Croats) in West Germany in the early 1960s, about 280,000 Yugoslavs were counted in 1973 and over 600,000 by 1989.[39] Of these perhaps one-third were Croats. By contrast, Christopher Molnar cites more official figures which do not take into account illegal immigrants. According to Molnar, 'in 1960 there were 8,800 Yugoslav labor migrants in [West Germany]; in 1968 there were 119,100; and by 1973 they reached a peak of 535,000', or approximately 700,000 if dependents are included.[40] The Yugoslavs were until the early 1970s the largest group of *Gastarbeiter* in West Germany before being eclipsed thereafter by Turks.

It must be briefly noted that a certain segment of present-day Croatian publicists and public opinion insist on portraying the second, economic wave of migration as a specifically Croatian 'tragedy', or even as a sinister attempt to shift the demographic balance in Yugoslavia in favour of the Serbs. Although there were undoubtedly many Croats who left in the 1960s and 1970s out of a mixture of economic need and political dissatisfaction, claims by Bože Vukušić and others that a 'second Bleiburg' occurred starting in the early 1960s are hyperbolic and decontexualized silliness.[41] Moreover, such rhetoric represents a continuation of the nationalist myth of a Croat nation eternally bedevilled and martyred by Serbs – and after 1945 by 'Serbo-Yugo communists', a myth that was of course nurtured by many Croat émigrés.[42] Nor is there any indication that the Yugoslav State Security Service systematically regarded *all* Croat émigrés as extremists or enemies of the state, as some latter-day Croat historians have claimed.[43] Even in 1972, which as will be seen was arguably the peak of the Udba's concern about Croat émigré extremism, the Udba maintained dossiers on about approximately one thousand émigrés.[44] Conversely, it must be emphasized that the vast majority of Croats (and émigré Yugoslavs of other ethnicities) were not particularly interested in political extremism. For many of them, the trials and tribulations of the *Gastarbeiter* existence were exhausting enough and for a wide variety of reasons they shied away – consciously or unconsciously – from engagement with political engagement, especially of a radical or extreme nature.

From the very outset of the economic migration phase, the Yugoslav authorities exhibited concern about the risk that the *Gastarbeiter* would become contaminated by the political emigration and/or by the intelligence services of Western countries. Given the already stated fear that NATO countries were in effect 'weaponizing' the most extreme émigrés, it was a logically related concern that the *Gastarbeiter* might also be recruited by the intelligence services of these countries. And, in practice, Yugoslav citizens who applied for political asylum were subjected to extensive debriefings by members of Western intelligence agencies in refugee camps such as the one at Zirndorf near Nuremberg or Traiskirchen near Vienna.[45] In addition, the already established émigrés invested great effort in recruiting newly arrived persons from Yugoslavia, including using 'blackmail, extortion, and even bodily harm' against new arrivals.[46] Thus, near Essen 'a former Ustaša lieutenant and ally of Pavelić oversaw a system of … so-called "Croatian Divisions." These divisions trained at weekends in preparation for the "coming conflict" against socialist Yugoslavia.'[47] Paradoxically, the West German authorities in the 1950s were – notwithstanding the 1948 Tito-Stalin split – extremely concerned that the *Gastarbeiter* were the vanguard of a communist revolution. Christopher A. Molnar cites fears of an 'infiltration of potential communism-infected Tito workers' in 1955.[48] The West German authorities also viewed with suspicion the efforts of Yugoslav diplomatic and consular personnel to nurture the loyalty and identity of the *Gastarbeiter* towards the Yugoslav state and ideology through associations and cultural work.[49]

The growing number of émigrés and their political activity required new bureaucratic structures. In January 1955, the Third Department of the Croatian branch of the Yugoslav State Security Service issued instructions regarding the necessity of better organizing the available intelligence on both economic and political migrants.[50] The instructions also pertained to persons repatriating to Yugoslavia and to the relatives in Yugoslavia of émigrés. Two years later, a desk (*referat*) was created within the Second Administration of the SSUP SDB for the purpose of monitoring the activities of émigrés.[51] This desk was specifically charged with the monitoring of émigrés in Western Europe, because the (political) émigrés in Eastern Europe and the Soviet Union – predominantly supporters of the 1948 Cominform Resolution – posed qualitatively different challenges.[52]

In 1962, Yugoslavia proclaimed a general amnesty, which resulted in the return of numerous émigrés, but also sought to effect the distancing of moderate and apolitical émigrés from the more extreme elements in their midst.[53] The amnesty offered those who had illegally left Yugoslavia, regardless of whether they had done so for economic, political or other reasons, a chance to return or to regularize their status as emigrants. However, those persons who had fought in the armed forces of occupying powers during the Second World War or for the quisling forces including the Ustaša movement were not encompassed by the amnesty.[54]

In the early 1960s, the federal organs of internal affairs began to develop more systematic and detailed forms of documentation for those Yugoslav émigrés who 'engage in hostile activities towards the FNRJ, as well as those for whom some operational interest exists'.[55] At the end of 1961 and beginning of 1962, the Federal State Secretariat for Internal Affairs issued instructions regarding the establishment and maintenance of centralized documentation of the Yugoslav emigration.[56] Available documentation shows that the SSUP maintained standardized questionnaires for émigrés in a sort of giant database, with the Eighth Administration of the Federal State Security Service responsible for maintaining accurate records. Each questionnaire listed which organizational unit of the State Security Service was primarily responsible for a particular émigré.[57] These questionnaires were very extensive in nature, including forty-five separate fields that were to be completed, of which many contained subfields. In addition to the standard biographical information and data on the geographical movements of the émigré, there were fields provided for the political activity of the émigré, political views, level of estimated influence and participation in espionage, terrorism and propaganda. The final two fields in the questionnaire asked for an analytical evaluation of the 'overall political attitude of the emigrant' towards Yugoslavia and whether 'an operational interest' existed and, if so, 'with which service'.

Three categories of emigres were envisaged by the instructions circulated to create a centralized database of émigrés.[58] The first category comprised those to whom admission to Yugoslavia was to be denied. The second category consisted of those individuals against whom no operational activities could be undertaken without the permission of those authorities who had asked for these individuals to be included in the database. This included all informants as well as those émigrés under current operational treatment. The final category encompassed those émigrés whose requests (for passports, consular assistance, etc.) could be granted, but with notification given to the proper authorities.

In 1970, the Slovenian State Security Service, the SDV, estimated that there were approximately 230,000 émigrés, of whom approximately 120,000 had fled from Yugoslavia at the end of the Second World War.[59] Almost 50 per cent of the émigrés were Croats, who in the estimation of the State Security Service for the most part supported the establishment of an independent Croatian state.[60] From the perspective of the Yugoslav authorities, many émigrés had acted consistently and continuously in a hostile manner, and this hostility justified the vigilance and proactive stance of the Yugoslav State Security Service towards the émigrés.[61] Conversely, both Croats in Yugoslavia and in the diaspora correctly suspected the Yugoslav State Security Service of recruiting Croats as informants both at home and abroad in order to monitor the activities of the more politically active émigrés.[62] Meanwhile, Savka Dabčević-Kučar, the president of the Central Committee of the SKH, stated at a meeting in March 1971 that 'we have 400,000 workers from Croatia abroad. And we regard them as our ambassadors in those countries, and not as the booty of the hostile emigration. And we want our [diplomatic and consular] representations to act accordingly towards these people.'[63]

In February 1973, the members of the SFRJ Presidency examined security issues related to Yugoslav *Gastarbeiter*. In their conclusions, they emphasized the need to protect 'our workers from all forms of hostile activity of foreign intelligence services and the extreme emigration'.[64] *Gastarbeiter* were, 'very frequently, exposed to the pressure of reactionary circles and intelligence services, blackmail by the hostile emigration as well as systematic enemy propaganda against our country'.[65] By contrast, more should be done to ensure that migrant workers remembered to support the solidification of 'the full mutual solidarity of our workers, equality, [and] brotherhood and unity of our peoples'.[66] Efforts on this front were to be coordinated by the SSUP and the SSIP, and more broadly by the SKJ. The concerns expressed in these conclusions from 1973 remained relevant until near the end of the existence of socialist Yugoslavia.

The further political evolution of the Croat emigration

During the first two and a half decades of Yugoslavia's existence, those operations of the Yugoslav State Security Service employing armed force outside Yugoslavia primarily targeted those individuals who were alleged to have been major war criminals. Indicative was the attempted assassination of the *Poglavnik* of the NDH, Ante Pavelić, in an attack in Argentina in April 1957. Pavelić was wounded by the assailant but survived.[67] After that attack, Pavelić relocated first to Chile and then moved to Spain, where he died in 1959, in part as a consequence of the wounds suffered during the attack. As a condition of receiving sanctuary in Franco's Spain, Pavelić had to promise to withdraw from all political activity.[68]

Prior to his death, Pavelić had in 1956 founded the Croatian Liberation Movement (*Hrvatski oslobodilački pokret*, HOP), whose irredentist goal was to reestablish a Croatian state covering the entire 'historical and ethnic territory between the Mura, Drava, Danube, Drina and the Adriatic Sea'.[69] The HOP replaced the HDS, which had remained moribund since its founding. Although it was regarded by the CIA as 'the most radical Croat émigré organization', as long as Pavelić was alive, the HOP did not engage in any violent activities.[70] Pavelić claimed that the time for doing so was not ripe, and that the reestablishment of a Croatian state would have to take place with Western support. With the establishment of the HOP, Pavelić succeeded in staunching the flow of support away from himself and towards Luburić and Jelić. Yet at the same time, Pavelić was never completely able to surmount his serious credibility problems in the West because of the atrocious record of the NDH, and the rapprochement between Tito and the West had created new challenges.[71] The HOP was according to Vukušić until 1974 the largest

Croat émigré organization, and it existed until the establishment of Croatian independence in 1991.[72]

After Pavelić's death, a number of émigrés including Stjepan Hefer, Rafo Medić, Srećko Pšeničnik and others vied to take control of the HOP, with Hefer proving successful. However, Luburić also continued to assert himself as the rightful heir to the NDH and to appeal to those émigrés who had been disappointed by Pavelić's disavowal of armed struggle. By contrast as the new head of the HOP, Hefer stayed Pavelić's course.[73] According to Mate Nikola Tokić, already by the mid-1950s, younger Croat émigrés had come to regard Luburić 'as the only leader capable of continuing the uncompromising struggle for Croatian independence'.[74] Unlike Luburić, whose fate will be discussed below, the Yugoslav State Security Service seems to have targeted neither Hefer nor Pšeničnik for assassination.

The cycle of violence accelerates

Mate Nikola Tokić has demonstrated that the younger generation of émigrés – whom he calls semi-émigrés – turned to violence as a means to surmount their frustration with what they viewed as the meagre fruits of the older generation's political strategy.[75] In the course of the second half of the 1960s and the first half of the 1970s, the increase in violent attacks of a terrorist nature inspired the Yugoslav authorities to consider reprisal operations, and also operations of a preventative nature against extreme émigrés.

Indicative of the new trend was the Croatian Revolutionary Brotherhood (*Hrvatsko revolucionarno bratstvo*, HRB), which was formed in 1961 in Australia by four émigrés – Jure Marić, Geza Pašti, Ilija Tolić and Josip Oblak.[76] That same year, Croat émigrés in Munich created what they called Secret Revolutionary Ustaša Formations (*Tajne revolucionarne ustaške postrojbe*, TRUP), as a splinter of the HOP.[77]

Geza Pašti, the leader of the HRB, was born in 1934 in Čepin near Osijek.[78] He was apparently a restive young man who as a teenager enrolled in secondary school came into contact with nationalist classmates who formed an illegal nationalist organization in 1950.[79] Although the first organization was quickly discovered and disbanded by the Yugoslav authorities, who also prosecuted some of the members of the organization, Pašti founded his own organization 'Young Croatia' (*Mlada Hrvatska*) in 1952. This organization, as well, only existed briefly before the authorities uncovered it and prosecuted its members.

Pašti, however, evaded arrest and succeeded in fleeing to Italy in January 1953 before then subsequently moving on to Australia, all the while broadening his network of contacts with émigré organizations. This trajectory was quite typical for a number of émigrés who would later become prominent.

The founders of the HRB were strongly dissatisfied with the lack of progress made towards achieving Croatian independence. They believed that it was quixotic to believe that the West would assist Croatia, particularly given that the West had since 1948 normalized its relations with Tito's Yugoslavia. As Mate Nikola Tokić expresses it, the founders of the HRB and their subsequent members and supporters had divined 'the simple, if painful, truth ... that the Croatian nation was not – and never would be – a consideration in global politics'.[80]

Therefore, the situation called for a new strategy in which Croats relied upon themselves and took matters into their own hands. The use of conspiratorial and even illegal means had to be included, including in the countries which hosted the emigration. Most importantly of all, armed violence was to be included actively in the arsenal of the emigration if they were to make any progress towards independence.[81] The 'Basic Principles' of the HRB referred specifically to the use of 'all available means, including the use of weapons in order to achieve the final goal'.[82]

In 1962, Pašti produced a handbook on guerrilla and sabotage activities entitled 'Freedom or Death' (*Sloboda ili smrt*). Already in July 1963, Tolić and Oblak led a sabotage group into Yugoslavia.[83] After very limited success in carrying out sabotage against their planned targets, all nine members of the group were arrested within two weeks of infiltrating the country. All of them were sentenced to prison sentences of between six and fourteen years. Two subsequent attempts by HRB members at infiltration and sabotage also ended unsuccessfully, ensuring only that the HRB now occupied a prominent and permanent place on the Yugoslav State Security Service's radar.[84]

For Pašti himself, it would appear that the HRB's aggressive approach would have fatal consequences. Although not part of the HRB's ill-fated missions, he returned to Europe from Australia in July 1963.[85] The fact that Pašti was not among those who infiltrated into Yugoslavia that summer – he apparently got as close as Trieste but did not enter Yugoslavia – caused other members of the HRB to suspect him of betraying the group to the Yugoslav authorities. In order to rid himself of this suspicion, Pašti worked on planning a new mission that would lead to sabotage actions in Yugoslavia and also pondered the possible assassination of top Yugoslav officials like Aleksandar Ranković. In the meantime, Pašti spent some time in prison in West Germany in the second half of 1963 and the beginning of 1964. After a prolonged period in which he peripatetically circulated in émigré circles across Western Europe (West Germany, France, Sweden, Switzerland, Italy and Spain), allegedly with the purpose of establishing and training terrorist cells, Pašti ended up in Nice in France. From Nice, Pašti made an excursion to Spain with fellow émigré Marijan Šimundić to meet Maks Luburić. This visit turned out to be a serious disappointment, as their idol regarded the two young émigrés as immature and suggested instead that Pašti enrol in the university at Madrid.[86] After completing a university education Pašti could according to Luburić – perhaps – aspire to a role in émigré activities. One can only imagine how frustrating this message would have been to Pašti, who had already been involved in planning sabotage operations and was by all accounts both zealous and ambitious.

It should be emphasized that during all the years that Pašti spent abroad, the Yugoslav State Security Service availed itself of various measures to monitor and counteract him and his activities – 'towards the goal of disruption, pacification and positive influence'.[87] Pašti's acquaintances and relatives back in Yugoslavia were under various levels of surveillance, their postal correspondence was controlled and intercepted and they were frequently contacted by the police or by the SDB inquiring about their knowledge of Pašti's whereabouts. Informants were also recruited from among his acquaintances.

At some point in 1965, Pašti disappeared without a trace, and was considered by the émigrés to have been a victim of the Yugoslav State Security Service. Bože Vukušić, based on the statement of Ivan Ćurak, who was the chief of the SDB Centre Doboj, alleges that Pašti was kidnapped and brought to Yugoslavia, where he was interrogated, tortured and murdered by the SSUP SDB.[88] In an operational diary of SDB Centre Osijek from January 1965 regarding Pašti, the possibility of physical liquidation is indeed mentioned.[89] Specifically, the following points were among those listed in the 'processing plan' (*plan obrade*) for Pašti: 'Work towards the goal of liquidation abroad, or capture upon arrival to the country. …. Through suitable informants place compromising material about Geza in the ranks of the emigration with the goal of provoking a reaction [leading] to his physical liquidation.'[90]

The SDB's plan for exploiting divisions in the HRB certainly did not lack basis. As has already been mentioned, Pašti had as early as 1963 been suspected by other émigrés of having betrayed the groups infiltrated into Yugoslavia. After his imprisonment in West Germany, Pašti also faced restrictions on his movements, which meant that Šimundić had to handle some of the training and operations of the HRB. They also disagreed vociferously about strategy and goals. According to an SDB informant, Pašti had wanted to assassinate Tito during his visit to East Berlin, while Šimundić wanted to target someone else. Generally speaking, Šimundić wanted to launch spontaneous attacks, where Pašti put more weight on preparation. The informant described how both gathered mutually opposing cliques within the HRB, with tensions growing.

> Geza intends to remove Šimundić from [his] leading position in the HRB. He does not say how he will accomplish this. Their intolerance has grown to the point that they are threatening to kill each other. Šimundić calls Geza a coward who has fallen under the influence of [other émigrés Franjo] Pavičić and [Mirko] Škrinjarić, while Geza says that Šimundić is tied to the American or German intelligence service, whence he draws financial means.[91]

In provoking a potentially fatal settling of accounts in the HRB, the SDB evidently would have found abundantly fertile soil.

Despite this rivalry and the statement of Ćurak, conclusive evidence regarding the killing of Pašti remains elusive. According to a West German federal police report from February 1967, Pašti had at the end of August 1965 disappeared without a trace from his hotel in Nice, leaving his belongings behind. His friends assumed that he had been killed or kidnapped by the SDB.[92] Yet the SDB operational diary for Pašti shows that as of 3 August 1966, well over a year after Pašti's disappearance, the SDB continued to make plans regarding him, including again 'liquidation abroad or capture upon arrival to the country'.[93] On 3 August 1966, the State Security section of the police in Osijek repeated that the desired goal was 'liquidation abroad or arrest upon an eventual arrival to Yugoslavia'.[94] On 8 August 1966, the same section listed Pašti's location as unknown, noting that he had left France in the second half of 1965 in an 'unknown direction', and citing unconfirmed rumours that he had returned to Australia.[95] And as late as October 1966, the SDB sought to obtain information from Pašti's father about him.[96] According to one source at the time, Pašti had 'simply disappeared from Europe. He is located in the Republic of South Africa and is not in contact with anyone.'[97] Another source claimed that Pašti had gone underground and had sought refuge with Vjekoslav Luburić in Spain.[98] Although the Yugoslav State Security Service never explicitly even in its own top secret documentation admitted responsibility for the assassination of any émigrés, there is no reason why the Udba would have kept trying to ascertain the whereabouts of Pašti had they actually killed him. That having been said, one must allow for the possibility that some employees of the Udba, including those writing this report, were not privy to the fact or details regarding his demise.

In the meantime, the Australian authorities looked in vain for confirmation of Pašti's violent death, about which they had heard rumours.[99] They learned that Pašti had been declared persona non grata by West Germany and had left the country 'voluntarily' instead of serving a seven-month prison sentence on charges of possessing firearms illegally and membership in a secret organization.[100] In January 1965, the Canadian Department of External Affairs forwarded to Canberra information, provided by the German authorities, that Pašti belonged to the HRB. 'He has within this organisation been appointed to special duties in a leading staff and had, obviously been sent to Germany to prepare acts of terror in order to do away with the Yugoslav Regime.'[101] Therefore, the Australian authorities sought to deport Pašti and, when they received information later in 1965, suggesting that he had been arrested by the French authorities, the Australians sought to strip him of his Australian passport. Moreover, the Australian authorities had determined that the HRB was a 'terrorist organization' and furthermore expressed dismay that the Croats had violated the trust and faith of Australia. Citing an intercepted communication among HRB members, 'Australia has realised that those who adopted Australian nationality did not do so for sentimental reasons but because it facilitated leaving the country whenever they wished.'[102]

The strange trajectory of Pašti's close associate Josip Senić is also worth examining. Like Pašti, Senić had immigrated to Australia and become a member of the HRB. According to the Australian Security Intelligence Organisation (ASIO), Senić 'assumed command of the HRB in Europe' after Pašti's disappearance.[103] Senić had in secondary school in Yugoslavia in the 1950s become active in an illegal Croat nationalist movement, leading to his arrest in March 1956.[104] He served six months in prison, and then went to Pula, whence he emigrated to Italy and then on to Australia in 1959.[105] After the failed HRB mission to infiltrate Yugoslavia in 1963, the Yugoslav State Security Service obtained information from the captured HRB members that Senić had in March 1963 'trained terrorists for the execution of sabotage missions'.[106]

Almost as soon as he was naturalized as an Australian citizen, Senić applied for a passport. He declared that his intent was to travel as a businessman to the United States, but that he also wanted to visit relatives in Europe. The Australian authorities, having heard about the HRB and Senić's membership in it, were reluctant to issue a passport. Their suspicion of his intentions was heightened by their knowledge that the HRB had recently sent nine Australian Croats to Yugoslavia on the aforementioned sabotage missions. In August 1964, the Commonwealth Police cited indications that Senić 'ran explosive and mine handling courses at [the] Croatian Welfare Centre' prior to the departure of the participants in these missions.[107] The New South Wales police wrote, 'It is submitted that because of SENIC's [*sic*] background, and in view of the previous activities of Members of the Brotherhood whilst overseas, a high level policy may be required as to whether or not he should be prevented from leaving the country.'[108] The Australian authorities were keen to avoid any further such 'embarrassments'. In the event, therefore, Senić received a passport that was only valid for travel to the United States.

Senić reacted angrily to this decision, protesting that 'due to my political ignorance, [I] assisted Croats in their struggle against communist tyranny, while I was not myself [a] member of any political organisation'.[109] Yet a search of his premises in September 1964 uncovered documents about guerrilla warfare inspired by Che Guevara and Mao – somewhat ironically given Senić's fervent anti-communism – which Senić admitted to writing.[110] Rubbing salt into his wound, the US authorities, having received adverse information from their Australian colleagues, refused to issue a visa. Hence Senić was stuck with a passport that was for all intents and purposes useless. Senić felt that he had exchanged Yugoslav for Australian oppression, writing 'Am I a slave of tyranny from which I suffered since early adulthood … or am I free among free men in a free count[r]y, so that I can voice my opinion, or am I among cowards who are afraid even of their own shadow?'[111] Senić tried in vain to abandon Australian citizenship.

Feeling stuck, Senić resorted to illegal means, apparently at some point in late 1964 obtaining an illegal passport and stowing away on a ship sailing for Italy. In July 1965, the Australian Embassy in West Germany received an anonymous letter, sent from Monaco, from 'one real and true friend' advising that Senić was now in Stuttgart and was in the possession of 'plastic bombs and explosives because he wants to destroy some Yugoslav consulate'.[112] By September 1965, the Australian authorities had decided that 'it was beyond reasonable doubt that Mr. Senić has linked up in Europe with Geza Pašti for the purpose of engaging in the undesirable activities which formed the ground for the cancellation of the latter's Australian passport'.[113]

In the meantime, the Yugoslav consulate in Munich had also received an anonymous letter – also sent from Monaco – stating that Senić was in West Germany, had recently met with Pašti and intended to murder the Yugoslav consul in Munich.[114] Moreover, the killing of the Yugoslav consular officer Sava Milovanović in Stuttgart on 30 August 1966 by Franjo Goreta, a member of the HRB, had caused the West German police to increase their vigilance regarding the HRB.[115] Goreta had come to West Germany in 1962 as a *Gastarbeiter* and had earlier in Yugoslavia been a boxer, with Josip Senić as a coach.[116] Goreta had a criminal record, but he received an official certification of a clean record based on an assurance that he would cooperate with the Yugoslav State Security Service. In July 1966, Goreta and an émigré named Božidar Konjević met with two agents of the Udba in Karlsruhe, who tasked them with the killing of three other émigrés, one of whom was Senić. The reward for doing so was 2,000 German marks. However, Goreta reported this offer to the West German police.[117] Meanwhile, the West German police arrested Senić on 6 August 1966 and sentenced him to three months in prison for membership in a secret organization – the HRB – and for illegal possession of a firearm.[118] Senić was released on 26 August 1966 on the condition that he leave West Germany within twenty-four hours, which he apparently failed to do.

Playing a double game, Goreta had two days earlier met with Milovanović, who provided Goreta with a gun and ammunition for the agreed-upon task. On the same day, Goreta handed the gun over to the police in Stuttgart.[119] At a second meeting, on 30 August, Goreta shot and killed Milovanović in the Hofbräukeller in Stuttgart after Milovanović had allegedly threatened Goreta's family if Goreta were to refuse to follow through on the killings. Goreta claimed not to have planned the killing or to have carried it out on the orders of the HRB. The following year, Goreta was sentenced to eight years in prison, of which he served approximately six.[120] He was himself subsequently the subject of an assassination attempt.

The Yugoslav State Security Service later obtained information that Goreta had received the task of killing Milovanović from Senić.[121] According to the DSIP SID, Goreta and Senić had met in Karlsruhe on 1 May 1966.[122] Strangely, Goreta himself shortly thereafter voluntarily approached the Yugoslav consulate in Munich and informed them that he had been recruited into the HRB.[123] Goreta also subsequently provided the police in Zagreb with information concerning Senić. Indications are that Goreta in the weeks and months leading up to his decision to kill Milovanović had been vacillating between extremism and cooperation with the Yugoslav authorities. As of early June, Goreta was reported to be in a 'difficult psychological state', having experienced legal and existential problems in West Germany and having left his wife.[124]

By the spring of 1967, the SDS Centre in Osijek had compiled a quite comprehensive portrait of the hostile activities of Senić. In particular, there could be no doubt that he played a leading – if not the leading – role in the HRB. The SDS Centre assessed that, given Senić's location in Australia, it would be difficult to pressure him, and disappointment was expressed with the insufficient results of the work on his case to date. The stated intent was clear: 'The goal of the [operational] processing is the liquidation of Senić or his eventual capture upon arrival to the country.'[125] This formulation was identical to that used for Senić's predecessor, Geza Pašti, back in January 1965. In Senić's case, the case officer was even more concrete in his formulation of what was to be done, specifying that 'towards the goal of liquidating Senić work towards locating [him], respectively selecting the most suitable individual and preparing him for such an operation; secure the necessary financial means for the execution of the planned [redacted?]'.

Meanwhile, also as in the case of Pašti, the Australian authorities now attempted to ascertain the whereabouts of Senić. In the summer of 1966, they received notification that Senić had been involved in a car accident in Verona, Italy. Firearms were found in the vehicle.[126] Senić then apparently left for West Germany, but was also expelled from that country. Afterwards, he absconded to Sweden, whence he was finally deported upon Australia's request back to his new 'homeland', despite the mutual antagonism existing between the two.[127] Barely back in Australia, and notwithstanding his legal travails, Senić reapplied for a new passport. Yet in September 1967, based on his behaviour hitherto, the application was rejected.[128] Surprisingly, after Senić told the Commonwealth Police 'that he has learned his lesson and he would do nothing to embarrass the Australian Government', it was recommended that he receive a 'Document of Identity'.[129] This document would enable him to travel but would have him to seek a visa from each country to which he travelled.[130]

It is not clear whether Senić actually received the document, but he continued to press in the coming years for a regular, unrestricted passport, even as he persisted in illegal activities. Senić was suspected of participating in the bombing of the Yugoslav consulate in Sydney in June 1969 and was 'as deeply involved as ever with the Croatian extremist organisations in Australia'.[131] Senić himself confessed that he was 'so hopelessly involved in world Croatian activities that, even if he wished to, he could not divorce himself from them'.[132] In September 1970, SDS Centre Split received information that Senić was transforming the HRB into the Croatian Revolutionary Youth (*Hrvatska revolucionarna mladež*, HRM). He allegedly moved in the constant company of bodyguards, had trained in martial arts and was preparing to travel to Europe to meet with Branko Jelić.[133]

In the meantime, the SDS continued to display a keen interest in Senić. On the one hand, the SDS considered establishing contact with Senić, perhaps to dissuade him from further hostile activities. But in May 1969 after a meeting in Osijek attended by Srećko Šimurina of the republican SDS regarding operational-technical means to be applied towards Senić, the following was noted in his operational diary located in Senić's SDS dossier:

> Basic task: liquidation as the only correct measure. To that end work on finding suitable persons in the country and Australia. The possibility of the connection 'Friend' [*Prijatelj*] is being considered. Therefore resume written contact because of the verification of the address. If he responds, then in a suitable form send him messages as to how we are interested that Senić's hostile conduct be stopped completely. We are ready to receive him most nicely and to ensure a pleasant stay. Undertake all other measures towards that goal.[134]

On 2 March 1971, the SDS put together an operational plan for 1971 for Senić.[135] From the operational diary, it is clear that the SDS for years employed a number of informants and kept a close eye not only on Senić's activities abroad, but also on his communications with his family and on their own attitudes towards him.[136] All of this was standard operating procedure. According to the entries for 10 November and 17 December 1969, at least two émigrés who came from Australia to Yugoslavia on personal visits offered the SDS to assist in the 'liquidation' of extreme émigrés, probably including Senić.[137] One of them specifically stated that 'it would be enough to mention an amount, e.g. 5,000 dollars, and we would not have to worry further'. The other emphasized that he personally was not ready to kill anyone, but 'money can buy anything', so someone would be found to do the job. 'This was reported to the chief', who agreed to keep in touch with the émigré who had made this offer. The other émigré appeared ready to do the job for free and personally. However, his background as a gambler and 'adventurist' who also happened to be the brother of a high-ranking official in the DSIP made it necessary to think the offer over at some further length. Another émigré had already in June 1967 offered to 'settle accounts' with Senić either directly or by contracting the job out to professional criminals. The émigré told the SDS that he merely had to send a message that the person in question was "'seriously ill, he needs to be treated immediately and be hospitalized." This would be the signal that [redacted] needs to liquidated.'[138]

It is worth pausing here to consider the terminology used in the SDS's documentation. As we have seen, the term 'liquidation' (*likvidacija*) was specifically and explicitly used to describe the possible goal of the SDS's operational processing of both Pašti and Senić. Yet the SDS's dossier on Senić shows that a shift away from this term took place. Whereas the operational diary noted the offers of other émigrés to liquidate Senić, the operational plan for Senić for 1970 stated that the goal of the operational processing was the 'carrying out of a special task' (*izvođenje/izvršenje specijalnog zadatka*).[139] Given that one of the two émigrés who had earlier offered to kill Senić was mentioned as a candidate for carrying out the 'special task', the only possible logical conclusion is that the term 'special task' had been adopted as a euphemism for the previous, explicit term 'liquidation'. The operational plan noted that the émigré had volunteered to perform the 'special task'. The case officer regarded the émigré as an 'adventurist' and as a suitable candidate for the job. The émigré was leaving for West Germany, 'and he would be checked over thoroughly during six months and in the end an assessment would be made if he is suited for carrying out the special task'. However, the case officer also noted that the physical distance of Senić and 'other objective difficulties significantly complicate the successful course of the processing'.

Illustrating that the objectives and terminology in the 1970 operational plan were no aberration, the plan for the following year reiterated the objective: 'Directly related to the goal of the processing – the carrying out of the special task – work on locating a suitable person for the carrying out of this task.'[140] An evaluation of the suitability of the aforementioned émigré was still pending.

It is not clear exactly what happened thereafter, but at some point Senić seems to have illegally left Australia a second time, probably in the autumn of 1970, making his way to West Germany.[141] In the spring of 1971, the SDS received reports of Senić traveling to both the United States and France; he allegedly met with a prominent émigré named Bruno Bušić in Paris.[142] The final entry in the operational diary was 23 March 1971. In August 1971, SDS Centre Split reported that Senić had been spotted in Sweden but was currently located somewhere in West Germany.[143] During his stay in Sweden, Senić had expressed particular interest in who had planned the raid on the Yugoslav embassy in Stockholm, which had cost the Yugoslav ambassador his life.[144] Senić was also reportedly interested in visiting Yugoslavia covertly in order to assess the situation there with his own eyes; he seemed to be less predisposed to 'the roughest operations' than earlier. The following month, the SDS Centre Split received information indicating that Senić might instead be in France, and SDS informants were asked to help identify his precise location.[145] Senić kept moving, however, and was already at the beginning of October back in Sweden.[146]

Josip Senić was assassinated on 9 March 1972 near Heidelberg.[147] In an official note from SDS Centre Osijek dated 18 April 1972, it was reported that the news of his death had reached his native village on 17 March. Bizarrely, Senić's father for some reason told people that his son had been killed by lions in a zoo somewhere in West Germany. Other versions told by relatives were that he had been shot in the back at an émigré demonstration or, 'closest to the truth,' had been found dead in a hotel room in Mannheim. According to the SDS Centre in Osijek, 'it appears that it was a conflict of opposing émigré groups in the ranks of the extremists of the HRB'.[148] At the very least, the phrase 'closest to the truth' indicated that the author of that report possessed precise information regarding the actual killing of Senić. On the main information sheet for Senić filed with SDS Centre Osijek, under 'reasons for cessation of [operational] processing', the following was drily stated: 'On 9–10 March 1972, in Heidelberg, Federal Republic of Germany, Josip Senić was killed in a settling of accounts of extreme émigrés of the HRB, and thus the reasons for carrying out the processing ceased.'[149] In an émigré magazine, Senić was remembered as a 'Croat revolutionary' who had been killed by 'agents of the Yugoslav Udba'. The magazine proclaimed that 'nothing will be able to stop the Croatian revolution! From the blood of Josip Senić new Senićes will be born, and if tomorrow one Croat revolutionary falls, five new ones will take his place'.[150]

The assassination of Vjekoslav 'Maks' Luburić

Before concluding this chapter, it is necessary to return briefly to the end of the 1960s and to Vjekoslav 'Maks' Luburić. After the death of Ante Pavelić in 1959, Luburić was, both despite and because of his disagreements with Pavelić, one of the premier Croat émigrés. As we have seen, young HRB members idolized Luburić and saw him as an inspiration for the continuation of the armed struggle for an independent Croatian state.

As seen earlier, as when Geza Pašti and Marijan Šimundić visited him, Luburić was notably wary of his admirers and lived in constant fear – expectation even – of assassination. And he did not only fear the Yugoslav State Security Service. After the Mossad's kidnapping of the leading SS official Adolf Eichmann, Luburić also had to consider the possibility that the Israelis might come hunting for him as well.[151] Indeed, the Australian authorities later cited six unsuccessful attempts at assassinating Luburić.[152]

In the end, however, Luburić did not prove vigilant enough. In September 1967, a young Bosnian Croat named Ilija Stanić arrived at Luburić's Spanish estate in Carcaixent, not far south of Valencia.[153] Stanić was the son of Jozo Stanić, who had fought for Luburić. Stanić's initial stay at Luburić's home was brief and tumultuous, and ended with Luburić expelling Stanić. He went to Paris but then returned to Spain, where Luburić made the fateful decision of accepting him back into the fold.

The subsequent events are, notwithstanding some concerns regarding the provenance of the relevant sources, worth recounting in detail. Namely, the publicist Bože Vukušić through his contacts in Sarajevo and Belgrade later came into possession of 'the original tape recording of Ilija Stanić, the Udba's killer under the pseudonym *Mungos* [Mongoose], which he gave to Mićo Japundža, agent of the Sarajevo Udba in the headquarters of the Sarajevo Udba, on 30 April 1969, ten days after the murder of Luburić in Spain'.[154]

In the period between Stanić's return to Spain and the murder, he had worked as a sort of assistant for Luburić. Then in mid-April 1969, Stanić met with a courier from the Yugoslav State Security Service, who brought Stanić some kind of poisonous material in the form of a thick powder. The plan was for Stanić to place this powder in Luburić's coffee. However, when Stanić did this, the poison did not have the desired effect on its intended victim, but rather merely made him feel ill. Therefore, Stanić instead decided to bludgeon Luburić with a metal rod, then forsook this for an axe. Yet after having hit Luburić with the axe, causing him to collapse, Stanić to his considerable astonishment saw Luburić rise. This recurred even after another direct blow to the head with the axe. Stanić then resumed bludgeoning Luburić with the metal rod, finally culminating in Luburić's death.

Having accomplished his mission, Stanić took a taxi to Valencia, whence he fled to Yugoslavia. Thus concluded the only Yugoslav State Security Service assassination for which direct positive testimony from the actual perpetrator has been identified. According to Vukušić, Stanić was in Belgrade amply rewarded with an apartment, a car and a monthly allowance. Allegedly, however, all of this did not prove sufficient in Stanić's opinion, and he became a nuisance to his handlers.

In 1972, the CIA in a brief on Croat émigré activity wrote that Luburić had been killed in an 'émigré feud'.[155] Had their colleagues in the Yugoslav State Security Service been able to read this brief, they would have been quite content to read this conclusion. From the point of view of the Yugoslavs, the most desirable outcome of every assassination was for it to appear, at least in the eyes of Western governments and their intelligence services, as the result of an internal settling of accounts in émigré circles. But the CIA was also correct in another respect, noting that 'the Yugoslav Intelligence Services and the ustashi [*sic*] emigres have already engaged in a gangland-style fight in Munich and in Spain over an eight-month period in late 1968 and early 1969. Six lives were lost then; a similar gang war may thus lie ahead.'[156]

Conclusion

As will be further explored in the following chapter, the actions of the HRB in the 1960s made it abundantly clear for the Yugoslav State Security Service that this organization and other extremist elements in the Croat diaspora posed a profound threat to Yugoslavia's security. In addition to the incursions mentioned above, the HRB was also linked to the attacks on the Yugoslav consular officials Andrija Klarić in June 1965 and the aforementioned killing of Sava Milovanović in August 1966. And in May and July 1968, explosive devices killed one and injured numerous people when they were set off at Belgrade's train station and in a Belgrade movie theatre.[157] There were incidents elsewhere as well, including multiple attacks against Yugoslav embassies, consulates and the offices of companies such as the Yugoslav national airline, JAT. One of the most notorious was the brazen attack by two Croats, Miro Barešić and Anđelko Brajković, on the Yugoslav embassy in Sweden in April 1971, apparently launched in part to avenge the killing of Vjekoslav Luburić. The Yugoslav ambassador Vladimir Rolović – himself like many Yugoslav diplomats a former employee of the Yugoslav State Security Service – was killed in the course of the attack. And shortly after the arrest and conviction of Barešić and Brajković, three other Croat terrorists kidnapped a Scandinavian Airlines flight and successfully demanded the release of several jailed Croats, including the convicted duo.[158] At the outset of 1972, a bomb exploded aboard a JAT flight from Copenhagen to Belgrade as it was flying over Czechoslovakia; on the very same day, a bomb also exploded on a train travelling between Belgrade and Ljubljana. In the aftermath of these attacks, the CIA did not mince words, writing that 'these terrorists mean business', and their assessment was definitely shared by their colleagues in Yugoslavia.[159]

At the same time, the bitter internal rivalries that emerged in the Croat emigration in the course of the 1950s and 1960s provided a golden opportunity for the Yugoslav State Security Service. Mate Nikola Tokić notes that the 'situation so degenerated that competing groups even drew up liquidation lists for members of rival émigré organizations'.[160] For the Yugoslav State Security Service, factionalism and chronic internal strife were among the most desirable outcomes for the Croat emigration. But the frequency and intensity of attacks perpetrated by extremist émigrés provoked Yugoslav reprisals. In 1972, this interrelationship would take a dramatic turn.

Agents, Infiltration and Surveillance: The Methods of the Yugoslav State Security Service in Émigré (Diaspora) Communities

This book's first chapter outlined the structure and the role of the Yugoslav State Security Service, and the chapter that followed provided an initial exploration of the 'war' between the Yugoslav State Security Service and Croat émigrés. In the pages that follow, we will take a break from the chronological approach and delve into the more specific rules and instructions that governed the actual operations of the Yugoslav State Security Service abroad.

Counterintelligence operations abroad

One of the most significant archival finds as regards the overall guidelines and considerations affecting the operations of the Yugoslav State Security Service abroad is a set of instructions for the counterintelligence work of the SDB abroad.[1] Although the document bears no date, based on the authorizing signature it can be assessed to be from the mandate of Federal Secretary for Internal Affairs Radovan Stijačić, which lasted from 18 May 1967 until 30 July 1971.

The guidelines described the work of the Yugoslav State Security Service abroad as a logical and constituent part of the effort to counter foreign intelligence services and the 'hostile emigration'. These threats were perceived to be intricately interrelated, not least because NATO members were (rightly) suspected of gathering intelligence from and recruiting émigrés as agents, and therefore fit logically together as part of the counterintelligence mandate. 'From abroad the organized activity of the hostile portion of the Yugoslav emigration evolves through certain organizations, groups and individuals, who in addition to politically propagandistic operations also organize and undertake terrorist operations against the SFRJ, its representatives and citizens abroad.'[2]

The guidelines emphasized, as did other later instructions, that the SSUP was responsible for all activities abroad in order to ensure efficiency, coordination and consistency in all operations.[3] Information about the work which the Yugoslav State Security Service performed abroad could be shared with other Yugoslav security and intelligence services (the UB SSNO, the Second Administration of the JNA General Staff and the SSIP UID), but this could only occur through the SSUP SDB.[4]

In addition to actual agents who were employees of the Yugoslav State Security Service, a healthy, reliable and carefully curated network of informants was a further prerequisite for successful operations abroad. The SSUP SDB could as needed provide forged passports and similar documents in order to facilitate the work of agents abroad.[5] The guidelines identified the following categories of informants abroad:

- informants embedded in sources of hostile activity;
- informants in 'double combinations' (i.e. double agents);
- informants with connections to sources of hostile activity;
- informants in positions of research, verification, observation and surveillance;
- informants operating as 'bases', supplying technical or other assistance to those carrying out tasks abroad;
- informants-connections;
- informants-residents;
- informants for the performance of especially sensitive operations abroad.[6]

The guidelines specified that detailed records should be maintained regarding all informants.[7] As regarded physical surveillance abroad, this could be performed either by agents or by trusted informants, but as always only with the express permission of the SSUP SDB. If a republican state security service was not capable of carrying out necessary surveillance operations abroad, then this task could be performed instead by the SSUP SDB.[8] It is worth emphasizing here that the final category was the only one of the above categories that was not more precisely described in the guidelines. In other words, no specification whatsoever was provided for what 'especially sensitive operations abroad' might entail.

For security reasons, all contacts with informants abroad had to be realized either when they visited Yugoslavia – vacations provided a suitable alibi – or a third country, i.e. a country other than the one in which the informant usually resided and worked.[9] Encounters in the country of residence were only permitted in exceptional circumstances. Thus, for example, in January 1967, the Udba met with their informant 'Djani' in Zurich, although Djani apparently resided in or near Cologne.[10] Counterintelligence measures were undertaken – in practice this meant that one operative met with the source while another performed countersurveillance, and it was noted that it seemed that the Swiss police had not observed the meeting between the informant and the operative. Every contact with informants abroad had to be justified and approved.[11]

Contacts between Yugoslav diplomatic and consular representatives and informants were also frowned upon.[12] Oral reports were to be preferred when obtaining information from informants, but encrypted reports or radio communications could also be utilized if the informants had received the necessary training and had sufficient experience.[13] Particularly trusted informants could with the permission of the SSUP SDB receive unidirectional radio transmissions.[14]

The guidelines further elaborated upon the use of various technical and chemical means abroad.[15] The republican secretary for internal affairs, having obtained the approval of the federal secretary, could authorize the utilization of 'fixed technical means and means for especially sensitive operations'.[16] Applications for 'the use of fixed technical means for covert listening, carrying out special operations, for photographic documentation and chemical means' had to include the following information:

- who (organizational unit, employee, informant) would use the [e.g. chemical] agents;
- the type of agents;
- the target person(s);
- the manner of the transportation and securing of the means across state borders;
- the time, place, conditions and manner of utilizing the means.[17]

A special code word existed for each chemical or biological agent that the Udba employed, and these code words had to be used whenever communicating in writing or orally about these agents.[18]

Financing operations abroad

Steven Spielberg's 2005 film *Munich* dramatically portrays the story of how the Israeli intelligence services hunted down the members of the Palestinian terror organization Black September. Early on in the film, a financial operations officer working for the Mossad carefully explains to the members of the assassination team that they will have access to ample amounts of cash which will be accessible to them in a Swiss bank account which will be replenished immediately once withdrawals from it are made. However, he strongly admonishes them; he needs to receive receipts documenting all expenditures.[19] Running agents and their informants in several Western European and other countries and engaging in various intelligence and counterintelligence operations did not come cheaply.

Although relatively little is known about the financial side of the Yugoslav State Security Service's operations abroad, the available documentation shows that agents requested and received funds from their supervisors. These funds of course had to be in hard currency in order to be usable outside of Yugoslavia, and could be used either directly for the operatives or to reward their informants or reimburse their expenditures. Documents testifying to these operational funds are relatively rare in archives, but a document from 1967 shows that SDS Centre Zagreb, the largest of the SDS centres in Zagreb, requested 9,000 US dollars for 1968.[20]

As will be described in more detail later, the Yugoslav State Security Service like many other intelligence services concealed some of its most sensitive operations behind euphemisms such as 'special operations' and 'special tasks'. Some insight into how the funding of such operations was regulated can be found in the 'Instructions on the Use of Means for Special Expenditures of the SDB in the SSUP' from April 1976.[21] According to these instructions, cash could be disbursed either in dinars or in hard currency for the following purposes:

1. operational work;
2. the remuneration and reimbursement of informants and operational connections;
3. the acquisition of special operational-technical means and equipment for special purposes abroad;
4. the training of informants and the specialization of operatives of the SDB for the implementation of certain tasks;
5. the reimbursement of expenses of operatives incurred in the course of protecting VIP's and delegations, operational contacts and meetings

with foreign security organs and the equipping of personnel for longer stays abroad;

6. the purchase, furnishing, maintenance and use of facilities for special purposes of the SDB.[22]

These activities pertained to the republican and provincial state security services as well as to the federal SDB. The Twelfth Administration of the SSUP SDB had the responsibility of coordinating all matters related to such expenditures.[23] Twice annually the republican and provincial state security services had to send a detailed report to the deputy secretary summarizing the expenditures for special tasks.[24]

A concrete example of the compensation of an informant can be found in the case of Milan Dorič, codenamed 'Hanzi'. In February 1975, the Slovenian SDV wrote:

> As regards the informant "Hanzi," who is acquainted with a broad circle of extremists, the dominant opinion is that he should be used for a specific operation aimed at an extremist known to him. He should then be called to the SFRJ, where he could be given financial means for the opening of a pub. It remains to be agreed against which extremist "Hanzi" should be directed.[25]

In extraordinary cases such as the one apparently described here for 'Hanzi' and for Ilija Stanić in the previous chapter, the informant could receive a one-time special assistance, such as 'the resolution of a problem of status, housing or other material problems for an informant who in the course of several years has successfully performed tasks for the security of the country'.[26] Such extraordinary compensation could be made on the recommendation of the undersecretary or a chief of an administration in the SSUP SDB or a comparable leader in the republican or provincial state security services.

Abduction, interrogation and prosecution: The case of Slobodan 'Bata' Todorović

The official documentation of the Yugoslav State Security Service describing the goals of its work and the means and methods over which it disposed in carrying out this work abroad leaves no doubt that the physical liquidation of the Yugoslav party-state's opponents through murder was a constituent part of the Service's arsenal. Yet as we shall see, there are numerous indications that killing was an absolute last resort, not least because of the high risk and potential cost that assassinations carried with them. Therefore, it is worth considering the fate of some of those émigrés who were instead abducted back to Yugoslavia.

Although there are several such cases, including among Croat émigrés – the case of the Jesuit priest Krunoslav Draganović being by far the most famous – this section will focus instead on the case of the Serb businessman Slobodan 'Bata' Todorović.[27] The choice of Todorović is in large part due to the fact that his case has been extensively detailed by the Slovene publicist Igor Omerza based on copious archival documentation from the SSUP SDB and the Slovenian SDB.[28] But summarizing Todorović's case also reminds us that while Croats may have overwhelmingly been the focus of the Yugoslav State Security Service, the strategies and tactics employed in principle applied to all émigrés who were identified by the party-state as 'extremists'. Perhaps the best reason for focusing on Todorović comes from a remark made by the SDS itself, which specifically referred to the Croat émigré Stjepan Đureković as a 'second Todorović'. Both were émigrés and businessmen suspected of economic crimes and treason, and both lived in Munich when their lives were violently interrupted by the Yugoslav State Security Service.[29] Indeed, there are indications that Đureković might have been slated for the same treatment meted out to Todorović, although this was in some ways only slightly less brutal than Đureković's murder.

Slobodan 'Bata' Todorović was a Serb businessman who left Yugoslavia legally in 1965. Prior to his departure from Yugoslavia, Todorović had among other jobs also worked for the Yugoslav State Security Service.[30] After the fall of the Yugoslav vice president and Tito's presumed heir to the throne Aleksandar Ranković in 1966, Todorović was suspected of being among those Serbs who continued to support Ranković.[31] He and others were the objects of an 'Operation X' conducted by the Yugoslav State Security Service, which had as its primary purpose the surveillance of all persons connected to Ranković.[32]

In the following years, the measures that the Yugoslav authorities took against Todorović escalated, betraying an extensive interest in his activities abroad. Precisely as in the later Đureković case, the civilian criminal police – the public security service – were also simultaneously investigating Todorović's alleged economic criminal activities.[33]

In November 1972, the Serbian SDB and the Slovenian SDV together with the SSUP SDB carried out Operation '*Vrh*' (Peak), whose goal was the secret surveillance of Todorović. The operation rapidly evolved further, as the organizers settled on the goal of his 'secret transfer' to Yugoslavia as the ultimate goal of their efforts.[34] Significantly, this 'secret transfer' was also described in a document of the Serbian SDB as an 'illegal transfer', indicating that the SDB was well aware that they were acting beyond the scope of the law.[35] The SDB and the SDV considered using Đorđe Anđelković, a business associate of Todorović, to organize his abduction.[36] This proposal was, however, not utilized, first because the criminals with whom Anđelković wanted to carry out the operation demanded a lot of money – approximately 1 million US dollars – and furthermore because Todorović for other reasons was not assessed to be available for abduction at that point in time.[37]

It is important to emphasize here that the strategy chosen in dealing with Todorović did not represent any kind of aberrant or maverick unilateral action by the Yugoslav State Security Service. For one thing, at least two republican services and the federal SDB were involved, completely in following with the valid guidelines regarding the work of the SDB on complex targets who were located abroad. Moreover, the party-state whose interests it was the primary job of the Yugoslav State Security Service to protect from domestic and foreign enemies was an integral participant in the decision-making process. In April 1974, the Extraordinary Commission of the Executive Bureau of the Presidency of the SKJ convened a session chaired by Jure Bilić. At the session, the participants discussed Operation '*Vrh*' and the aborted abduction of Todorović.[38] Among other things, the Federal Secretary for Internal Affairs Luka Banović was criticized for not being able to explain why the operation had not been successfully implemented. This led to a discussion of the conditions under which the state security services of the republics could be operationally active abroad.[39] The chief of the general staff Miloš Šumonja asked whether there were any rules for such operations since 1966, which prompted Slobodan Stević of the Serbian SDB to reply that operational measures abroad could only be carried out with the express permission of the SSUP.[40]

In May 1974, the senior management of the Slovenian and Serbian secretariats for internal affairs met in Belgrade in order to discuss the further development of operation '*Vrh*.'[41] A joint working group was established, and the decision was made to change the name of the operation to '*Magistrala*' (Highway). In addition, it was decided that the republican secretaries would henceforth report on the operation to the presidents of the presidencies of SR Serbia and SR Slovenia, the president of the Central Committee of the two republican leagues of communists, and to the federal secretaries for internal affairs and people's defence. Later in May, the working group decided that the code name for the operation would change once again, this time to 'Operation 55', and the name changed several times again thereafter, to 'Operation XY', 'Operation XX' and 'Operation *Jadran*' (Adriatic).[42]

Through its public agencies and diplomatic service, the Yugoslav authorities also took public steps against Todorović. His accounts in Yugoslavia were blocked, and Yugoslavia demanded his extradition from West Germany. Although this did not occur, the West German police did question Todorović in 1975.[43]

On 25 February 1975, the Yugoslav State Security Service finally acted and kidnapped Slobodan 'Bata' Todorović from Munich. The archives in Slovenia contain very detailed information about the operation, including sketches of the area of Munich where Todorović was located. Eight men participated directly in the abduction, while another seven handled the logistical and other aspects of the operation.[44] All were members of the Slovenian SDV, but as has been seen the Serbian SDB and the SSUP SDB had participated extensively in the larger operation aimed at neutralizing Todorović.

No more than two days later, on 27 February 1975, Todorović found himself in an apartment building in the centre of Ljubljana which had been rigged as an improvised illegal prison. At this point, Franjo Herljević, the new federal secretary for internal affairs, established an interrepublican working group for the execution of the operation, which was at this point known under the code name '*Atina*' (Athena).[45] The group consisted of employees of the SSUP SDB, the Slovenian SDV, the Serbian SDB and the Croatian SDS, and it remained active in Slovenia until the end of May 1975.[46] For months, Udba employees subjected Todorović to intense interrogation about his activities and his connections. Todorović remained in illegal detention until he was transferred to another city in October, after which the local police immediately received an anonymous tip regarding the location of this alleged fugitive from Yugoslav justice.[47]

The end of this operation was a textbook example of the process of 'legalization' (*legalizacija*): having used illegal means to obtain its goal, the Yugoslav State Security Service essentially laundered Todorović and enabled his prosecution by orchestrating his 'legal' arrest. On 29 August 1977, Todorović's trial began in Belgrade. At the end of his trial four months later, the judges – one of whom was a former employee of the Yugoslav State Security Service – sentenced Todorović to twenty years in prison for anti-state activities and for undermining the economic foundations of the Yugoslav state. Adding salt to the wound, the prison sentence of course commenced only with the day of the legalization of his detention in October 1975. Neither his abduction nor his time spent in illegal detention between February and October of that year was recognized. Todorović died in 1984 of chronic health issues likely aggravated by his experience at the hands of the Yugoslav State Security Service.

Operation Tiper (Argus)

Another operation from the mid-1970s further supports the conclusion that the Udba's activities in the Todorović case were not an anomaly. The goal of Operation Tiper, which the Udba hatched in 1974, involved the kidnapping of the émigré Vladimir/Ladislav Šoprek from Italy. Šoprek was born in 1903, but had lived outside Yugoslavia since 1941.[48] The Udba believed that Šoprek was working for or on behalf of the West German intelligence service the *Bundesnachrichtendienst* (BND) as well as the British and the Italian intelligence services, and he had apparently during the interwar period worked as an intelligence agent for the Kingdom of Yugoslavia.[49] The Udba had been keeping their eye on him almost since the end of the Second World War, and assessed that they could abduct Šoprek without incurring too much damage abroad.

Operation Tiper, which is notable for being one of the very best preserved operations hitherto uncovered in the archives, included the SSUP SDB along with participants from the Croatian SDS and the Slovenian SDV.[50] The SDS was designated as the 'bearer' (*nosilac*) of the operation, and it is clear that information about the ultimate goal and target of the operation was kept highly confidential on a 'need-to-know' basis.[51] The plan entailed performing extensive surveillance and countersurveillance on Šoprek, studying his surroundings and possibilities for his abduction and also introducing systematic checks on postal items sent to and from locations relevant to Šoprek. Based on Šoprek's alleged espionage and in particular reasons of state security, the Udba assessed his abduction to be necessary and tentatively scheduled it for August 1975.[52] Notably, the documentation regarding the plan explicitly and repeatedly mentioned an 'illegal transfer', a very conspicuous recognition by the Udba that they were manoeuvring on the wrong side of the law.[53] The Fourth Sector of the SDS was put in charge of identifying an adequate and safe method of rendering Šoprek unconscious for the purposes of the transfer, though they later coordinated with the SDV, which was particularly experienced with anaesthetics. Several vehicles types – a tourist van, a hearse, a (refrigerated) lorry and a van with diplomatic plates – were considered for the transfer. Care would be taken to ensure that the vehicle with Šoprek would be able to pass through customs.[54] The informant 'Lukrecija', who was a Yugoslav double agent 'working' for the BND, would be used to lure Šoprek to a meeting in Rome, though the actual abduction was to occur in Brunico/Bruneck in Southern Tyrol, which had been codenamed 'Trsteno'.[55] Upon the arrival of Šoprek in Brunico, a team consisting of two women was to head there. The team consisted of one elderly woman and one younger woman playing mother and daughter on a trip for the mother's health, though the informant 'Vicko' accompanied by a physician would take the lead in carrying out the actual operation. A team of seven operatives including three drivers would undertake the transfer. Once in Yugoslavia, Šoprek had to be housed in an adequate secure facility.[56] All the preparations were paid for out of the 'special funds' (*specijalna kasa*) of the SSUP SDB.[57]

While the ultimate responsibility for the operation of course resided with the SSUP SDB, the Croatian SDS and the Slovenian SDV were in charge of the actual operational management of Operation Tiper. Three teams of operatives were established consisting of eight employees of the SDS and the SDV, including one anaesthesiologist. 'The teams will be specially trained, prepared, equipped with means of communications, fake documents, etc. Three cars with Yugoslav licence plates will be used.'[58]

As in the contemporaneous case presented above, the SSUP SDB contemplated a covert operation concluding with a retroactive 'legalization' where the actual steps taken during the operation would be hidden from the view of both the public and other Yugoslav authorities. However, in the case of Šoprek legalization was regarded as inopportune. Only in the case of a 'sharp reaction on the Italian side' would the SSUP SDB 'prepare and implement an appropriate legalization in such a manner that it would leave the impression that his arrival in the country was "voluntary".'[59] The SSUP SDB was in charge of ensuring that the operation would succeed and remain covert.

Operation Tiper was linked to a second operation, Argus, which among other things encompassed future operational measures against individuals identified during the planned interrogation of Šoprek.[60] In a 27 June 1975 letter from the chief of the First Administration of the SSUP SDB Nikola Nikolić sent to Srećko Šimurina, the chief of the First Sector of the SDS, it was stated that the operation would take place in the 'foreseeable future'.[61] However, a month later it seemed that Šoprek would not come to 'Trsteno' until August.[62] Once he did, the informant 'Žiško' was to awaken Šoprek's interest and motivate him to go on an excursion together or to come to Rome or Trieste at a later date.

The preparations for the 'illegal transfer' of Šoprek, who was first given the code name 'Carlo' (later 'Tatar'), were thorough.[63] The assessment of the utility of the operation performed by the First Administration of the SSUP SDB on 9 June 1975 constitutes a classic cost-benefit analysis.[64] On the positive side, the architects of the operation estimated that the operation would seriously disrupt the activities of the BND in Italy, which also affected Yugoslavia, as well as the activities of its Munich centre focused on Yugoslavia. The envisaged interrogation of Šoprek would likely reveal the identities of numerous agents and informants of Western intelligence agencies and detailed information about their activities, as well as information about Yugoslav agents and informants whose cover might have been blown. The risk of Šoprek divulging no information at all was estimated to be minimal. On a deeper level, the assessment showed that the SSUP SDB was also interested in obtaining information about the operation of Western intelligence services in Yugoslavia for the entire postwar period and even for the period of the Second World War.

On the negative side, Šoprek's intelligence value also meant that his disappearance would not go unnoticed, particularly in Italy. The operation could therefore create problems of a 'broader political dimension (official state intervention and protests, broad publicity in means of public information, the discrediting of Yugoslavia and its politics at the international level linked to similar operations, etc.)'.[65] The risk of reprisals by Western intelligence services was also calculated. 'Because with such an operation we directly attack sensitive points and interests of the services mentioned, reciprocal actions can also be expected, primarily from the Italian service (towards positions of the SDB, towards identified operatives of the SDB, towards Yugoslav citizens abroad, through forms of strengthened support for the extreme emigration, etc.)'.[66] In addition to these risks if the operation proceeded successfully, there were of course also considerable risks attached to various things that could go wrong in the course of the operation. These risks included the arrest of SDB operatives.

Weighing the risks against the benefits, the planning team composed of employees from the SSUP SDB, SDS and SDV concluded in favour of kidnapping Šoprek.

> Taking into consideration all elements, the operation should be carried out because we estimate:
> a) that the information obtained will be very useful for the security of the country;
> b) that he will not be able to misinform or disorient us in the wrong direction;
> c) that the positions of the SDB will not be threatened, nor will our future opposition to the work of these agencies;
> d) that the West German and British agencies will not react against this measure of ours;
> e) that it should not be necessary to expect a more serious counteraction of the Italian agency; and

f) that although we cannot for certain and in a qualified manner determine and predict the reactions on the international and propaganda levels (particularly from Italy), it will be possible to remove the more serious consequences even in that case.[67]

It is important to emphasize that Operation Tiper once again confirms that the SSUP SDB cooperated with the republican security services in terms of information, logistics and all other aspects on a running basis during operations conducted abroad. The documentation speaks of a 'synchronized undertaking of appropriate measures' (*sinhronizovano preduzimanje odgovarajućih mera*), which were agreed upon at repeated meetings of the relevant state security services.[68] Relevant rulebooks and guidelines were cited, demonstrating that these were not just regarded as abstract distractions but were instead carefully consulted and applied operationally and in order to justify the necessity and framework of specific operations.

Taken together, the two cases of Todorović and Šoprek further corroborate that the Yugoslav State Security Service not only contemplated but in fact planned and carried out abductions of émigrés. Moreover, these operations were not aberrant departures from standard operating procedure carried out by mavericks or rogue elements, but rather carefully planned operations that were vetted and approved according to regulations by the leadership of the Yugoslav State Security Service. It is further worth emphasizing that the documentation pertaining to Operation Tiper refers to 'similar operations abroad, as well as operations that are planned'.[69] According to Federal Secretary for Internal Affairs Franjo Herljević, operations such as these should be carried out 'more subtly', and the repetition of the same operational tactics should be avoided. In particular, international incidents were to be avoided in the course of such operations.[70]

Bringing someone against their will across an international border was of course a highly risky operation, not least because the operation was so sensitive that even border control agents and the regular uniformed police would not be inducted into the operation. It was therefore necessary to transport Šoprek in such a manner that he could not create problems. It was decided that this could best be done by sedating him in such a manner that he would appear as merely a particularly drunk passenger in a vehicle with several occupants. A professional anaesthesiologist was to handle the sedation, and forged travel documents would provide the 'drunk friend' with an innocuous identity.

As in the case of Todorović, the plan further entailed keeping Šoprek in a secret and secure location for a longer period. A new team would be formed to handle his interrogation. However, the question still remained what was to be done with Šoprek once his protracted and intensive investigation finally concluded. Unlike the case of Todorović, the planners wrote that 'a trial and legalization would not come into consideration. Insofar as there were preemptive inadvertent reactions, then only some kind of semi-legalization (which would deny his liquidation and forcible bringing into the country) would come into consideration.'[71] In other words, the SSUP SDB apparently considered it certain or at least possible that they would kill Šoprek after the end of his protracted interrogation.

In this context, it is also worth noting that the planners of the operation had to take into serious consideration the risk which the sedation posed to Šoprek. Owing to his advanced age and possible previously existing health conditions, it was impossible to exclude that he might die during the operation.[72] Of course, his death would definitively put an end to any further espionage activities on his part, but that was only one of the desired results of the operation. As seen, the planners were much more interested in apprehending him and keeping him alive in order that they could extract as much information from him as possible. In the end, however, the death of Šoprek seemed to be the likely and acceptable outcome.

Šoprek arrived in 'Trsteno' on 5 August 1975, and 'Žiško' not only managed to achieve contact already on the next day, but also was able to assess Šoprek's health.[73] Within a few days, Šoprek had moved to recruit 'Žiško'. As the two continued to meet, the Udba worked on identifying a precise location for the planned abduction.[74] Meanwhile Šoprek seemed to continuously suspect 'Žiško' of being an Udba agent, and conspicuously declined every offer to be driven in 'Žiško's' car. Up until this point, 'Žiško' had not been told the goal of the operation, and expressed shock when it was revealed to him. 'Žiško' was apparently a physician of some reputation, and he feared for himself and his family if something should go wrong, asking that his wife be evacuated from Italy.

Finally, at the end of August 1975, the 'realization' of Operation Tiper seemed to be imminent. On 31 August, SDS Centre Rijeka wrote to their superiors at the SDS headquarters in Zagreb and the federal SDB that everything was ready for the arrival of 'Tatar'.[75] However, he failed to materialize.[76] A month later, on 25 September, the federal SDB wrote that, while the goal of the operation remained unchanged, the realization of it would now take place in Trieste or some other suitable town.[77] Yet it continued to be the case that Šoprek's own alert state and own counterintelligence training – his 'security culture' (*sigurnosna/ bezbednosna kultura*) in the Udba's parlance – apparently inhibited the final steps that would have led to his abduction.

From the available documentation, it is apparent that Operation Tiper was contemplated, planned and even implemented over a longer period of time, but the documentation is incomplete. There are tantalizing indications that the operation's cover was blown when a rental car hired by Yugoslav agents in Italy was stolen – perhaps even by their Italian counterparts wishing to warn them discretely against carrying out the operation.[78] In any case, the operation emerges again in November 1982 when the SRH Republican Secretary for Internal Affairs Pavle Gaži approved what was now called Operation Argus. Section chief Radoslav Bego had proposed the operation and Zdravko Mustač approved the operation in his capacity as the chief of the SDS.[79] Vladimir Šoprek was still identified as the main target of the operation. In addition to the engagement of informants to obtain intelligence about and monitor Šoprek, the SDS was to make use of 'all possible other operational and other actions as well as measures', though kidnapping was not specifically mentioned. Article 39 of the Rulebook on the Work of the State Security Service was cited as the foundation of this operation, which again proves that the SDS in its work adhered to relevant rules and regulations.[80] Yet the repeated references to 'illegal transfer' should also be kept in mind.

Between cooperation and opposition: The relationship between the Yugoslav State Security Service and Western intelligence services

In Chapter 1, brief mention was made of the cooperation that occurred between the Yugoslav State Security Service and Western intelligence services and law enforcement agencies. Although this topic will not be treated extensively in this book, some brief remarks are in order. Generally speaking, the relationship was a lot more complex than the standard East versus West Cold War dichotomy might lead many to assume. Many factors figured in this equation. Despite the fact that socialist Yugoslavia existed from beginning to end as a communist party-state, the obvious major factor was the split which took place in 1948 between Tito and Stalin. Although Tito did not overnight become a darling of the West, and although he never wavered from communist dictatorship internally in Yugoslavia, the mere fact of the break complicated the view of those – first and foremost nationalist Croat émigrés – who desired that the West should wholeheartedly pursue the dismantling of both communism and Yugoslavia. Conversely, Western intelligence agencies which were deeply informed by a strong anti-communist ideology did not immediately after 1948 sprint towards cooperation with their Yugoslav counterparts. Certainly as regards West Germany, law enforcement and intelligence agencies remained profoundly sceptical of the intentions of the Yugoslav state, and by extension of the *Gastarbeiter* who started to stream into the country.[81] In addition, although Yugoslavia and West Germany recognized each other in 1951–1952, Yugoslav recognition of East Germany led in 1957 to a break in diplomatic relations between Yugoslavia and West Germany pursuant to the Hallstein Doctrine. Only in 1968 would the two states reestablish diplomatic relations.[82]

Looking at the long term, an equally important factor for the complexity of the relationship was the use of violence by extremist émigrés. It is probably a reasonably safe assertion to state that peacetime states do not take kindly to private actors, in particular foreign nationals, who use the territory of their host states to prepare and launch armed attacks on the territory of other states. Considerable forbearance and a blind eye may be possible if the states targeted by such attacks are ideological opponents of the host country, but even then the risk of diplomatic scandal and by extension sanctions of some sort are considerable.[83] Yet an even more serious line is crossed if foreign nationals carry out attacks against diplomatic or other targets of their own states on the territory of the host state, particularly if those attacks claim lives, and even more especially if those killed are citizens of the host state. If such attacks occur, the wrath of the host state and its security apparatus will very likely come down on the suspected perpetrators regardless of previous ideological, moral, financial or other support.

Two such incidents in respectively West Germany and Australia must suffice to illustrate the above point as regards Croat émigrés, erstwhile Western supporters and the Yugoslav State Security Service. In broad daylight on 29 November 1962 in Bonn, twenty-six Croat émigrés identifying with the splinter group Croat Crusaders' Brotherhood (*Hrvatsko križarsko bratstvo*, HKB) attacked the Yugoslav trade mission.[84] Mate Nikola Tokić summarized what ensued:

> After setting off a bomb in the courtyard of the Mission – which functioned as socialist Yugoslavia's de facto embassy to the Federal Republic following the severing of official diplomatic ties between the countries in 1957 as a result of the Hallstein doctrine – the young radicals broke down the front doors of

the building and forced their way inside. Shouting slogans denouncing Tito and Yugoslavia, they proceeded to ransack the building, destroying furniture, equipment and documents before setting the wreckage on fire. The *Križari* – as the members of the HKB referred to themselves, drawing a stark connection to the postwar Ustaša guerrillas of the same name – also rigged a number of bombs inside the Mission that detonated upon their retreat. By the end of the short but brazen attack, the building was in ruins.[85]

The attack, which also cost the life of one employee of the mission and seriously injured another, was actually the second one that year against the mission, which had also been attacked with signal rockets in April. The incident at Bonn made it abundantly clear to the West German authorities that they could not ignore Croat extremists in their midst or count on them to confine themselves to attacks against targets in Yugoslavia.

Notwithstanding the radical and violent nature of the most extreme Croats in West Germany, the willingness of the West German authorities to intervene was also affected by changes in the political landscape. From Tito and the Yugoslav State Security Service on the one hand to rank-and-file members of Croat émigré organizations on the other, a general perception existed that the West German Social Democrats were significantly less tolerant than the conservative Christian Democrats of Croat extremists. Conversely, the Social Democrats were more likely to tolerate the reprisal actions taken by the Yugoslav State Security Service in West Germany. Thus, with the establishment of the 'Grand Coalition' between the Social Democrats and the Christian Democrats in 1966, a shift commenced. And with the advent of West German Social Democratic Chancellor Willy Brandt's *Ostpolitik* in 1969, Yugoslavia was afforded even more leeway because it served as an important intermediary between East and West.[86] By the early 1980s, the main West Germany domestic intelligence agency, the Federal Office for the Protection of the Constitution (*Bundesamt für Verfassungsschutz*) was monitoring ten émigré organizations, of which seven were Croatian, two were Serbian and one was (Kosovo) Albanian.[87] It should be emphasized, however, that this number represented a small fraction of well over one hundred such organizations legally operating in West Germany at the time.

In Australia, which also hosted a very significant number of émigré Croats, the most radical elements posed similar challenges. While the ASIO and Conservative governments had tolerated somewhat Croat émigré activity in the 1960s, the situation became untenable as this activity started to result in attacks in Australia as well and in 'embarrassments' of the type previously noted in secret Australian immigration and security documents, as will be seen in the next chapter.

Conclusion

This chapter has examined in more detail the guidelines affecting the work of the Yugoslav State Security Service outside the borders of Yugoslavia. From the available documentation, it is evident that these guidelines were not abstract or theoretical documents which gathered dust in the desk drawers of employees of the Yugoslav State Security Service. Rather, these documents were meant to guide actual work, and the examples offered here show that they were indeed utilized in the planning and execution of operations outside Yugoslavia.

It is also necessary to keep in mind that these operations occurred with the approval and at the behest of the Yugoslav communist party-state. In December 1977, the Federal Secretary for Internal Affairs Franjo Herljević met with the leadership of the SDS.[88] Herljević reminded his assembled subordinates that the SDS had received a 'programmatic orientation', and that the political guidelines set out in this document were binding.[89] Herljević demanded that the SDS engage its enemies with 'all its might'. 'The service stands in the function or, if you wish, at the service of the League of Communists, working people and social-political factors, and no abuses can exist. That is imperative. We must nurture communist ethics, communist morale, and I do believe that we nurture it [*sic*], that it is represented.'[90]

Political verification and political authorization were, so Herljević claimed, essential to the work of the Yugoslav State Security Service.[91] Not only were political guidelines binding, the Yugoslav State Security Service also had to ensure that the SKJ could verify and approve its operations.[92] Even after the necessary political approval had been obtained, the leadership of the SSUP SDB and the republican state security services had to keep their political superiors apprised on a running basis of how operations were proceeding.[93] This applied even to the federal secretary for internal affairs, a figure who had often rotated out of a leadership position in the SKJ – and often rotated back after his mandate in the SSUP ended. Herljević told his subordinates that 'I did not do anything in my jurisdiction without consulting the political leadership, including the representatives of the republics. And when I get a green light, then I start. You should stick to this.'[94] Herljević also called for more inventiveness in the Yugoslav State Security Service's work against the hostile emigration. 'We have been become a bit stereotypical, especially when we consider that all the services in the world are looking for the Yugoslav service, they are not looking for Ustaše or Chetniks.'[95] The leaders, operatives and analysts of the Yugoslav State Security Service had their work abroad cut out for them in the years to come.

4

Taking the Fight to Them: The 1972 Bugojno
Uprising and the Shift to an Offensive Stance

As seen in Chapter 2, the late 1960s and early 1970s witnessed the emergence
of a new and younger generation of Croat émigrés, more restive and prepared
to engage in violence than the remaining ageing members of the Ustaša regime.
The young radicals perpetrated a number of smaller attacks in Yugoslavia, but
they had greater initial success carrying out attacks outside the country. This
situation changed in 1972 and would have a major impact upon the Yugoslav
State Security Service's approach to confronting its opponents among the
émigrés.

The seminal event that seized the attention of the Yugoslav leadership
and the security services was the infiltration and attempted armed uprising
instigated by a group of nineteen émigré Croats in the summer of 1972. The
operation in question came to be known as the 'Bugojno Uprising' – and by its
respective codenames among its instigators – Operation Phoenix (*Feniks*) –
and on the part of the Yugoslav authorities – Operation Raduša. Already
before this incident, concerned about the upsurge in violent attacks, the
SSUP SDB had in February 1972 prepared an 'action plan' for the fight against
'the sabotage and terrorist activity of the hostile portion of the emigration'.[1]
Once again, Croat émigrés took top priority in the hierarchy of enemies of
the Yugoslav state. The document made it clear that the SDS of Croatia and
the SDB of Bosnia and Herzegovina shared responsibility for neutralizing the
threat posed by Croat émigrés.[2] One month later, the SSUP SDB produced a
set of theses regarding the work of the State Security Service as regarded the
emigration.[3]

The Bugojno Uprising occurred at a particularly delicate time in Yugoslav
history, and this timing helps to contextualize the regime's reaction. Beginning
with linguistic and cultural expressions of dissatisfaction in the late 1960s,
discontent in Croatia regarding centralized rule from Belgrade and alleged

discrimination of Croatian interests snowballed into a mass movement (*masovni pokret*, or *maspok*) led by Croat intellectuals and students. With a nod to events in Czechoslovakia in 1968, this phenomenon became known as the Croatian Spring (*hrvatsko proljeće*).[4] The *maspok* found strong allies within the League of Communists of Croatia and initially enjoyed some indulgence from Tito. However, by 1970 and 1971, some of the movement's leaders articulated increasingly nationalist – and in the view of Tito – 'counterrevolutionary' demands. In November 1971, at a meeting at his hunting lodge in Karađorđevo in Vojvodina, Tito initiated a massive purge of the League of Communists of Croatia. Many people in Croatia were dismissed from work and/or arrested, inaugurating the period popularly known as 'the Croatian silence'.[5] The SDS in Croatia and the SDB in Bosnia and Herzegovina subsequently closely monitored a sizable number of persons as potentially subversive 'internal enemies'. It is indicative that in the aftermath of the uprising, one of the SSUP documents dealing with the implementation of additional security measures mentioned the potential danger of 'various "mass movements"'.[6]

Hence by the time of the Bugojno Uprising, which began only seven months after the fateful Karađorđevo meeting, the sensors of the Yugoslav regime were hypersensitive to any expressions of Croatian nationalism. This chapter will provide a summary of the Bugojno Uprising and its consequences. In addition, the chapter will highlight a number of both Croat terrorist operations and, on the other side, Yugoslav state-sanctioned assassinations which occurred during the second half of the 1970s. These events and the spiral of violence set the context for the detailed examination of the case of Stjepan Đureković in the following chapter.

The Bugojno Uprising

In the spring of 1972, a group of HRB members stemming predominantly from Australia carefully planned an operation that would entail infiltrating Yugoslav territory in order to foment a popular uprising against the communist regime.[7] Several of the members had returned to Europe in the late 1960s with the intent of converting their passionate anti-Yugoslav thoughts into concrete actions. The group, composed exclusively of men, carried out the final preparations in Austria, not far from the Yugoslav border.[8] They also trained near Salzburg in anticipation of combating Yugoslav security forces, moving later to another camp at Garanas in Styria, not far from the Austrian-Yugoslav border. The training included loaded marches with full gear, handling and using weapons and explosives, daytime and night orienteering and other exercises.[9] The planned HRB operation was the largest infiltration of Yugoslavia by an armed group since the HRB's fiasco in the summer of 1963, although another failed armed infiltration had also occurred in 1967.[10]

The Yugoslav State Security Service had of course as seen earlier kept a close eye on the activities of the HRB. In December 1971, the Federal Secretary for Internal Affairs Luka Banović convened a meeting regarding the HRB.[11] On 15 January 1972, the authorities formed an interrepublican taskforce codenamed *'Venera'* (Venus) that would focus specifically on the HRB.[12] In February, the Udba met with representatives of the military security services, the UID of the SSIP and representatives of the regular police to discuss an action plan aimed at the HRB.[13] The security services agreed upon a wide spectrum of activities, including 'offensive operations'.[14] Ambroz Andrić and Josip Senić were listed as the top priorities, 'because they have already had established terrorist groups, contacts and points [bases] in other Western European countries and in Yugoslavia'.[15] It is worth noting that 'offensive actions' were mentioned alongside the need to take into account in the action plan 'the political interests of the country and its international position and reputation'.

The Yugoslav authorities were obviously concerned that something was brewing, but they apparently did not yet know exactly what the HRB was planning. The Yugoslav authorities did come tantalizingly close, however.[16] On 9 June 1972, they caused an explosion of some of the explosive materials located in the residence of HRB member Ambroz Andrić in Strasbourg, France. The intent was apparently to press the local authorities to investigate the activities of Croat émigrés such as Andrić who were associated with the HRB. While no one was injured in the attack, the incident did cause the French and German authorities to issue warrants for a number of HRB members, including Andrić.[17] But the HRB remained a few crucial steps ahead of the Yugoslav authorities.

In the end, nineteen HRB members, all but one of whom were under forty years old, participated in the actual operation.[18] Moving from their forest camp near Salzburg, they arrived at Austria's border with Yugoslavia by the morning of 20 June 1972, at a point not far removed from where the Bleiburg massacre had taken place approximately twenty-seven years earlier. Here it is worth noting that the HRB like all other zealous Croat émigrés styled themselves as *'osvetnici Bleiburga'* (the avengers of Bleiburg), which was in fact the title of a HRB manual.[19] They crossed illegally into Yugoslavia and then spent the day and a half near the village of Muta on the Drava River. On their second evening in Yugoslavia, they hijacked a truck transporting mineral water. Taking the Slovene driver as a hostage, they drove the truck to the area of Bugojno and the Raduša mountain in central Bosnia.

Once there, their plan was to incite a popular uprising among the local, predominantly ethnic Croat, population, which the HRB members of course assumed were oppressed and discontented. Things did not go as planned. Having sent the kidnapped driver back to Slovenia, the group had to decide how to proceed. Time was surprisingly on their side, especially as the authorities back in Slovenia initially believed that the driver had stolen his own truck and had made up the entire story about the hijacking. Naively, the young Croats detained a group of hunters near Raduša mountain and subjected them to a protracted ideological indoctrination session. Believing that they had convinced the hunters of the righteousness of their cause, the infiltrators allowed the hunters to return to their village, whence they promptly contacted the authorities who immediately sounded the alarm.

Within hours, the regular police (*milicija*), all State Security offices in Bosnia, the Territorial Defence (TO) forces and the army had all been mobilized. According to a later report prepared by the First Administration of the Main Staff of the JNA, the command of the Seventh Army received unverified notification of the existence of the armed group in the late evening of 24 June 1972.[20] The highest-ranking officials in the country, particularly those from the Secretariat for Internal Affairs and the Secretariat for People's Defence, held crisis meetings in order to prepare the counteroffensive. Needless to say, Tito was not only informed but was personally involved. Overall, during the coming weeks an estimated 30,000 members of the TO forces alone participated in the hunt for the insurgents. The commander of the Bosnian TO, Franjo Herljević, subsequently became the federal secretary for internal affairs, likely because Tito approved of the way the TO had handled this task.[21]

Soon the woods in the area were swarming with police and troops determined to crush the infiltrators. With their pleas to the local population finding little resonance, the group found itself completely on hostile territory and gradually became involved in firefights with the Yugoslav security forces. As Igor Omerza has pointed out, the police and TO reservists who in the coming weeks lost their lives fighting against the guerrillas were not fanatically indoctrinated members of the communist elite which the Croat émigrés despised but rather were themselves young men who had the simple misfortune of being in the wrong place at the wrong time.[22] In part because of the difficult terrain, the operation only concluded approximately a month later on 24 July 1972.

Although the 'Bugojno Uprising' lasted the better part of a month, it was a complete fiasco in terms of the goals its organizers had set. The group's incursion into central Bosnia did not ignite any broader uprising, and there are absolutely no signs that any Croats in the area took to arms and attempted to assist the nineteen would-be guerrillas. On the contrary, the Yugoslav security system, although it had failed to anticipate the attack, reacted relatively promptly and functioned as envisioned once the existence of the group was known and confirmed.

At a more personal level, the incursion was an unmitigated self-made disaster and tragedy for the nineteen participants in the operation. Several of them were killed in the fighting around Bugojno, others were extrajudicially killed after capture, while the remainder were imprisoned and sentenced to death.[23] There were losses on the other side as well, as eight members of the Bosnian TO were killed in combat. The desire for severe punishments of those insurrectionists who were captured stemmed from the very top. At a meeting of the SFRJ Presidency held on 19 September 1972, Tito spoke directly about the trials that awaited those who had been apprehended alive.

> I would like to deal here with just one thing, and that is the question of the trial of those whom we captured from the group of nineteen. Now is the best time to try them, the three of them, I don't know how many of them there are over there, in order that some things are understood a bit differently abroad. Because now from various sides we are being accused of organizing this ourselves, that those are very sinister workings of our UDBA, and these things are becoming overwhelming. I would like to suggest that we agree here that the judicial proceedings should start immediately for those who were apprehended. Those who are dead are dead, and as for those who have remained alive, we will try them as necessary, and it is known what the result of that should be.[24]

The trial of the four surviving insurrectionists – Đuro Horvat, Vejsil Keškić, Mirko Vlasnović and Ludvig Pavlović – commenced before a military court in Sarajevo in December 1972, and all four were sentenced to death. The choice of military jurisdiction and martial law conformed to the regime's views that the Yugoslav state found itself at war with Croat émigré extremists. The trial lasted less than two weeks, and as indicated by Tito's remarks, both the guilty verdicts and the death penalties meted out were foregone conclusions. The only surprise was that Ludvig Pavlović's sentence was commuted on appeal to twenty years' imprisonment because of his age, his lack of prior criminal conduct and the remorse he expressed at trial.[25]

The carrying out of the death sentences, which transpired in March 1973, significantly aggravated Yugoslavia's relations with Australia, as some of those executed possessed Australian citizenship.[26] Yet the anger felt in Australian official circles at the execution of Australian citizens was tempered by the significant embarrassment that the masterminds of the Bugojno operation stemmed from Australia. In addition, bombings perpetrated by Croat terrorists in September 1972 on George Street, the very heart of Sydney's commercial district, had injured over a dozen people and outraged the Australian public.[27] In an unprecedented occurrence, the Australian Justice Minister Lionel Murphy strode into the headquarters of the ASIO and demanded that he be given documents on Croat extremism which he believed that the ASIO had been withholding. A series of controversial police operations and trials of alleged Croat émigré extremists followed.[28]

Needless to say, in Croat émigré circles and in publicistic works by Croat authors, the nineteen Croats were portrayed as heroes and martyrs for the Croat cause. The deaths of many of them, whether during the operation or later pursuant to death sentences meted out by Yugoslav military courts, are taken as confirmation of the oppressive and morally repugnant nature of the Yugoslav communist regime. Such outrage is at least somewhat unjustified given the fundamental fact that these young men voluntarily and deliberately launched a premeditated armed attack on another country. Setting ideological considerations aside – and knowing full well that ideology is for many Croat observers the only relevant criterion – it must be recognized that any state's security forces would have reacted similarly when confronted with such an incursion. The group committed several felony offences even before arriving near Bugojno, and from the moment that they entered into armed altercations with Yugoslav security forces, it was a foregone conclusion that most of them would either be killed, wounded or receive draconian punishments.[29] This outcome had very little to do with any inherent traits of the Yugoslav system and rather more to do with the acts of the group's members.

Assuming an offensive stance

Although the size of the infiltrated 'Bugojno Group' paled in comparison to the massive numbers of police and soldiers which the Yugoslav authorities were able to deploy, and although the group was eliminated and did not even come close to realizing any of its goals, the events of June and July 1972 shook the confidence of Tito and his regime. All of the Yugoslav security services, both civilian and military, were ordered to undertake a thorough examination of what they called Operation Raduša. It is difficult if not impossible to overestimate the outrage and anger that Tito and his associates felt, or their desire to prevent at any cost a recurrence of such an embarrassing and threatening incursion. The émigrés had violated the sovereignty and security of the Yugoslav state and had embarrassed Yugoslavia in front of the entire world. If the émigrés wanted war, then Tito would ensure that war was what they would get – but on Yugoslavia's terms, not those of the émigrés.

On 21 July, a few days before the suppression of the would-be insurgency was accomplished, Tito issued a critical directive.[30] Within the context of the 'war' between Croat nationalist émigrés and the Yugoslav State Security Service, this document occupies a seminal place and therefore deserves close examination. The directive itself, including all actions and reports pursuant to its implementation, was classified as a state secret.

Perhaps the most striking aspect of Tito's directive is its wilful placement of the Bugojno incident in the epic context of a 'special war' (*specijalni rat*) which was being conducted against Yugoslavia, and against which Yugoslavia had to defend itself.[31]

> As the consequence of negative movements in the world in the past decade, small and unaligned countries are, in addition to local and limited wars and interventions, also exposed to a "special war" which is prosecuted against them through political, economic and military pressure and intervention, through subversive intelligence, psychologically propagandistic and other undermining operations, through the creation of a contemporary "fifth column" and the provocation of internal strife, coup d'états and other activities. As a rule, "special war" is also conducted by relying on the support of "internal forces" of these countries. Particular conceptions, doctrines and strategies have been developed for the organization and prosecution of "special war," special forces have been organized and measures have been taken towards the development of special weaponry and equipment.
>
> Already for many years, reactionary, anti-communist and anti-self-managing forces, in the context of which the internal enemy and the extreme political emigration increase the intensity of counterrevolutionary activity against our self-managing socialist community, have been applying various forms and methods of precisely this "special war." While their emphasis was earlier more on psychological propaganda, they later transitioned to subversive activity, above all attempts to destroy the unity of Yugoslavia through separatist-nationalist and similar movements. More recently that activity has escalated, making use of even the roughest types of activity – terror, sabotage, the infiltration of armed gangs, etc. They are attacking almost all areas of our socio-political activity – internal, external, defensive, economic, cultural policy, etc.

Tito made it clear that everyone, 'from the individual citizen to the organs of the Federation' had to take the danger of the 'special war' seriously and consequently engage and neutralize those who sought to destroy Yugoslavia. Tito seemed certain that the 'Bugojno group' had not acted alone, and events seemed to confirm his suspicions – already reinforced by the Soviet military intervention in Czechoslovakia in 1968, which Yugoslavia had opposed – that Yugoslavia continued to exist in a hostile international environment.

Tito ordered the SSNO and the SSUP to form special military and police units which would be able to effectively combat and eliminate attacking special forces, guerrillas, etc. Given that a large number of Yugoslav men eligible for conscription were located abroad, the SSNO and the SSUP were also to coordinate in order to ensure that they could play a role in defending the country and in the protection of Yugoslav citizens residing abroad.

The political emigration was among those external factors which harboured malignant intentions against Yugoslavia, and which could be deployed in the context of the special war. Therefore, the SSUP, the SSNO and the SSIP had to continue to factor in appropriate measures against the emigration when putting together their strategies. Pursuant to the directive and to similar directives from the SKJ, it was decided that 'the activity of the extreme emigration must be suppressed with all methods and means of the service in all areas and environments abroad where these are to be found. The emigration must not be allowed to bring their activity into the country.'[32] The Yugoslav State Security Service had to establish 'robust positions' in the internal structures of the extreme emigration and was to focus especially on 'the intellectual portion of the hostile emigration.'[33]

In March 1973, the Federal State Security Service prepared an extensive analysis of the 'sabotage and terrorist activity of the hostile emigration.'[34] Approximately half a year later, in October 1973, the SSUP SDB performed an assessment of the overall progress in the strengthening of the country's security.[35] The necessity of adopting an offensive role abroad was emphasized, because extreme elements in the emigration continued to display an interest in bringing the fight to Yugoslavia.[36] Among the objectives of the SSUP SDB were

> the acceleration of the implementation of the agreement regarding the more offensive approach of the service with the goal of moving the emphasis of the struggle abroad; to directly and as much as possible to engage in the infiltration of the most dangerous centres of terrorist activities in the emigration; given the fact that the political-subversive activity of the emigration has increased, to engage more broadly and systematically in the suppression of this activity and

particularly in the pacification [*pasiviziranje*] of the émigré-intellectuals [who act] as organizers and bearers of this activity and as the inspiration of terrorist activities.[37]

Therefore, it was necessary to define and create enabling guidelines for this 'more offensive' work abroad.[38]

The demand for a more offensively oriented stance also trickled down through other related elements of policy in the SSUP SDB. As was noted earlier, the danger that the 'hostile emigration' posed to Yugoslav *Gastarbeiter* in Western Europe had been a prime concern of the Yugoslav authorities ever since the first Yugoslav worker migrated to the West. And a number of those involved in the Bugojno operation had at least in part left Yugoslavia in search of gainful employment. Therefore, in an April 1973 analytical overview of the security aspects of the employment of Yugoslavs abroad, the consequences of the new policy could also be seen. The SSUP SDB noted the need to 'from the hitherto mainly defensive attitude move towards a more offensive stance in uncovering and stopping various forms of enemy activity through emigration'.[39] In addition to preventing the emigration of persons who had criminal records or for whom evidence existed that they harboured intent to damage Yugoslavia in any way, the SDB was also to look at how it could prevent the recruitment of Yugoslav émigrés into hostile organizations.

Also in October 1973, the SSUP SDB reported that it had established 'special units' which could be employed in the struggle against the hostile emigration.[40] Very little is known about the special units, though tantalizing hints regarding them can be found in the available sources. According to Jan Gabriš and Josip Perković, there was in the 1980s within the Second Administration of the SSUP SDB

> a group for so-called special operations [*grupa za takozvano specijalno djelovanje*]. This group independently planned and carried out various operations abroad and in the process of doing so made use of its own group of agents. It carried out psychological operations of intimidation, agitation and disinformation, produced various kinds of promotional material up to and including forgery of certain editions of some émigré magazines, planned and carried out burglaries in the offices of émigré organizations in order to steal documents, and according to certain indications the group also ordered the physical liquidation of individuals.[41]

The need for an offensive stance in the work (*ofanzivnost u radu*) of the Yugoslav State Security Service was explained thoroughly.

It is emphasized that the component of the offensive stance in the work of the counterintelligence sector in the country and abroad must be implemented consistently, and that it is a significant precondition for the realization of the confirmed orientation and for the implementation of the work plan. The offensive stance must be embedded in all aspects of our resistance towards the enemy and presupposes:

the broader and more organized presence of the means and measures of the state security service abroad (the embedding and infiltration of informant positions among groups and individuals who carry out intelligence and subversive activity, the formation of amateur and professional groups for the carrying out of operations, the creation of adequate bases, the broader and more organized engagement of Yugoslav representatives and workers on temporary assignment [i.e. *Gastarbeiter*], the planned organization of special operations with the goal of intercepting enemy activity or obtaining more significant intelligence, the embedding of SDB agents for the carrying out of special tasks, a more active relation towards specialists and stipend-holders who are located abroad)[.][42]

The leadership of the Yugoslav State Security Service wanted to ensure that a uniform stance was maintained as regarded the question of the hostile emigration. The 'undertaking of special operations to smash and destroy them' was discussed.[43] 'The successes hitherto in these operations must be analysed, in order to discover deficiencies and good aspects, and with more planning and continuity also to discover new means and methods.'[44] Psychological measures were to be increased, improved and to be employed better. In a nutshell: 'The planned and continued disruption and the destruction of sabotage points, of terror and subversive activity require the transfer of the main emphasis of our work abroad and more offensive penetration in the tops of the émigré organisations.'[45]

In addition, a broader coordination and exchange of information had to occur, with less interagency competition. For this reason, the establishment of 'control and coordination dossiers' (*kontrolno-koordinirajući dosjei*) was agreed upon in principle. However, it is unclear whether such dossiers were in fact created. The establishment of an interrepublican group for counterintelligence work abroad was also agreed upon.[46]

In an internal training manual of the SSUP from 1974, the offensive stance of the Yugoslav State Security Service was also emphasized. Indeed, this stance was even compared to the fight against guerrilla groups after the formal end of the Second World War:

However, in cases where sabotage, terrorism, or even the dissemination of illegal propaganda materials is being prepared, which is today characteristic for the activity of the hostile emigration and for some types of internal enemies, one has to intensify all the measures, methods and means of the service towards the goal of the realization of the processing so that such activity is prevented – and so even if not everything that was planned was attained – the uncovering of all participants and the documentation of [their] criminal activity. For example, at the end of the war, bandit groups were disrupted and liquidated at a more accelerated tempo. The measures in such a process and its tempo were subordinated to the aforementioned goal: the prevention of the carrying out of such activities, avoiding that it would come to harmful consequences.[47]

Although all of the official and operational documentation produced by the SSUP and its subordinate organs was of course highly confidential, the authorities made a considerable effort to acquaint the public with the nature of the terrorist threat. In 1978 the leadership of the Yugoslav party-state decided to publish a *White Book on Terrorism of the Fascist Emigration Stemming from Yugoslavia* (*Bela knjiga o terorizmu fašističke emigracije poreklom iz Jugoslavije*).[48] The SSUP was tasked to write the book. In the coming years, books and articles regarding terrorism and extremism among Yugoslav émigrés were disseminated broadly in Yugoslavia. The 'hostile emigration' was also treated as a feature in the official in-house journal of the SSUP, which referred to the existence of a 'sixth column' intending to destroy Yugoslavia.[49] Perhaps the most interesting book on the topic that was publicly available was *The Chronology of Anti-Yugoslav Terrorism, 1960–1980* (*Hronologija antijugoslovenskog terorizma, 1960–1980*), published in 1981.[50] At the outset of the book, written by Sreten Kovačević, the reviewer Vjekoslav Radović highlighted the term 'special war'. Citing Tito's aphorism that 'we should work as if there will be one hundred years of peace and prepare as if war will come tomorrow', Radović then proceeded: 'A special war, treacherous and perfidious, exposed in the form of the most callous terrorist acts, in which innocent people as a rule die, is carried out still today.'[51] Radović further referred to a nexus of the interests of 'the hostile terrorist emigration' and 'counterrevolutionary elements' in Yugoslavia, which were in turn interwoven with the irredentist or other nefarious plans of foreign powers, both large and small. In his own introduction, Kovačević counted numerous terrorist incidents:

> 34 acts of arson and placing of explosives at diplomatic and consular offices; 6 killings of diplomats and consuls; 10 officials and members of diplomatic or consular offices wounded; dozens of killed citizens, who fell only because

they were abroad and were loyal to their fatherland; the same amount of killed and wounded émigrés of Yugoslav origin, who fell because they still love their fatherland; seven times terrorist groups were infiltrated into the country; 25 times offices of Yugoslavia abroad were attacked, causing considerable material damage; in terrorist activities more than 200 of our citizens were wounded, both at home and abroad; in Yugoslavia approximately 15 acts of sabotage were carried out by members of the terrorist emigration; and it cannot be precisely established how many attacks there have been against diplomatic, consular, economic and other offices, unsuccessful assassination attempts, acts of sabotage on means of transportation, endangerment of air travel, killed and wounded members of the military, security organs and social self-defence personnel.

The bulk of Kovačević's book consists of very tedious but meticulous and terse summaries of confirmed and suspected terrorist incidents against Yugoslav targets both in Yugoslavia and abroad. The first listed incident is the attempted bombing, allegedly by 'one of the Ustaša émigré groups', of the Yugoslav consulate in Munich in February 1962. At the end of the book, over 120 pages later, we arrive at the arrest of Muse Hotija for the killing of Stojan Đerić, an employee of the Yugoslav Embassy in Belgium. The book concludes with a sombre statement noting that the author's original intention had been to conclude the book with the end of 1980. However, it seemed clear that the illness and death of Tito had led to a renewed upsurge in the number of terrorist attacks on Yugoslav targets.

The hunt for accomplices after Bugojno: Stjepan Crnogorac and others

As indicated above, the Yugoslav State Security Service at the outset of 1972 had accumulated intelligence that strongly suggested that the HRB was planning some kind of attack(s). However, the Bugojno operation was not discovered until after the nineteen participants had already infiltrated Yugoslavia and arrived at their destination. Their appearance and discovery left the Yugoslav State Security Service scrambling to identify any potential secondary cells or other potentially related operations and participants. Obviously, the place to start looking was among HRB members and sympathizers, particularly in Austria.

Even before the operation to suppress the 'Bugojno Uprising' started, the Yugoslav State Security Service had already taken concrete steps to neutralize one particular emigrant. Stjepan Crnogorac was a lapsed seminary student who had become increasingly involved with the activities of the HRB. As the leaders of what would become the Bugojno group engaged in training near Salzburg, a number of potential members dropped out because of illness or other reasons, and it seems that Crnogorac was among them.[52] Apparently, these persons were to reassemble around Crnogorac, who was to continue to train them in anticipation of a signal from the first group. Upon receiving this signal, Crnogorac was to have led them into Yugoslavia as the second wave of what would, they hoped, become a successful Croat uprising.[53] Several persons named Crnogorac appeared on a list from the beginning of July produced by the SDV based on the operation 'Venera – Duet I'.[54] At around the same time, Federal Minister for Internal Affairs Luka Banović passed on instructions based on his consultations with the president of the SIV, Džemal Bijedić. According to Banović, the Yugoslav authorities were to broaden their networks of informants abroad and especially to be on the lookout for terrorist training centres in neighbouring states that might be readying the infiltration of new armed groups.[55] Banović concluded, 'The State Security Service must counteract the roughest terrorist-sabotage operations of the extreme emigration with all available means and measures, including also special operations.'[56]

On 2 July 1972, while fighting raged in the hills and mountains close to Bugojno, Stjepan Crnogorac together with the well-known émigré cleric Vilim Cecelja and the brother of one of the nineteen participants participated in a traditional Roman Catholic pilgrimage between Salzburg and Linz. That evening, Crnogorac returned home and was subsequently never seen again by his acquaintances.[57] Among émigrés, the assumption was that Crnogorac was abducted by the Yugoslav State Security Service, tortured until his interrogators believed that he had revealed all relevant knowledge, and then subsequently killed.[58]

As in the case of Geza Pašti, the specific details regarding Crnogorac's death are not available. However, Crnogorac was apparently abducted into Yugoslavia using a fake identity and a forged passport which were later found in the archives in Slovenia.[59] In addition to this, and quite extraordinarily, a very long handwritten document written by the involuntarily detained Crnogorac was also found in the Slovenian state archives. In this document, Crnogorac described in precise detail the circumstances of his own abduction.[60] On 3 July, three men claiming to be members of the Austrian secret police had come to Crnogorac's residence in Salzburg. They had accused him of smuggling narcotics. Handcuffing Crnogorac, they led him to their car and then drove towards Villach near the Yugoslav border. Once there, they drugged him before proceeding into

Yugoslavia, aided and abetted by an Austrian customs officer who had been recruited by the Yugoslav State Security Service. Thereafter, Crnogorac was brought to Ljubljana where he was subjected to extensive interrogation.[61]

No one has seen Stjepan Crnogorac since he disappeared from Salzburg on 3 July 1972. Although the Udba's abduction of Crnogorac can be proven beyond a reasonable doubt, there is also no positive evidence proving that Crnogorac was killed. Some unrepentant veterans of the Slovenian State Security Service continue to claim that Crnogorac absconded or even received a new identity in exchange for becoming an informant or agent working for Yugoslavia.[62] However, such claims are not credible, nor has any documentation been produced to support such claims. As with other victims of the Udba, rumours swirled in émigré circles regarding his fate, with some speculating that he had been murdered, and others suspecting that he had the whole time been working for the Udba.[63]

Finally, it is worth noting that Stjepan Crnogorac did not disappear from the documentation of the Yugoslav State Security Service after July 1972. On the contrary, almost precisely a year after his kidnapping he was mentioned in a listing of HRB members and associates in Western Europe.[64] The impression given is that Crnogorac is still alive and poses a threat. Yet this publication was an official and therefore secret document issued by the SSUP SDB. It was therefore not intended to convince the public – for whom Crnogorac was at any rate largely unknown – of his continued existence, but rather showed the lengths to which the Udba went even internally in terms of disguising, or at the very least heavily compartmentalizing, its involvement in extrajudicial killings. It may simply have been the case that only a very few employees of the Udba (and their political masters) were privy to Crnogorac's final fate and the Udba's involvement in it – and that such knowledge was never put in writing.

The case of the kidnapping and alleged murder of Crnogorac has been investigated by the Austrian authorities with a view to examining the role of former members of the Slovenian State Security Service based on a criminal complaint filed by the Slovene publicist Roman Leljak.[65] However, no one has been formally charged.

Apart from Austria, once it became apparent that a large number of the participants in the Bugojno operation were Croats from Australia, any other Croat émigrés with known extremist views and links to Australia quickly came under suspicion. A number of persons were for this reason arrested, convicted and sentenced to long jail terms in Yugoslavia for their alleged criminal associations.[66] Together with the measures apparently taken against Crnogorac, these measures show the Yugoslav state adopting a more aggressive stance even as the operation in Bosnia wound down.

Cooperation with Western security and intelligence services

Before moving further along in the history of the 'war' between the Udba and extreme Croat émigrés, it is worth pausing to consider the relationship between the Yugoslav State Security Service and its counterparts abroad in Western European countries. Although most of these countries were members of the NATO alliance, numerous Croats also resided as *Gastarbeiter* in neutral states such as Switzerland and Sweden. The topic of cooperation between the Udba and Western security services could easily be the subject of a separate book, but a few brief comments are in order here.

Historically speaking, Yugoslavia had gone from being at the vanguard of Stalinism in Europe immediately after the Second World War to its eventually famous status as a leader of the Non-Aligned Movement. Yet from the very early postwar years when the Yugoslav authorities suspected Western intelligence services of aiding and abetting the escape of Ustaša and other war criminals to Austria, Italy, South America and Australia, an extreme suspicion existed that the West was in fact allied with Croat extremists.

As has been shown repeatedly, the Yugoslav authorities did not believe that the governments in the West were serious about cracking down on extremists in the emigration. For starters, too many Western governments tended to regard anti-Yugoslav activities first and foremost as anti-communist activities, and hence as something to be condoned. Certainly, various Western countries seem to have turned a blind eye to the pressganging by well-established Croat émigré extremists of new Croat arrivals into various Croat nationalist organization, including those involved in paramilitary activities.[67] Equally certainly, Western intelligence organizations did not harbour any illusions about the pacific nature of some Croat organizations and societies, as shown by a study of the ASIO from 1963 entitled 'Activities of the Ustashi [*sic*] Terrorist Organizations'.[68] However, it was only when the activities of the extremists turned violent, and when that violence started to claim non-Yugoslav victims that even the more conservative elements of Western agencies began to realize that the time had come to crack down on extremism. Certainly there are plenty of indications that both West German and Austrian authorities increased their surveillance of émigrés and quickly advised their Yugoslav counterparts in those cases where, for example, the émigrés had acquired or sought to acquire explosives.[69] Yet even then the line between law enforcement and political enforcement remained difficult to navigate for Western states. Moreover, the real and alleged activities of the Udba and other Yugoslav intelligence services in Western countries raised the attention and ire of numerous intrepid journalists and anti-communist politicians.[70] Many of the latter, acting alone or in association with émigré activists, used their positions as members of parliament to pose official questions of their own governments and law enforcement agencies regarding the Udba.[71]

This Yugoslav frustration with the Western stance was on clear display at a meeting of the SSIP in Krapinske Toplice in July 1971. Noting the assassination of ambassador Rolović in Stockholm the previous April and the occupation of the consulate in Gothenburg two months before that, Branko Karadžole, the chief of the consular administration in the SSIP, expressed his dissatisfaction that other states did not wish to cooperate with Yugoslavia regarding the suppression of 'political propaganda activities because, so they say, the expression of political convictions is in harmony with their system and "democratic liberties." From experience we know that the authorities and the police are willing to, more or less consistently, cooperate with us when violence is used against Yugoslav citizens and representations, but that they energetically reject cooperation with respect to so-called political activities of individuals and groups'. Karadžole later commented in a surprisingly subtle manner that

> it must be kept in mind that foreign organs differentiate substantially between the expression of opposing views and acts of terrorism. And we will also not be convincing among our workers [i.e. Yugoslav citizens abroad] if we proclaim to be terrorists [those] persons who have never been engaged in such activities and who publicly, even if only for tactical reasons, distance themselves from violence as a method of struggle.[72]

Once the events around Bugojno commenced, the Austrian authorities cooperated closely with their Yugoslav colleagues in investigating the origins and suspects in the entire operation, and emphasizing their readiness for further cooperation.[73] And the Yugoslav authorities did not hesitate to appeal publicly and through diplomatic channels for Austria to implement 'decisive measures … in order to stop subversive and terrorist activities from its territory against Yugoslavia', in the words of the president of the Yugoslav government, Džemal Bijedić.[74] In October 1972, the Austrian Ministry of Internal Affairs issued a report on 'the infiltration of an armed Croat group through Austria into Yugoslavia'.[75] From the point of view of Austria, it was necessary to prevent any further deterioration of the bilateral relationship with Yugoslavia.

Nonetheless, the events of the summer of 1972 and in particular the Australian and other Western 'origins' of the participants in the Bugojno operation only served to confirm the suspicions of the Yugoslav authorities. Moreover, the Yugoslav State Security Service continued to obtain information indicating that Croat émigrés were communicating with disgruntled Croat nationalists and common criminal elements in Yugoslavia in an effort to carry out further acts of sabotage and terrorism.[76] The activities of the hostile portion of the extremist emigration were identified by the SSNO in 1974 as a constitutive part of the 'special war against the SFRJ'.[77] The authorities in Yugoslavia were convinced that Western intelligence services exploited the émigrés as part of an overall attempt to weaken Yugoslavia. From the mid-1970s, in part because of greater concern and awareness among Western governments regarding terrorism, cooperation between the West German and Yugoslav authorities increased. This trend of course distressed the émigrés, who on occasion complained that the West German police were allegedly behaving like 'the Gestapo'.[78] The leadership of Yugoslavia generally remained convinced, however, that the degree of cooperation was related to whether Social Democrats or Christian Democrats were in power in Bonn.[79]

Murder and attempted murder in Paris: The cases of Dane Šarac and Bruno Bušić

Two of the émigré Croats who would quickly feel the consequences of the offensive Yugoslav stance were Dane Šarac and Bruno Bušić. Šarac, who had as a mere teenager fought for the NDH and had later been imprisoned in Yugoslavia, was a TRUP and HRB member residing in Karlsruhe. He had fled Yugoslavia in April 1960.[80] Šarac was a dedicated planner and executioner of sabotage and terrorist acts.[81] Indeed, in August 1968, the SSUP SDB even described Šarac as one of the 'organizers of all acts and acts of sabotage against our country, its representatives or our citizens'.[82] He was regarded as the leader of his own group, and as such was a suitable target for the Yugoslav State Security Service.

Through the TRUP Šarac was linked to Mile Rukavina, Nahid Kulenović, Franjo Goreta and other dangerous émigrés.[83] Mile Rukavina and his associates Krešimir Tolj and Vid Maričić were all killed, allegedly by the Udba, in Munich

on 26 October 1968.[84] The death of Rukavina and others was later mentioned in
the operational textbook of the SSUP SDB.

> For example, in the ranks of the emigration there are great conflicts and friction
> among opposing groups and organizations who are subject of processing. The
> escalation of these conflicts to extreme limits should be the constant focus of the
> SDB. Conflicts are often of such a character that they lead to internal physical
> settlings of accounts and killings [*fizički obračuni i ubistva*]. For example, in
> 1969, several prominent émigrés from Ustaša organizations were killed: Maks
> Luburić in Spain, Rukavina and others in West Germany, because of which
> more discord was created, mutual incriminations arose, threats of vengeance,
> fear among individuals, etc.[85]

Given that it is known for certain that an informant working for the Udba
killed Luburić, this excerpt from the Udba textbook leaves little doubt that
the Udba and its informants were involved in Rukavina's assassination as well.
The dossier of the Slovenian SDV agent, Milan Dorič 'Hanzi' also contains
several documents indicating his involvement with an operation against
Rukavina and demonstrating that the SDV supplied Dorič with pistols and
other weaponry.[86]

As for Kulenović, the son of Džafer Kulenović, who was a minister in the
NDH, the Udba regarded him as a particularly dangerous member of the TRUP.
As early as the autumn of 1964, Kulenović had allegedly been gathering names
of Udba officers whom he and his associates attended to kill.[87] According to a
March 1969 report, Kulenović wanted to expand the TRUP to all (presumably
West) European countries as a kind of elite, radical émigré organization.
Kulenović's ambition was that the TRUP would, financially assisted by émigrés
worldwide, train saboteurs and terrorists who would be capable of carrying
out attacks against Yugoslav targets both in Western Europe and in Yugoslavia
itself.[88] While Kulenović had earlier wanted to carry out such attacks only if
the international political climate allowed it, he had allegedly become more
radicalized and now favoured carrying out armed operations as soon as
possible. However, other members disagreed with Kulenović's course. Kulenović
would later be found dead, with the Udba suspected of his murder. In the
available documentation, the responsible operative laconically notes that the
reason for the end of operational processing was that 'on 30 June 1969, Nahid
Kulenović was found dead in the bathroom of his apartment'.[89] At his funeral,
the mourners condemned West Germany for cooperating with Yugoslavia and
called for vengeance, with one mourner advocating the bombing of all Yugoslav
consulates.[90] Ivan Galić, a former associate of Kulenović's who was believed to

be responsible for his assassination, was allegedly rewarded with property near Vinkovci in Croatia, but was later himself killed.[91]

After the July 1968 bombing of the movie theatre '20th October' in Belgrade, Šarac was arrested by the West German police and, although he was initially released, he subsequently served several years in prison.[92] Although briefly released in December 1972, Šarac was arrested once again on suspicion of having organized the murder of another émigré whom Šarac suspected of working for 'the Udba'. After finally being released from prison, Šarac remained on the radar of the Yugoslav State Security Service and allegedly continued to plan attacks on and in Yugoslavia.[93] In July 1973, Šarac disappeared for some time, leading to great anxiousness that he had gone underground in order to prepare new operations.[94] The authorities were particularly worried that Šarac would try to enter Yugoslavia and carry out attacks during the tourist season, and his description was therefore circulated to all organs of internal affairs in Croatia. When a bomb went off at the Belgrade train station in August 1973, Šarac was instantly suspected.[95] In January 1974 more reports surfaced of Šarac's adverse intentions, including the possibly planned assassination of a Yugoslav diplomat.[96] Similar reports continued to accumulate, with specific details hinting at concrete planned attacks.[97]

In 1975, Šarac's activities took him to Italy and France. In March 1975, an assassination attempt took place against the Yugoslav deputy consul in Lyons, which certainly would have increased the already high state of alert surrounding Šarac, who was subsequently held to be responsible.[98] In addition, a Croat émigré, Vinko Barišić and a West German woman named Barbara Pachetka were arrested in Split on 21 June 1975 and were found to be in possession of seventeen explosive devices. During interrogation, Barišić stated that he had obtained the explosives from Šarac.

According to the information obtained by Bože Vukušić, Barišić further agreed to call Šarac, who was in Paris, and to tell him to await a phone call at a specific location on 17 July 1975.[99] On that date and location, Dane Šarac was shot over twenty times by an unknown assassin. Miraculously, Šarac managed to survive, though he was permanently partially paralyzed. Federal Secretary for Internal Affairs Franjo Herljević allegedly personally informed Tito of the successful operation, only to have to later that same day sheepishly admit that Šarac had survived.

A key document located in the archives of the SFRJ presidency appears to confirm the allegations regarding the attack on Šarac made by Ivan Ćurak, a former high-ranking official in the Bosnian SDB. On 31 August 1975, Tito met with all of the secretaries for internal affairs from the federal, republican and provincial levels. According to the minutes of the meeting, Herljević held a speech which among other things briefed Tito on specific developments linked to the emigration. Herljević started this portion of his speech rather innocuously, stating that there were an estimated 30,000 émigrés worldwide who held hostile views towards Yugoslavia and that, of these, 4,000 to 5,000 were 'more extreme and active'.[100] According to Herljević, 'the terrorist portion of the emigration … is constantly prepared and is preparing itself for the staging of terrorist acts in the country and against our citizens and institutions abroad'.[101] But after this information, Herljević moved on to highlight some recent successes of the Udba in its struggle against the hostile emigration, and here he provided tantalizing information. Among other things, said Herljević,

> the service has carried out a series of operations which have resulted in the provocation of conflicts, discord and mutual settlings of accounts in some of the most dangerous organizations and groups, as well as among terrorists. In the settlings of accounts that have arisen, 12 known criminals from the ranks of Ustaša and Chetnik extremists have lost their lives, and two have suffered serious bodily injury – Šarac [is] in a hopeless situation – paralyzed. These measures have brought uneasiness and fear and mutual distrust among extremists and have significantly contributed to the current pacification of some groups and individuals. The conditions are being created for further mutual settlings of accounts in the ranks of the extreme emigration. Currently a few operations and combinations of the SDB are underway which should contribute to the further sowing of fear, disorganization and mistrust among extremists.[102]

Herljević further rather naively assessed that in its operations hitherto against the emigration, the Yugoslav State Security Service had not even once been compromised. In any case, Tito reacted positively, stating that he was satisfied with the work of the organs of internal affairs, which he characterized as '*the weapon of our working class and the League of Communists*'.[103] Meanwhile, Stane Dolanc, secretary of the Executive Committee of the SKJ Central Committee, who himself would succeed Herljević in 1982 as federal secretary for internal affairs, praised the Yugoslav State Security Service for bringing the fight abroad to the emigration, as Tito had directed in 1972.[104]

The report delivered by Herljević and the reaction of Tito represent an almost explicit admission at the very highest level of the practice of assassinations of extreme Croat émigrés. Although euphemisms such as 'mutual settlings of accounts' are still used, and although there is no explicit admission of agency on the part of the Yugoslav State Security Service, it beggars belief that the head of the Yugoslav state and the head of the public and secret police discussed anything other than the assassination of émigrés by the Yugoslav State Security Service. It must be kept in mind that the HRB and other extremist Croat émigré organizations were heavily infiltrated by Yugoslav agents and informants. Considering that many members of these organizations became informants, it was only slightly disingenuous to speak of 'mutual settings of accounts in émigré circles.' Informants in this sense acted as a very real and potentially lethal force multiplier for the Yugoslav state. In any case, there can be no doubt that the violent deaths of émigrés or extensive injuries to them represented a source of satisfaction to both Tito and Herljević.[105] Certainly neither of them had any reason to wonder who might be behind this outcome, and both hoped that such successes would recur in the near future.

Moving back to Šarac, after the failed assassination attempt against him, the Yugoslav State Security Service sought to ascertain how badly he had been injured. Given the attention which the assassination attempt had focused on Šarac, not least among the French authorities, this proved to be difficult. Rumours abounded that other émigrés might kidnap Šarac from the hospital in order to prevent him from divulging confidential information about their networks and impending plans, or that the French authorities would try to use some kind of injections in order to force Šarac to tell them about his plans.[106] Unfortunately for the Yugoslav State Security Service, by February 1976 Šarac had already recovered significantly enough, at least psychologically, to the point where he was once again

> full of plans for the future in the sense of continuing terrorist activity. … He is sorry that the planned operation was not implemented, that the "material" was wasted, but he does not feel sorry for himself. He has decided to continue with the commenced activity, he will not take into account whether he or others will die, the important thing is that an attack into the country is made for the affirmation of the emigration. The prison hospital permits him to work on the preparation of new operations. … In the country [i.e. Yugoslavia], are seven undiscovered persons who were included in the aforementioned [unsuccessful] operation, he has unlimited faith in them and just needs to connect them. … The requisitioning of new "material" will not be a problem, because the emigration is ready to lend support without limit, both with respect to money and personnel.[107]

Moreover, through what one senses were gritted teeth, Stanko Čolak, the chief of the Second Administration in the SSUP SDB, reported that Šarac was quite satisfied with his treatment in prison. Indeed, he felt flattered by the attention representatives of the French police and state were paying him, and by their assurances that he would not be extradited to Yugoslavia. Some of them even went so far as to 'encourage' him, telling him that he would return to his country 'as a hero' after the death of Tito. In this sense, the outcome of the Šarac case was far from satisfactory for the Yugoslav authorities, and they had to keep monitoring him for years to come.[108]

If one were to conduct a survey in contemporary Croatia, asking people to name Croat émigrés (allegedly) murdered by 'the Udba', there is a fair likelihood that the name Bruno Bušić would be mentioned first or would receive the most frequent mention. Bušić came to be regarded by both émigrés and the Udba as one of the leading Croat émigré intellectuals, passionately committed to the Croatian cause.[109] Latter-day Croatian portrayals of Bušić are usually hagiographic, where he appears as an innocent martyr, but for the Udba at the time, Bušić's influence and frequent contacts with émigrés with known violent intentions proved sufficient to render him a target.

Born in 1939 as Ante Bruno Bušić in a village near Imotski, Bušić like many other Croats in the Dalmatian hinterland and in Herzegovina had a difficult relationship with the socialist Yugoslav state from a quite early age. According to his biographer and close associate Anđelko Mijatović, Bušić showed up in the documentation of the Yugoslav State Security Service already in 1956, when he was attending secondary school in Imotski.[110]

Unfortunately, there does not appear to be an SDS dossier for Bruno Bušić available in the Croatian State Archives, despite evidence in the available SDS documentation that such a dossier existed, so his case has to be reconstructed based on other documentation.[111] Bušić became active in a group called the 'Secret Organization of the Croat Intelligentsia' (*Tajna organizacija hrvatske inteligencije*, or TIHO) and was detained and questioned by the Croatian State Security Service in 1957.[112] Thereafter, Bušić and his like-minded classmates were expelled from their secondary school and subsequently remained under surveillance, with some of them inevitably being recruited as informants.[113] Despite this and a spell in prison, Bušić later resumed his education and graduated from secondary school in 1960.[114] Bušić managed to go on and pursue an education in economics at the University of Zagreb and later found gainful employment.

Bušić's fate crossed paths with the future president of Croatia, Franjo Tuđman, when Bušić in 1965 became employed at the Institute for the History of the Workers' Movement of Croatia, which Tuđman directed.[115] Yet only two months after starting his new job, Bušić was arrested for alleged anti-state activities.

After being sentenced to ten months in prison (with a two-year suspended sentence) and with the prospect of losing his job, Bušić decided to do what many other Croats in a similar situation did – he fled abroad, initially to Vienna.[116] An appeal from Tuđman persuaded Bušić to return to Yugoslavia and his job at the institute, although this proved short-lived as Tuđman was dismissed from the institute in 1967. This turn of events prompted Bušić to once again leave the institute. He ultimately settled in Paris at the beginning of 1970, socializing there with Vice Vukojević and other well-known émigrés. As the SDS later put it, 'Upon his arrival in the emigration, Bušić immediately became a person of interest for all émigré groups and organizations, so they all competed for him as an ideologue and a journalist.'[117] As of April 1970, the SDS had at least three informants, 'Marko', 'Žan' and 'Lazo' who reported on the activities of Bušić and Vukojević.[118] 'Marko' described the two as a 'tandem' in which Vukojević was the 'interpreter' of Bušić's thoughts given that Bušić suffered from a speech impediment.[119]

Although Bušić had established himself as a respected authority among Croat émigrés in Western Europe, his existence there was precarious. Without sufficient financial means or employment, and dissatisfied with his situation abroad, Bušić decided in April 1971 to return to Yugoslavia. Bušić did so knowing that his return might be greeted negatively by the authorities.[120] During the Croatian Spring, Bušić became an editor of the *Hrvatski tjednik* (Croatian Weekly), but he failed to fulfil his wish of becoming a member of Matica hrvatska – the cultural institution which helped to initiate the Croatian Spring – or to be appointed to any other positions of note.[121] However, in 1972 he was put on trial together with Franjo Tuđman and received a sentence of two years' imprisonment, which he served up until the end of 1973.[122]

In September 1975, using a fake passport Bušić arrived in London, where he successfully applied for political asylum and started working for the publication *Nova Hrvatska* (New Croatia).[123] While in the UK and later in West Germany and France, Bušić wrote prolifically and met frequently with other leading émigrés. Bušić also founded *Hrvatski List* (Croatian Newspaper). Notable among Bušić's projects was a documentary film, '*Hrvati – teroristi ili borci za slobodu*' (Croats – Terrorists or Freedom Fighters), which Bušić succeeded in having broadcast on Swedish television in February 1978.[124] Besides his publicistic activities, the Yugoslav State Security Service was thoroughly convinced that Bušić was collaborating closely with terrorists, e.g. Tomislav Naletilić, Stanko Nižić and Nikola Miličević. Moreover, in respect to the September 1976 hijacking of a Trans World Airlines flight from New York by Zvonko Bušić (no relation), Bruno Bušić was said to not only have supported that action, but to also be telling other émigrés in early 1977 that he was planning something even bigger.[125] Indeed, he had spoken of the need to transform something which he called 'Croatian liberation forces' into a 'Croatian IRA' (Irish Republican Army), in part with the assistance of the HRB.[126]

Certainly Bušić was a person of great interest to the Yugoslav State Security Service, and it is clear that agents and informants of the SDB and SDS were keeping an eye on him and his activities. In particular, they wanted to prevent him from uniting into a strong and coherent organization with the aforementioned émigrés and Ante Butković, another major figure in the emigration, into a strong and coherent organization.

Bušić himself was aware that he posed a threat in the eyes of the Yugoslav State Security Service, and that he was therefore at some risk. At the end of 1976, Bušić had told fellow politically active émigrés, including Naletilić, that he had reliable information from Zagreb according to which 'the Udba' had sent three persons to West Germany and France in order to kill him.[127] On the same occasion, Butković had warned that 'the Udba never sleeps'.[128] Naletilić also claimed to possess information regarding the presence of assassins in West Germany.

As a consequence of the aforementioned film having been shown, Bruno Bušić became even more convinced that his name was on the Yugoslav regime's hit list. And it certainly seems that he surmised correctly. At a meeting held in the headquarters of the Croatian RSUP in January 1977 and which was attended by among others the chief of the Second Administration of the federal Udba, 'the terrorist group around the émigré Bruno Bušić in France and West Germany' appeared at the top of a list of extreme émigrés. The attendees concluded that 'all preliminary actions' be undertaken 'so that the actor [*sic*] of the operation listed under number 1 be neutralized or respectively that his hostile activity be made impossible for a longer period. With respect to this we ask that this proposal be examined by authoritative persons [*od mjerodavnih*] and be adopted because it is – in our opinion – the only outcome for the existing situation. ... After the competent authorities have approved the proposed measures, these will be agreed upon again – especially after each operation, so that the realization of these operational treatments is as successful as possible.'[129] At the end of August 1977, the Second Administration of the federal Udba concluded that 'all conditions have been met for the Service to move more offensively and purposefully in the realization of the programmed tasks' with respect to the struggle against the 'fascist emigration'.[130]

Bušić was killed in Paris on 16 October 1978.[131] He had returned to Paris at the end of September and had spent the last weeks of his life meeting with fellow émigrés as usual. Late in the evening of 16 October, as Bušić was returning to his rented apartment, he was shot to death by an unknown perpetrator or perpetrators. Bušić had told another émigré, Petar Brnadić, that he was going to visit another friend, and that he would return that evening. According to a SSUP SDB report, 'on the basis of this, those [émigrés] present concluded that this friend whom Bušić did not mention had accompanied Bušić back to Brnadić's apartment and had then shot him.'[132] The French authorities investigated the killing but closed the investigation in 1982 without identifying a perpetrator.

As was the case with other killings, the Udba monitored the reactions of émigrés to the death of Bušić. Without taking any responsibility for the death of Bušić, the Yugoslav State Security Service at the end of October 1978 analysed the comments of other prominent émigrés regarding the consequences of his demise.[133] A report filed shortly after his death noted that 'some individuals from the leading portion of the emigration emphasize how a second [Stjepan] Radić has disappeared, that the emigration without Bušić is like a bomb without a detonator, and that with Bušić's disappearance the hope of the emigration in the imminent liberation of Croatia and similar [things] has also disappeared'.[134]

The Udba seems to have sown a sort of panic among the deceased's associates, with the informant 'Marko' reporting in February 1979 that 'many extremists have moved apartments and changed telephone numbers. An unprecedented fear and distrust among them prevail[s], no one trusts anyone and there are almost no visits among them like earlier. There exist several versions about his death, but not one of them excludes the participation of the Udba in it.'[135] Many émigrés were busy pointing the finger of blame for the assassination on other émigrés and organizing informal investigations, and in some cases even violent interrogations of suspects.[136] They viewed Bušić's death as a nearly insurmountable defeat. The hard work of Bušić was now falling apart 'like a house of cards', with no obvious successor to replace him.[137] In what must have been a development of concern to the Udba 'Marko' also believed that the older generation of Ustaša émigrés would now be ascendant. Yet the Udba perhaps believed that the older generation was less likely to transform their profound antipathy for Yugoslavia into armed operations.

Fourteen years later, in 1992, a documentary film about Bruno Bušić was shown on state television in the now independent Republic of Croatia.[138] The film, produced with the sponsorship of the Sabor's Commission for the Confirmation of Wartime and Postwar Victims, projected a hagiographical portrait of Bušić. As we shall see later, this film is in some circles credited with further inflaming the tense relationship between those émigrés who had repatriated to Croatia and those who had entered Croatian state service after spending most of their careers in the service of the Yugoslav state.

Conclusion

The Yugoslav regime had engaged in assassinations of its enemies among the émigrés since the late 1940s. Conducting such operations outside Yugoslavia carried with it significant risks both for the Udba and for the international reputation of Yugoslavia. However, the leadership of the Udba believed that the benefits outweighed the risks, brushing aside the criticism of those who saw 'special operations' as 'illegal work' which would damage Yugoslavia and merely result in revenge attacks from extreme émigrés.[139] And as Bernd Robionek has noted, the authorities' militaristic language during the month of the unsuccessful Bugojno Uprising, including the pervasive use of the term 'liquidation', harkened back to anti-guerrilla suppression of the late 1940s and early 1950s.[140] For Tito and his top security officials, Yugoslavia was once again in existential danger. The Croatian Spring, the Bugojno Uprising – and outside Yugoslavia also the Soviet invasion of Czechoslovakia in 1968, which Yugoslavia had condemned – all left no doubt about that.

Tito's directive of 21 July 1972 to the Udba and other Yugoslav security services to move to an 'offensive stance' in the wake of the Bugojno Uprising merely represented a reinvigoration of the assassination campaign and a (renewed) official stamp of approval. And there can be no doubt that a link exists between Tito's directive and subsequent deaths among émigrés. To take but one example, the SSUP SDB on the second page of a report issued on 18 September 1972 about 'the newest indications of possible sabotage-terrorist operations of the extreme portion of the emigration and our measures' mentioned groups led by the brothers Krnak in Paris, Stipe Ševo in Stuttgart, Gojko Bošnjak in Karlsruhe and Stjepan Crnogorac and Marko Logarušić.[141] The SSUP SDB boasted of having already acted against these groups. As we have seen, Crnogorac disappeared from Salzburg in July. Ševo had in fact already been killed together with his wife Tatjana and his stepdaughter Rosemarie in Italy in August, and Gojko Bošnjak survived an apparent assassination attempt in late Karlsruhe in late 1972. At the same time, the SSUP SDB also highlighted the need to focus more on the most dangerous émigrés and to direct the efforts of the Service towards

> the undertaking of offensive operations; on the continuation of measures in Yugoslavia against confirmed contacts of the emigration; on the faster creation of informant networks in the centres of extreme activity in European and especially in transoceanic countries; on the more systematic research of the foreign factor in the subversive activity of the emigration; on the more professional use of available operational sources and the more serious selection of received intelligence; on the faster creation of complete operational documentation and on the more intensive use of the possibility of engaging sabotage-terrorist activities of the emigration. Simply put: on the consistent implementation of the Directive of the President of the Republic.[142]

The assassination of Bruno Bušić showed that the Yugoslav authorities believed in the threat of the written word, and in the power of incitement to armed action against the Yugoslav party-state. A little over a decade after the Bugojno Uprising, this increased focus on intellectuals would have fatal consequences for a man named Stjepan Đureković.

Murder in Munich: The Assassination of Stjepan Đureković

Like other socialist countries, Yugoslavia had its own political, economic and social elites. Predominantly members of the ruling League of Communists, these elites occupied the leading positions in the country, running its institutions and largest companies. Particular notable among the many leading companies was the Croatian oil company INA (*Industrija nafte*), which was established in 1964 when the refineries in Rijeka and Sisak merged with the company Naftaplin Zagreb (literally: Oil-gas Zagreb).[1] INA was by far the largest company in the Socialist Republic of Croatia, and the significance of INA only increased with the oil crises of the 1970s. Moreover, as the largest Croatian company, INA played an important role in the persistent power struggles between Croat communist political elites and predominantly Serb political elites based in the Socialist Republic of Serbia and in the federal Yugoslav institutions in Belgrade.

It was not just the size and turnover of INA that gave the company its importance, but even more so its involvement in the business of oil, gas and petroleum derivatives. These products have strategic significance for all modern countries. For Yugoslavia, whose defence doctrine in principle entertained the nightmare scenario of fending off simultaneous invasions by the Warsaw Pact and NATO, the need to secure adequate access to oil was even more acute. For this reason, both the military and civilian security and intelligence services in Yugoslavia took a keen interest in INA, as did, of course, foreign intelligence services.

Before proceeding on to Đureković, the fragility of the Yugoslav economy and the political situation need to be emphasized. Tito died in 1980, the Yugoslav state was de facto bankrupt and unemployment was increasing, particularly in the less developed areas of the country.[2] Inflation reached 45 per cent in 1981, and the country had a very pronounced trade deficit. In addition to inflation and unemployment, average citizens of Yugoslavia also began to experience shortages of various goods, and the state implemented various restrictive policies in order to suppress consumption.[3] In this context, it was clear that a major scandal in Croatia's largest company would contribute to the sense of crisis.

INA and its secrets would come to play an important role in the case of Stjepan Đureković. Born in 1926 in Petrovaradin in Vojvodina in present-day Serbia, Đureković joined the Partisans during the Second World War. In 1951, he finished his studies in economics at the University of Belgrade. In 1956, he became the director of finances at the refinery in Sisak. Đureković's career was off to a very promising start. In the meantime, Đureković married Gizela and in 1955 their son Damir, their only child, was born.

In 1964, Đureković was promoted to sales director of the company's newly created division, INA Trade. In May 1980, Đureković was again promoted, this time to be the marketing director for INA. In sum, Đureković belonged to the management of INA and all indications were that he would spend his entire career working for the company.[4] As a successful manager in INA, Đureković spent quite a lot of time travelling both within Yugoslavia and abroad, and he had relatively easy access to hard currency.

The from all appearances prosperous and busy but normal existence of the Yugoslav businessman Stjepan Đureković took a surprising turn in the second half of April 1982. On Thursday, 22 April 1982, Đureković came to his office, but then went home midday complaining of illness. The next day, Đureković did not show up to work, and the following week he again failed to show up at his office.[5] Unbeknownst to his wife and his employers, Đureković had on that Friday driven to Austria together with his mistress Snježana Brkić/Jakšić. Although she eventually returned to Yugoslavia, Đureković travelled on, reaching Munich at the end of May. On 1 June 1982, Stjepan Đureković filed an application for political asylum in the Federal Republic of Germany.[6] In his application, which was approved at the end of October 1982, Đureković expressed a fear that he would be held responsible for the economic crisis that Yugoslavia was at that point experiencing. Đureković's son Damir had already arrived in West Germany in July 1981 and had received asylum based on his stated opposition to serving his mandatory military conscription in Yugoslavia. Reunited in Munich, they resided together.

Đureković's departure from Yugoslavia turned out to have been very well prepared. As would soon become apparent, Đureković had in the previous years worked secretly but diligently writing several books in which he severely disparaged the leadership of socialist Yugoslavia and the way in which the

Yugoslav economy was being (mis)managed. Such writings, had Đureković attempted to publish them, would almost certainly have led to his arrest and the pressing of criminal charges. Đureković was well aware of this risk.

Even more dangerous were Đureković's connections with the West German authorities. Starting in April 1975 and until January 1983, Đureković had worked as an informant for the West German civilian intelligence service, the *Bundesnachrichtendienst* (BND). Given his background and access to confidential information, Đureković was in a position to supply very sensitive and accurate information regarding not just the economic situation in Yugoslavia but also militarily strategic information about the oil supply and the Yugoslav army's supply requirements. In 1982, Đureković spoke openly about this sensitive subject in the London émigré newspaper *Nova Hrvatska* (New Croatia). Although he claimed not to possess any confidential documents, Đureković nonetheless indicated that the JNA's strategic oil supplies were small and he divulged the (alleged) locations of several secret oil depots.[7]

Operation *Brk*

Đureković did not waste any time after arriving in Munich before getting involved in the political activities of the city's vibrant Croat émigré community. Given the high degree to which the Yugoslav State Security Service had infiltrated this community, it was only a matter of time before Đureković's whereabouts would become known to the SDB/SDS, a prospect which Đureković seems to have recognized.

Đureković first appeared in the available SDS documentation towards the end of June 1982. On 25 June, the informant 'Stiv' (i.e. 'Steve') reported that Dr Ivan (aka Juan) Jelić had established contact with a man from Zagreb.[8] Jelić was at the time the leader of the Croat National Council (*Hrvatski narodni odbor*, HNO), which had been established in West Germany at the beginning of the 1950s by his brother Branko, and which aspired to be the umbrella organization for all politically active Croat émigrés. 'Stiv' was one of two known code names of Krunoslav Prates – 'Boem' (i.e. 'Bohemian') being the other. Prates was a Croat émigré residing in Munich who had already been active for years as an SDS informant; Josip Perković had recruited Prates back when Perković had worked for the SDS Centre in Osijek.[9] Perković continued to work with Prates after being promoted to the chief of the Second Department in the headquarters of the SDS.[10] For his role in the killing of Đureković, Prates was sentenced in 2008.[11]

Meanwhile, in June 1982, an investigation was being mounted in Zagreb to ascertain the circumstances of Đureković's disappearance. On 28 June 1982, the chief of the First Administration of the SDS wrote to SDS Centre Zagreb in order to inform them that Đureković was suspected of embezzling funds from INA Marketing.[12] Therefore, it might be necessary to initiate operational processing of Đureković, and it was suggested that this could take place within the scope of an already existing operation regarding financial crime in Yugoslavia. That operation was codenamed 'Lugano'. There are, by contrast, ample indications that the embezzlement investigation against Đureković was designed at least in part to make him a scapegoat for the general malaise of INA and the Yugoslav economy at this time.[13]

In the meantime, another code name appeared for the first time: '*Brk*' (i.e. 'Moustache'); Đureković himself wore a moustache. '*Brk*' was mentioned in the context of an official SDS note regarding Đureković's son, Damir.[14] In their later reconstruction of the work of the SDS from 1980 to 1990, Josip Perković and Jan Gabriš stated that '*Brk*' encompassed Đureković and his activities allegedly aimed at undermining the Yugoslav economy, and that the SDS Centre Zagreb was the authority responsible for leading this operation.[15] The exact timeframe for the operations *Brk* and Lugano is not known, but both were definitely active during the fifteen months that Đureković spent in West Germany.

In addition to embezzlement, the SDS also worked to uncover what if any state secrets Đureković might have divulged to foreign intelligence agencies. The SDS quickly concluded that there was a significant likelihood that Đureković had detailed knowledge regarding the JNA's fuel needs in both peacetime and wartime.[16] However, there were no signs that Đureković had taken confidential documents with him; the extent of his work predating his departure would only later become clear.[17]

Here it is important to reiterate that, given the nature of Đureković's work and his knowledge, a number of the secrets he had been privy to were of a military nature. And for this reason, the Yugoslav military intelligence and security services would or should have shared jurisdiction with the SDS on this aspect of Đureković's activities. Yet the available archival material reveals very little about any role of the military services, and the relevant military archives remain inaccessible even today. Therefore, the precise nature and extent of the military's role will remain unknown for the foreseeable future. That having been said, all indications from the available documentation are that the SDS retained primary responsibility for Đureković after he absconded from Yugoslavia.

The SDS Centre Zagreb began to gather information about the family and acquaintances of Đureković. The Centre proposed wiretapping of the relevant telephone lines – 'secret control of telephone conversations' (*tajna kontrola telefonskih razgovora*, TKTR).[18] The SDS also initiated other measures from its toolbox, including surveillance and background checks, as well as so-called 'informational conversations' (*informativni razgovori*) – i.e. interrogations or interviews – with persons who were somehow connected to Đureković.[19]

On 7 July 1982, the SDS Centre Zagreb completed and approved a proposal for the operational processing of Đureković.[20] In his capacity as the chief of the SDS Centre Zagreb, Franjo Vugrinec proposed the measure.[21] Josip Perković, as chief of the Second Department of the SDS, supported the proposal, and Zdravko Mustač as chief of the SDS granted final approval. The initiation of operational processing was justified by contacts between Đureković and the émigré Ivan Jelić and by Đureković's proposal to publish a book about the political and economic situation in Yugoslavia. The justified suspicion also existed that Đureković would provide foreign intelligence services with confidential information.

As a person subjected to operational processing (*operativna obrada*) a formal SDS dossier was now established, initially bearing the number 249482. The abbreviation 'OO' would henceforth appear next to the first mention of Đureković's name in SDS documents.[22] Đureković's son Damir was put in the category of preliminary operational processing (*prethodna operativna obrada*) and was hence designated as 'POO'.

In the coming months, information about Đureković gathered in Munich accumulate rapidly in the filing cabinets of the SDS Centre in Zagreb. As part of the standard operating procedure of the SDS, much of this information was collated and summarized in informational reports. These reports were cleared by Franjo Vugrinec as the chief of the SDS Centre and sent on to the chief of the SDS, Zdravko Mustač.[23] In addition, during the period in which the SDS was working intensively on the Đureković case, the SDS produced several special informational reports (*specijalne informacije*) which dealt specifically with Đureković and INA.[24] Although no distribution list is included in these special reports, the members of the Croatian Council for the Protection of the Constitutional Order were definitely among the recipients. This conclusion is supported by a statement by the SRH Secretary for Internal Affairs Vinko Bilić in April 1980, who reminded the members of the Council of the regularly issued special informational reports which offered the 'leadership of the republic' an overview of current security issues.[25]

The number of special reports devoted to Stjepan Đureković illustrates his great importance for the SDS and its political masters. Although not all such reports are available from the relevant time period, the numbering of the reports leads to the conclusion that the SDS had produced only seven such reports from the beginning of 1982 until the end of August. By contrast, in the subsequent two months between 9 September and 4 November, the SDS produced nine further reports, of which five dealt with Đureković and INA.

On 2 September 1982, the SDS Centre Zagreb summarized its findings to date in Operation 'Brk'.[26] Besides the background for the flight of Đureković and a reconstruction of his journey to Munich, the SDS listed the persons with whom Đureković had been in contact with since arriving in West Germany. The SDS also had obtained information concerning Đureković's ambitious publishing plans. He allegedly had four or five books in various states of completion, and the purpose of these books was to depict socialist Yugoslavia in a very negative way. In addition, the SDS had heard rumours that Đureković aspired to establish a radio station which would broadcast hostile information into Yugoslavia. Đureković would finance the radio station personally and his son Damir would run the programming. Contrary rumours, meanwhile, held that both of them were preparing to flee to South America.[27] Together with the existing contacts to émigré circles in Munich, the portrait which the SDS drew was clearly a negative one of a person engaged in high-profile hostile activities aimed directly against the interests of socialist Yugoslavia. In a memo written only a few days after the summary of Operation 'Brk' was produced, Vugrinec recapitulated the hostile activities of Đureković, noting again the alleged contacts between Đureković and Western intelligence services.[28] And by the end of September, the SDS had received information that the Croat émigré Vladislav Musa was preparing a terrorist attack in Yugoslavia and that he was in touch regularly with Đureković. These reports more than sufficed for the SDS to regard Đureković as a member of the extreme portion of the Croat emigration.[29] Moreover, it might be considered that the SDS leadership must have also to some degree been affected in their stance towards Đureković by their frustration at not having detected his hostile activities in a timely manner before he could defect to West Germany.[30] This failure had also caused the SDS to lose face vis-à-vis the federal Yugoslav State Security Service.

As the SDS suspected and feared, Đureković was indeed prolific in his publications during his time in Munich. In the approximately fifteen months from his arrival there until his death, he in rapid succession published five books with the assistance of veteran Croat émigrés in Munich such as Ivan Jelić.

Significantly, Đureković seems to have written at least large parts of these books in Yugoslavia and to have smuggled them out of the country prior to eloping to West Germany. The titles were *Ja, Josip Broz Tito* (I, Josip Broz Tito), *Crveni manageri* (Red Managers), *Komunizam: velika prevara* (Communism: A Grand Deception), *Slom ideala* (Collapse of the Ideals) and *Sinovi Orla* (The Sons of the Eagle). All of the books appeared in printings of several thousand copies.[31] A mixture of pulp fiction and shrill political polemics, the very titles of these books were designed to provoke the Yugoslav party-state. Besides attacking the very principles of socialist Yugoslavia and openly mocking and attacking the memory of Tito – who was still considered to be untouchable and beyond reproach in Yugoslavia – Đureković in the latter book also explicitly aligned himself with the Kosovo Albanians. Doing so was particularly provocative given the riots and state of emergency that had occurred in Kosovo soon after Tito's death.[32]

In addition to the books, Đureković maintained a public profile by granting interviews to émigré and West German newspapers and also gave speeches to émigré organizations. In an interview with the tabloid *Bild am Sonntag* on 5 December 1982, Đureković stated that the information included in his books stemmed from knowledge which he had accumulated through his previous job. Đureković vehemently denied the accusations flourishing in the Yugoslav press according to which he had committed massive fraud and absconded with a large fortune.[33]

Portions of the printing of Đureković's books took place in a small printing press installed in a garage in Wolfratshausen, a sleepy but picturesque village approximately 30 kilometres south of Munich's centre. Đureković rented the garage and from it he distributed his books through the HNO and through his growing network of other Croat émigré connections. In what can only be regarded as an act of deliberate provocation, Đureković also sent copies of the book to Yugoslav journalists and officials.[34] Publishing and distribution were demanding work and Đureković received assistance from Krunoslav Prates, who had been for years working closely with Jelić. Unbeknownst to both Jelić and Đureković, Prates was also an informant for the SDS.

The anti-regime nature of Đureković's activities was therefore no secret, and the SDS reported on the publication and distribution of his books. In a special informational report dated 11 October 1982, the SDS focused on *Communism: A Grand Deception*, the first book published by Đureković, noting that it was selling very well.[35] The report confirmed that Đureković had previous to his flight from Yugoslavia smuggled manuscripts abroad 'in which he openly and hostilely writes about the highest leaders and the situation in the

SFRJ'.[36] The SDS provided a very detailed summary of the book in the eight-page informational report. Đureković aimed with his book, the publication of which he had financed himself, to 'create the impression of the collapse of the socialist system from within. The main thesis is directed against communism: communism as a social system itself creates its enemies and destroyers.' The SDS noted that among numerous other angles of criticism, the book also characterized the SFRJ as a 'police state'. The author's use of a 'base and vulgar vocabulary' added insult to injury. The SDS further saw the similarity between the arguments of Đureković and those of the émigré press as evidence that 'Đureković has during his stay abroad been constantly connected with the extreme emigration'.

Đureković's second publication, *I, Josip Broz Tito*, received an equally detailed seven-page 'review' by the SDS in an informational report issued on 26 November 1982.[37] Đureković had once again financed the publication himself, which was a demolition of the personality, role and legacy of Tito. With disgust, the SDS wrote that Đureković created a 'monstrous portrait' and that he 'on every one of the 368 pages ascribes to him [i.e. Tito] countless depravities, vulgar and inhumane characteristics which he then emphasises to absurdity'. The SDS noted that Đureković had 'impudently sent individual high-ranking political leaders of the SFRJ and SRH' copies of the book, which he claimed to have written during the course of the past decade. Translations of the book were underway to English, German, French and Spanish. Two further books were in preparation for publication. In the foreword to the book, Đureković claimed that he had a 'moral obligation and patriotic duty' to write the book, but that he had also had to flee Yugoslavia because of the expected consequences of the book's publication. Đureković told his readers that he knew that he was not safe abroad and that the Yugoslav authorities would continue to pursue him. The SDS concluded that the goals of Đureković's activities abroad to date were to contribute to the destruction of Yugoslavia. Đureković's positive comments about both Croatian independence and certain figures associated with the wartime quisling state did not escape the SDS's attention.

At the end of September 1982, the steering council of the SDS met in 'expanded composition' – i.e. with special guests – with Zdravko Mustač chairing the meeting. Mustač emphasized the need to continue the struggle against both internal and external enemies of Yugoslavia and cited the 'Đureković case' as an example that 'certain forms of economic crime' paralleled 'hostile political activity'.[38] The highest instances of the party-state demanded that such matters be investigated and resolved, and therefore the SDS had to prepare and executive relevant operations.[39] In the concluding discussion at the meeting, the 'Đureković case' was mentioned as being 'instructive,' illustrating that the SDS had to act more decisively.[40]

In October 1982, the SRH Council for the Protection of the Constitutional Order discussed the Đureković affair. Mustač highlighted the matter and the ongoing investigation of the company INA Commerce as among the most important security-related matters facing the Croatian leadership.[41] It should be noted that Mustač portrayed Đureković and INA as separate but interrelated subjects. The council was told that the investigation into Đureković revealed his 'current very intensive hostile activity' in West Germany.[42] The council concluded that it was necessary to accelerate the investigation as much as possible.[43] As regarded the investigation into INA, the members of the council expressed their dissatisfaction, as the political and public climate was negatively affecting the investigation and impeding the normal work of the company. Therefore, this investigation should also be duly accelerated so that it could be properly concluded as soon as possible. Interestingly, and despite what Mustač had stated, it was concluded that 'in doing so, one should vigorously strive to ensure that this case is not related to the Đureković case'.[44] Illustrating the importance of INA to the SRH leadership, the council also received relevant information directly from the management of the company.[45]

On 1 November 1982, an urgent meeting of the SRH Council for the Protection of the Constitutional Order was held to discuss the INA affair.[46] Prior to the meeting, the council had received a new special informational report from the SDS.[47] During the meeting, the necessity of keeping the two investigations separate was once again emphasized, and the suggestions in the press regarding the interconnections between the two were criticized.[48] There was also talk of an attempt to manipulate the investigations conducted by the federal authorities for accounting and hard currency control in a way that the leadership of the SRH would be discredited. This rumoured attempt must be seen in the context of chronic struggles for power and economic primacy in Yugoslavia. These struggles pitted the federal authorities (sometimes aligned with the authorities of the Socialist Republic of Serbia and the giant trading company Geneks) against the Croatian authorities and INA.[49] The political and public interest in the INA affair as such threatened negative consequences not just for the company but for the entire standing of Croatia in Yugoslavia. Therefore, the council decided that the leadership and employees of INA had to double the intensity of their efforts. The Đureković investigation was to continue but separately from that into INA.[50] It was very obvious that the council would not hesitate to micromanage both investigations. However, it should be noted that the council claimed that there had in connection with the investigation of INA Commerce been no pressure from the federal authorities, including the SSUP.[51]

Also in November 1982, the SDS obtained information indicating that Ivan Jelić was looking to promote Đureković for a prominent post in Croat émigré circles.[52] This news seemed to confirm the SDS's worries that Đureković was rapidly ascending to the top of the 'hostile emigration' in West Germany. Yet as of 10 November 1982, the SRH Council for the Protection of the Constitutional Order noted that there were no significant new revelations in the Đureković investigation.[53]

In December 1982, the SDS Centre Zagreb constructed an overview of the activities of Đureković hitherto.[54] The SDS believed that Đureković continued to be engaged in hostile activities towards Yugoslavia. In order to better understand Đureković and his motivations, the SDS sketched three trajectories for its future work on this case. First, the SDS wished to gather intelligence in order to create a reliable profile of Đureković's personality. The SDS wanted to analyse his flight from Yugoslavia and the reasons for this flight and also to examine his activities immediately before he eloped. The emphasis was on identifying which types of confidential information he could have taken with him. Secondly, the SDS wanted to investigate Đureković's allegedly criminal activities in Yugoslavia and his suspected self-enrichment. Thirdly, the SDS of course continued to monitor the further activities of Đureković in West Germany and in particular to identify and monitor any possible contacts he had not only with other émigrés, but also with any persons remaining in Yugoslavia, especially in INA. These priorities for the SDS's handling of Đureković were reiterated in March 1983.[55]

On 14 December 1982, the SRH Council for the Protection of the Constitutional Order received further information regarding the 'hostile and otherwise criminal activity' of Đureković.[56] It was concluded that this information should be forwarded to the Presidency of the Central Committee of the SKH. It was further concluded that the SDS should produce a report which would include 'the most sensitive questions and information', and that this report should be distributed exclusively to four addresses: the president of the SRH presidency, the president and the secretary of the CK SKH and the president of the Council for the Protection of the Constitutional Order.[57]

On 27 December 1982, the SRH social accounting agency overseeing financial matters and hard currency filed a criminal complaint with the district prosecutor in Zagreb.[58] According to the complaint, Đureković had committed a number of financial irregularities from which he had derived considerable personal financial gain. The Yugoslav authorities were therefore operating on two tracks, displaying an interest both in Đureković's financial activities prior to his flight from the country and in his publishing and other activities in West Germany.

At the beginning of February 1983, the council criticized the course of the INA investigation, noting that it still did not conform to the wishes expressed by the council. In order to remedy this situation, the council established an extraordinary commission which received a mandate to audit and analyse the work of all investigative organs hitherto. On the basis of the conclusions of this commission, the council would take 'relevant measures to eliminate the currently unacceptable situation'. The members of this extraordinary commission were Tode Ćuruvija, Vinko Bilić, Martin Špegelj and Milorad Viskić, who were to receive assistance from Pavle Gaži, Zdravko Mustač and Josip Šlibar.[59] On 1 June, the council discussed the work and findings of the commission.[60]

In the meantime, on 15 or 16 February 1983, the SDS Centre Zagreb sent the prosecutor and the superior court in Zagreb an indictment of Đureković for anti-state activities.[61] These activities included the contacts between Đureković and Ivan Jelić, Đureković's books and the interviews which he had given to various émigré newspapers and magazines. The indictment of Đureković left open the question of how he was going to be prosecuted, and no mention was made of his having passed state secrets to the BND. It is almost certain that the Yugoslav State Security Service must have contemplated kidnapping and subsequently prosecuting Đureković based on the template used for Slobodan 'Bata' Todorović. This option would also have had the added attraction of permitting a thorough interrogation of Đureković which would have uncovered the extent of his cooperation with the BND.

Đureković remained very active in Munich throughout this period, but even as he agitated against Yugoslavia and rose in prominence in the Croat émigré community, his anxiety regarding possible reprisals grew.[62] Apparently, Đureković initially seemed to think that his publicistic activities and his newfound fame would protect him.[63] However, by November 1982 Đureković had, according to the émigré Vladislav Musa, begun to see 'an agent of the Udba' wherever he looked.[64] By March 1983 at the latest, Đureković allegedly lived in 'great fear' and had acquired two bodyguards who could protect him from attack.[65] Around this time, Đureković had also supposedly fatalistically stated that he wanted to publish just one more thing, then he could be killed.[66] Đureković also stated that the SDS had considerable resources but was ineffective but nonetheless dangerous because of its 'bloodthirst' (*krvoločnost*).[67] Đureković also later told a German acquaintance that he had learned that there was allegedly a bounty on his head of half a million Deutschmarks.[68]

On 10 April 1983, the Croat émigrés in Munich commemorated the anniversary of the establishment of the so-called Independent State of Croatia in 1941. This particular edition of the annual commemoration was of particular significance, as it would turn out to be the only such commemoration in which Đureković would participate in Munich. As had been the case in previous years, the SDS received detailed reports about the commemoration from its numerous informants embedded in the Croat emigration.[69] Jelić presented Đureković as the keynote speaker, and Đureković spoke of his future publications and other plans. His prominent role in the commemoration confirmed that Đureković was being groomed for, and aspired to, a leading position in the Croat emigration.[70] It certainly seemed that this assessment was shared by both the most politically active Croat émigrés and the SDS and the SSUP, whose analysts wrote that Đureković 'is attempting to position himself in multiple ways: as an individual who is capable of attracting and gathering around himself all émigré groups, moreover as an all-round connoisseur of all structures and the general state of affairs in Yugoslavia, whose assessments are perfect, and also as a mobilizer of the emigration to undertake concrete operations.'[71]

On 15 April 1983, the SRH Council for the Protection of the Constitutional Order convened in an extraordinary composition. Besides the regular members, prominent guests had also been invited, of whom Mika Špiljak, the vice president of the Presidency of Yugoslavia, was undoubtedly the most prominent.[72] It is worth noting that the tape recording of this particular meeting of this session of the council was labelled as a state secret, although the other recordings or minutes of these meetings were usually classified instead as 'very secret'.[73] The session had been convoked at the behest of Špiljak.[74] At the meeting, a dramatic confrontation took place between Špiljak and the Croatian secretary for internal affairs, Pavle Gaži, because Gaži had allegedly told the federal secretary for internal affairs Stane Dolanc that Špiljak and others were blocking the investigation into INA. The presumed reason for this was that Vanja Špiljak, Mika's son, as well as the sons of some of other prominent officials, were employed by INA.[75] Dolanc had allegedly provided this information to the President of the Yugoslav Presidency Petar Stambolić. Špiljak angrily demanded that Gaži reveal from whom he had obtained these allegations, and why he claimed that the investigation had been obstructed.[76] From the context of the further discussion, it is visible that the federal authorities – both the SSUP and the Yugoslav presidency – had received reports regarding the investigations into INA.[77] Gaži claimed that he had not passed along any information but had rather merely stated that the investigations were focusing on Đureković, and that the council wanted to complete the investigations as soon as possible.[78] Špiljak said that it might be best that the entire matter be handled by the federal investigative authorities so as to avoid any appearance that he was somehow interfering. Here it is necessary to underline that Špiljak was, according to the logic of the rotating presidency that had come into effect after the death of Tito, supposed to be the next president of the Yugoslav presidency after Petar Stambolić.[79]

By the end of the council's discussion, the participants agreed that the investigations into INA should be neither delayed nor interrupted, but that public opinion had on the other hand meanwhile come to the conclusion that various actors were seeking to impede or stop the investigations. Tode Ćuruvija emphasized that the SDS continued to investigate Đureković.[80] Zdravko Mustač reminded the council that the SDS had not had any activities directed towards Đureković until after he had left the country, as he had succeeded in keeping his activities well camouflaged.[81] Mustač said that the investigations up until that point had shown that Đureković was greedy, but that there were no indications of major crimes. It was possible that Đureković had accumulated his hard currency wealth legally through savings.[82] By contrast Milorad Viskić, who headed the judicial and administrative committee in the Sabor, claimed that Đureković had used his trips abroad to carry out tasks for foreign intelligence services.[83] Mustač explained that the investigative reconstruction of Đureković's activities in Yugoslavia was intensive and ongoing, and that the SDS had identified thirty-six persons linked to Đureković. Mustač further claimed that 'we today know almost everything about Đureković, about what he is up to today, what he is up to abroad, almost everything'.[84] The SDS possessed information according to which Đureković possibly had embezzled several millions of US dollars. However, the accusations against Đureković for economic criminality were very weak compared to those regarding his anti-state activities.[85] Mustač persisted in his opinion that there was no direct link between the two investigations.[86]

Mustač further stated that he had spoken twice confidentially and directly with Secretary for Internal Affairs Dolanc, and that Dolanc had shown a particular interest in Đureković.

> He was very concerned, because we know very little about the intelligence background of the Đureković case, he was very critical because we did not in advance have an operational interest in him, etc. He asked how we could deploy

the service systematically so that such things could be prevented in large systems. Naturally we also spoke about how Đureković could evolve as a problem in the emigration. I was quite pessimistic in the view, and I still believe this, that he is evolving in an extreme manner there, as we can anyway also see.[87]

Mustač also remarked that the investigations into Đureković continued to focus on his books. Dolanc had read all of the books and wanted to know who the sources for the books were. Dolanc's curiosity was piqued by his conclusion that the type of information contained in the books was not accessible to 'mortal human beings'.[88]

On 1 June 1983, the INA affair was once again on the agenda of the SRH Council for the Protection of the Constitutional Order.[89] The extraordinary commission of the council had produced its report. The earlier questions regarding impediments or sabotage of the investigations were assessed to be misunderstandings, and Dolanc had now apparently decided that the SSUP would examine the work of the Federal Hard Currency Inspectorate.[90] The SDS would continue its investigation of INA. Đureković was not mentioned in the abridged minutes of this session of the council.

This was the last session of the SRH Council for the Protection of the Constitutional Order that was held before the death of Đureković. The next session was not held until 9 September 1983, and at that session Pavle Gaži was removed from his position and was replaced by Zdravko Mustač, who became acting secretary for internal affairs in Croatia.[91]

On 9 June 1983, the SDS reported about its further plans for Đureković, who allegedly had still more material ready for publication soon.[92] Less than a month later, the SDS further learned that Đureković had in fact passed on confidential information – presumably to the BND – regarding the petroleum requirements for the Yugoslav military, thereby confirming Đureković's status as an enemy of the state.[93]

In the weeks and months preceding his violent death, Đureković lived in fear. As we have seen, the SDS was well aware of Đureković's anxiety. On the very day of his murder, the SDS Centre Zagreb produced an informational report according to which Đureković had switched residences in Munich four times within the past two months due to his fear of being kidnapped or killed. The source for this information was the informant 'Dukat', who had allegedly heard this from Vladislav Musa. The SDS instructed 'Dukat' to ascertain Đureković's address.

This instruction raises the question of whether the SDS could plausibly be behind Đureković's murder when they were still trying to pinpoint his location on the day of his murder. Yet there are other plausible explanations. For one, the SDS was probably trying to establish the location of all the houses or apartments that Đureković was using. And the case officer handling 'Dukat' might not have known that others in the SDS (or the federal SDB) had obtained the correct location. It is also possible that the SDS or others had located Đureković, but still wanted to confirm this information.[94]

Operation *Pismo*

Before proceeding to a description of Đureković's murder, another related SDB operation must be mentioned. As has been mentioned in previous chapters, the Yugoslav State Security Service made frequent use of information and disinformation campaigns in the struggle against the hostile emigration. In 1981, the SSUP SDB initiated Operation *Pismo* (Letter) which was designed to produce such disinformation. The operation was therefore not limited to Đureković but came to encompass him after his departure from Yugoslavia in April 1982.

Operation Letter was run from Belgrade in coordination with relevant republican state security services. Božidar Spasić, who worked as an operative in the Second Administration of the SSUP SDB, was apparently in charge of carrying out the part of the operation that most specifically affected Đureković. Spasić has a history of being quite self-aggrandizing in his own publications about his previous SDB activities, but it is clear that he played a role.[95] According to Spasić, the operation included the 'writing of forged personal letters, flyers, invitations, newspapers, brochures, even books'.[96] Spasić also placed threatening phone calls to émigrés in the middle of the night in order to increase their sense of fear and anxiety.[97]

Spasić claims that Stane Dolanc, in his capacity as the chief of the SSUP, at an unspecified time ordered the liquidation of Đureković.[98] Further actions targeting Đureković should according to Spasić have been connected to an operation named *Dunav* (Danube), but very little information is available to corroborate this claim.[99] Likewise, Spasić claims that he already at the time possessed detailed knowledge regarding the espionage activities of Đureković, whereas relatively little specific information about this is available in Đureković's dossier. It is hardly credible that such information would not have been shared between the SSUP SDB and the SDS.

In the spring of 1983, Spasić organized the printing and sending to émigrés of a large number of postcards that purported to come from Đureković. The postcards depicted Bleiburg, the site of the largest Yugoslav postwar massacre of Croats, and on the other side 'Đureković' offered a discount on his books.[100] Among the possible desired effects of this particular act of disinformation was the placing of Đureković in an uncomfortable position in which he would be forced to sell his books at a discount, or in which he would be accused of exploiting a national tragedy in order to increase his book sales. On the other hand, if Đureković were to announce publicly that the postcards were forgeries, he would risk ridicule or – another consequence that the SDB would not have deemed undesirable – it would have dawned on the many recipients of the postcards that the SDB possessed their mailing addresses. As for Spasić, he paradoxically wrote that 'we did not take too much care to hide that this was our doing, because we intended to make Đureković relax, to expose him as much as possible publicly, to reduce his alertness and to liberate him of the fear of liquidation'.[101] In any case, Đureković complained to the Munich police in April 1983 that the fake postcards were an attempt to discredit him.[102]

A more ambitious forgery perpetrated by Spasić was the printing of an entire forged issue of the émigré magazine *Nova Hrvatska* (New Croatia), including a fake interview with Đureković. Spasić personally brought thousands of copies of the forged magazine to Dortmund, whence they were distributed.[103] Needless to say, the execution of this operation was also quite expensive for the Yugoslav State Security Service, although the available documentation does not reveal how much money was spent on the disinformation campaign. In any case, the effect of this particular tactic was questionable given that the forgery was done in such a manner that a casual glance at the magazine would make it clear that it had been written by illegitimate authors.[104] Namely, the authors of the forgery used many Serbian words and expressions which would never have been used by the Croat nationalist authors usually featured in the magazine.

Taken in their entirety, the elements in Operation *Pismo* were designed to cast aspersions on the reputation of Đureković, who clearly had leadership ambitions in the Croat émigré community. Equally importantly, Đureković at least in theory had the potential to unite an otherwise fractious community, which could have presented further danger to Yugoslavia. By damaging his reputation, the Yugoslav State Security Service hoped to sow further discord in the community and therefore make it plausible that any unfortunate developments that might befall Đureković could have resulted from internal rivalries and factionalism.

The assassination of Đureković

It is necessary to repeat that the state of the available documentation is such that there is no single original document stemming from the Yugoslav State Security Service or from any other Yugoslav government agency that explicitly reveals a decision to assassinate Đureković or casts detailed light on this decision-making process or on the actual operation that resulted in the murder of Đureković. It may be doubted whether such documentation still exists, or indeed whether it has ever existed. Numerous witnesses testifying in the Munich trial of Zdravko Mustač and Josip Perković testified that they believed that decisions to assassinate émigrés abroad were communicated verbally and were not recorded in any documents. The brief summary provided here regarding the actual assassination will therefore necessarily rely on the findings of the trial chamber in Munich, which itself is based largely on witness testimony, and in particular that of insider witnesses. While the reliance on witness testimony is certainly not optimal, it is by no means uncommon when courts deal with crimes committed by organized criminal enterprises. Moreover, the reliance on witness testimony must also be considered within the context of a robust and voluminous collection of structural documentation which leaves no doubt that the Yugoslav State Security Service repeatedly and over the span of several decades engaged in the assassination of émigrés.

As has been seen above, based on its own internal rationale the Yugoslav State Security Service did not lack reasons to justify killing Đureković. Not only had he committed treason and economic crimes, he had single-mindedly worked since his arrival in West Germany on publications and other activities designed to discredit and undermine the Yugoslav party-state. Although there was little direct evidence linking him to current or planned émigré terrorist activities against Yugoslavia or Yugoslav targets abroad, he met and socialized with one of the most hostile Croat émigré scenes. Numerous persons with whom he came into contact were among those of the highest operational interest for the Yugoslav State Security Service. Moreover, Đureković openly aspired to a leadership position in the Croat émigré diaspora, wrote about the plight of ethnic Albanians in Kosovo and also had plans of establishing a radio station that would broadcast hostile propaganda into Yugoslavia. Đureković's flight and treasonous and hostile activities both before and after his flight to West Germany also constituted a major embarrassment to the SDS and, by extension to the SKH. Given the sensitivity of these matters and the importance of INA to the political leadership in Croatia, the elimination of Đureković also made sense from this angle.

As has been seen, the SDS possessed an extensive network of informants in the Munich area. An examination of the SDS's documentation creates the impression that it was impossible for any substantial group of Croat émigrés to meet without there being at least one SDS informant present. These informants provided the SDS with highly detailed and often very accurate information on a running basis.

Beyond the gathering and provision of actionable intelligence, a smaller group of informants also played a specific role in the operation leading to Đureković's murder. Foremost among these was the aforementioned Krunoslav Prates, who worked as Josip Perković's informant. In June 1983, in accordance with the proper procedure for contacting informants abroad, Perković travelled to a third country, Luxembourg, to meet with Prates.[105] At this meeting, Prates provided Perković with a duplicate key to Đureković's garage in Wolfratshausen. At a later point, Perković then handed this key either directly to the team responsible for the operation or to those persons who were in contact with that team. Perković remained in contact with Prates after the meeting in Luxembourg regarding the activities and location of Đureković. In this manner, Perković was able to ascertain that Đureković would be present in the garage on the morning of 28 July 1983.

On 24 July 1983, Stjepan Đureković met with several prominent Croat émigrés including Ivan Jelić at the restaurant Simbacher Hof in Munich.[106] According to Petar Kegalj, who worked there as a waiter, the main topic of conversation that evening was the candidacy of Đureković for the leadership of the Croatian National Council (*Hrvatsko narodno vijeće*, HNV), a leading émigré body. They also discussed the forged issue of *Nova Hrvatska*. Krunoslav Prates was also among those present, and was thus there when Đureković told Jelić that he would bring a draft article to the improvised print shop in Wolfratshausen on 28 July. Only a small number of people knew that Đureković was using the garage there as a print shop.

On the morning of 28 July 1983, a sunny and pleasantly warm Bavarian summer day, Đureković departed from the apartment in St Cajetan-Strasse in Munich, where he resided together with his son.[107] He intended to check his mailbox at the post office in Wolfratshausen, and thereafter to leave his article in the garage before heading to meet his friend Herta Stossberger for a boat ride on the Isar River. According to her, Đureković called her during the morning to tell her that he was running late, and that they would meet at noon, half an hour later than planned. Using his own car, Đureković drove a roundabout route in order to shake any potential surveillance teams.

Using the duplicate key provided by Prates to Perković, the hit team consisting of at least two men gained access to the garage in Wolfratshausen in the early morning of 28 July. They then hid themselves awaiting Đureković's arrival. At some point that morning, Đureković arrived on foot. He had as always parked his car some distance from the garage in order to try to mitigate the discovery of his destination by any agents of the SDS that might be following him.

Entering the garage, he left the door open to let some daylight in, as the only light switch was located in the middle of the garage's three rooms. He deposited a document entitled '*Zašto sam se kandidirao za HNV*' (Why I Ran for the HNV) on a photocopier in the garage. Portentously, the typed text of the draft article concluded with the following words:

> The only thing I am afraid of is that the UDB-a will from now on even more relentlessly search for me in order to kill me. But as regards this I do not fear death but only that they will thereby make it impossible for me to together with our people return to a free Croatian State and to partake of that great moment of our national history.[108]

The text bore numerous handwritten revisions and corrections. Among other things, Đureković had added 'and my son', expressing a fear that the Yugoslav State Security Service would also pursue and kill Damir Đureković.[109] Stjepan Đureković had also added his hope that he would come to play an important role in the newly independent Croatian state.

Having deposited his draft in the garage, Đureković then apparently headed for the exit, but as he did so, he was shot from behind by the perpetrators – of which there were at least two and most likely three – using a Czech 7.65-mm automatic pistol and another 22-mm automatic weapon, possibly a Beretta.[110] Eight shots were fired in all, of which five struck Đureković from behind. Not content with the damage caused by the shooting, the perpetrators struck Đureković's head repeatedly with a sharp tool. According to the subsequent report of the medical examiner, Đureković died of head and lung injuries at some point between 10.50 and 11.30 am on 28 July 1983.[111]

After carrying out the assassination, the perpetrators left the crime scene, closing the garage door in order to conceal the murder. In all likelihood, the direct perpetrators of the killing were assisted by a larger logistical team, as was the case in kidnapping operations for which detailed documentation is available.[112] The identity of the perpetrators has to this day not been determined, but numerous witnesses in the Munich trial expressed the belief that the Yugoslav State Security Service had hired seasoned Yugoslav criminals residing outside of Yugoslavia to carry out the assassination. This hypothesis is to some extent supported by the available archival documentation, which makes it clear that the Yugoslav State Security Service repeatedly contemplated making use of such criminals to carry out tasks such as kidnapping and murder.

The most convincing explanation provided at the Munich trial of Josip Perković and Zdravko Mustač for the involvement of Yugoslav criminals in the liquidation of Đureković came from Dušan Stupar, who served in the 1980s as the head of the SDB Centre in Belgrade. The Belgrade centre was commonly perceived within the Yugoslav State Security Service as the *primus inter pares* of all SDB centres. Stupar is one of the few high-ranking former SDB or SDS officials who have since the collapse of Yugoslavia spoken publicly about the Yugoslav State Security Service's assassinations abroad. Appearing in 2008 in the documentary series '*Službena tajna*' (Official Secret) which was shown on the Serbian television channel B92, Stupar stated that the federal SDB had used 'members of the criminal underground for the carrying out of certain tasks' abroad.[113] Three years later, Stupar gave an extensive interview to the controversial Serb journalist Milomir Marić in his programme '*Ćirilica*' (Cyrillic [Alphabet]). In that interview, Stupar confirmed that the Yugoslav State Security Service had regarded assassinations of state enemies abroad as part of its arsenal.[114] Stupar referred to the killings as 'neutralizations', while emphasizing that these were a measure of last resort which was used only when all other measures had been exhausted.

Testifying in court in Munich in May 2016, Stupar repeated these assertions and elaborated further.[115] Stupar stated that he had been closely acquainted with the Yugoslav career criminal Željko Ražnatović 'Arkan', who during the wars of Yugoslav succession gained particularly notoriety as a leader of a Serb paramilitary formation.[116] Ražnatović is among those names most frequently mentioned when the alleged role of Yugoslav criminals in covert Yugoslav State Security Service operations is discussed, although it sometimes seems that this has more to do with his later notoriety than with any actual evidence. Nevertheless, Stupar in his testimony stated that he had heard directly from Ražnatović that he had been directly involved in the operation against Đureković. Ražnatović claimed that the goal of the operation had been not the assassination but rather the kidnapping of Đureković.[117]

As regards the involvement of career criminals in assassinations perpetrated by the Udba, rumours of this circulated contemporaneously in émigré circles. In April 1984, Milan Dorič, who as previously noted was an informant for the Slovenian SDV with the codename 'Hanzi', reported on such rumours, which included the street names of several notorious Belgrade-based criminals.[118]

And Josip Manolić, who has in the course of his career held several important positions in the Udba and in Yugoslav and Croatian political life, claims that Ražnatović was a 'state killer' (*državni ubojica*).[119]

In his testimony Stupar also spoke about the preparations that the Yugoslav State Security Service undertook for operations abroad, including cooperation with other Yugoslav intelligence and security services. He confirmed that the orders for especially sensitive operations were given orally and that debriefings were subsequently conducted to assess the success of such operations.

Around ten o'clock in the evening of 28 July 1983, Krunoslav Prates returned to his home in Geretsried near Munich.[120] Upon his arrival, his wife informed him of several instances in which the telephone had rung twice but no one had answered when she picked up the receiver. After Prates had arrived, the phone rang once again, and Prates took it as a signal that his handler Josip Perković wanted to speak to him urgently. Prates therefore went to a public phone booth and called Perković. In their conversation, Perković asked if there was anything new and wanted to know why Prates had not recently been in regular contact with him as was their agreement. Two days later, Perković and Prates spoke over the phone again. Perković wanted to confirm the dates of a meeting they had planned for Mallorca the following month. According to Prates, Perković had already heard of the death of Đureković and asked Prates how he was doing. In the following days, Perković tried to keep abreast of the murder investigation by talking to Prates.

Post-mortem disinformation campaign

News of the murder of Đureković was also received in Belgrade. According to Ivan Lasić, who was at that point relatively new in the position of the chief of the Second Section of the Serbian SDB, Sreten Aleksić, the chief of the Second Administration of the SSUP SDB told him that 'you have one less [émigré]'.[121] In response to Lasić's query, Aleksić made it clear that he was referring to Đureković. Lasić subsequently spoke with the Federal Secretary for Internal Affairs Stane Dolanc, who nonchalantly asked how 'the team' had fared, an apparent reference to the hit team responsible for the actual murder. Lasić later heard from his boss Srđan Andrejević that the 'team was complete'; that is, that its exfiltration had been successfully completed.

After the murder of Đureković, the SDS received several reports from their informant network as regarded the alleged circumstances of his death and the people behind it. Already on 30 July 1983, the informant 'Ivo' reported that Đureković had been killed the previous day.[122] The informant 'Jerko' also called with the same information. The SDS learned that the German media were reporting that the Yugoslav State Security Service was responsible for the murder. 'Jerko' and 'Ivo' were instructed how to behave and were asked to gather information about Đureković's death.[123] On 1 August, the SDS Centre Zagreb produced a report collating the available intelligence on the death of Đureković.[124]

At the beginning of September 1983, the acting SRH Republican Secretary for Internal Affairs Zdravko Mustač sent a letter to Franjo Vugrinec, the head of SDS Centre Zagreb.[125] The purpose of the letter was to agree about a list of (dis)information that should be provided to the BND by the informant 'Viktor'. The second point on the list was (dis)information about the death of Đureković. 'Viktor' was to argue that the killing of Đureković would not have served the interests of the Yugoslav State Security Service. It was therefore far more plausible that Đureković had been the victim of (yet another) internal settling of accounts in the often violent émigré scene. No available documents from the SDS provide corroboration of this version of Đureković's death.

A later report from the end of September 1983 shows that 'Viktor' in fact met with his contact from the BND, a certain Neumann, and provided him with the above disinformation.[126] 'Viktor' reported that the meeting had the desired effect. Neumann stated that Đureković had gained many enemies among other émigrés quickly after arriving in Munich. Although Neumann thought that the idea of neutralizing could stem from Yugoslavia, Neumann did not believe that Đureković had been killed by the Yugoslav State Security Service. Neumann was 'rather predisposed to believe that this was the doing of émigrés themselves'. Neumann had read various accounts about the killing in the newspapers, but he believed that the émigrés had much more motive for killing Đureković than did the Yugoslav authorities, as there was a bitter ongoing power struggle for the leadership of the Croat émigrés.[127]

In the Munich trial, neither of the accused testified. However, based on previous statements made by the accused, it was clear that they denied any connection with the assassination and believed instead that others, in particular the SSUP SDB, had organized the assassination or had, at the very least, carried it out in a manner that was objectionable to the accused.[128] It should here be noted that it would have been highly unusual and in contravention of standard operating procedures at the time for the SSUP SDB to undertake operations aimed at émigrés stemming from Croatia without coordinating this with the

SDS. Moreover, no documentation has to date emerged to support a solo operation by the SSUP SDB, although it should also be noted that the relevant archives in Belgrade remain closed to researchers.

It bears repeating that no hitherto available official document of the SDS or any other Yugoslav government source explicitly and specifically proves that the Yugoslav State Security Service carried out or ordered the murder of Stjepan Đureković in Wolfratshausen on 28 July 1983. If such a written document were ever composed, which is in itself doubtful, it will probably never be found, or it was shredded or otherwise destroyed some time ago. Yet any analysis of the murder of Đureković must take into consideration that the SDB/SDS definitely considered the killing of émigrés to be a legitimate and constituent part of its arsenal in the 'war against the hostile emigration'. That fact is amply demonstrated by the available documentation.

Furthermore, such analysis must at a minimum find noteworthy that although the SDS did gather intelligence about the death of Đureković, the available documentation does not reveal any great concern about the reasons for his murder or about the identity of the perpetrator(s) behind the crime. No investigation was launched to ascertain these facts. On the contrary, the SDS seemed more interested in obtaining information about Đureković's funeral and about attendees at the ceremony, including whether his widow Gizela planned to attend.[129]

A similar pattern emerges when the killings of other émigrés are examined. These murders were duly noted by the SDS which had been meticulously tracking their movements, activities, public and private lives, contacts and communications for months or even years. In most cases, the SDS tersely entered findings into the relevant dossiers according to which the émigrés had been the victim of an 'internal settling of accounts in extreme émigré circles', or similar formulations. Little if any investigation was launched prior to the issuance of such findings, and the SDS seemed most interested in hearing whether anyone was blaming the SDS for the killings. This on the surface paradoxical contrast between the degree of interest shown by the SDS for the émigrés while they were living and the near-complete lack of interest in their murders can only implausibly be explained by the fact that dead émigrés no longer posed a direct threat to Yugoslavia. The contrast becomes much more understandable if one considers the culpability of the SDS for these murders. A perpetrator has an interest in covering up his crime and in casting aspersions of guilt onto others, but very little if any interest in investigating their own crimes. After all, they know who the perpetrator was, and they know why the crime was committed.

As we have seen, there are numerous indications that after the murder of Đureković, the SDS took steps to blame the killing on someone else and draw the attention away from themselves. The SDS wanted the émigrés to be scared, so rumours that the SDS was responsible served a useful purpose, but on the other hand the SDS did not wish to have such rumours rise to the level that it would cause problems with the West Germans or lead to meaningful investigations that might point towards Yugoslavia.

On 2 September 1983, the district prosecutor in Zagreb asked the SDS to confirm whether the newspaper articles claiming that Đureković had been killed by the 'Ustaša emigration' were true or not.[130] SDS employee Goran Ljubičić received the task of responding to the prosecutor's query, but the archives do not contain his reply.

Although Đureković was killed on 28 July 1983, the SDS did not immediately close his case or that of the operation '*Brk*'. As late as March 1984, the SDS Centre Zagreb produced a summary of the intelligence obtained during the operation, including a plan for further measures related to the thirty-four persons who had been identified as having links to Đureković.[131] The possible added value for the SDS of a continuation of the operation after the death of Đureković is not entirely clear, but it seems that they wanted to make sure that any possible accomplices of Đureković had also been identified and neutralized.

The SRH Council for the Protection of the Constitutional Order also did not cease to be interested in Đureković after his death. After approximately half a year in which Đureković was absent from the council's discussions, he showed up again on the agenda of the council's session on 6 February 1984.[132] Prior to the meeting, the council had received a report from the SDS regarding Đureković's contacts in Yugoslavia.[133] After its discussion the council decided that the SDS should continue to attempt to work towards laying the Đureković affair completely bare, with a special focus on the uncovering of his collaborators in Yugoslavia.[134] For its part, the INA affair retained the attention of the council until at least June 1985.

In March 1985 a meeting of the INA was held between representatives of the company and the SRH RSUP. 'The meeting took place at the initiative of the INA and had as its purpose the protection of matters, persons and information in those matters which the INA carries out for the JNA.'[135] Vilim Mulc, the secretary for internal affairs of the SRH, represented the RSUP at the meeting, and his deputy Zdravko Mustač was also present. Mustač emphasized that the SDS had a considerable interest in the development of adequate security measures in INA. Interestingly, Mustač added that the Đureković affair had been an 'atypical' case for both INA and for Yugoslavia as a whole.[136] No further explanation of this qualification was provided, however.

Conclusion

Although the amount of original SDS material available regarding Operation '*Brk*' and Stjepan Đureković is voluminous, it must be emphasized that the documentation is incomplete, and that this inevitably limits any analysis of the SDS's involvement. Among other things, the dossiers which the SDS maintained for informants embedded in the Đureković case (and all other cases) remain inaccessible, if they indeed still exist at all. And the disinformation campaign that it ran against Đureković, and which included the printing of forgeries of the émigré magazine *Nova Hrvatska*, is barely mentioned in the available SDS documentation.[137] Needless to say, there are also several reasons for retaining healthy scepticism regarding the subjectivity of the SDS documentation.

The Đureković case is in some ways an outlier compared to other cases in which Croat émigrés were assassinated. Having spent most of his career in socialist Yugoslavia and having occupied several prominent posts in INA, Đureković had a quite distinct profile compared to both fascist émigrés from the immediate postwar period and also the disillusioned and angry young men who had left Yugoslavia for distant shores in the 1950s and 1960s. Also, compared to Croats like Vjekoslav Luburić, Bruno Bušić or Josip Senić, who engaged years or even decades in activities highly antagonistic to the Yugoslav state, the time elapsed between Đureković's arrival in Germany and his murder was astonishingly brief. A mere fifteen months separated Đureković's disappearance from Zagreb and his demise in a garage in Wolfratshausen. Nevertheless, the choice of the Đureković case is amply justified, not least because it was the subject of a major recent trial in Germany, and has therefore been subjected to more scrutiny than most other assassinations. Moreover, Đureković's activities were of a primarily propagandistic and publicistic nature, and that even in the records of the SDS there is very little indication that he personally had any intentions of committing violent acts against Yugoslav targets. Hence his assassination indicates the lengths to which the Yugoslav state was willing to go to neutralize a prominent émigré who from their point of view had libelled the Yugoslav regime and who aspired to unite and lead the Croat emigration. When all is said and done, amongst the hundreds of pages which make up the SDS dossier of Stjepan Đureković, one particular detail catches the eye. On the same form which the SDS Centre Zagreb used to apply for the operational processing of Đureković in July 1982 – the form signed Franjo Vugrinec, Josip Perković and Zdravko Mustač – the last field in the form was reserved for 'reasons for the cessation of processing, date' (*razlozi za obustavu obrade, datum*). In October 1983, someone concisely wrote 'Processing is deleted because Đureković has died'.[138]

Conclusion and Epilogue

The Revenge of the Émigrés in the Collapse of Yugoslavia

The low-intensity war that pitted the Udba against the émigrés lasted for the entire duration of socialist Yugoslavia's existence. This epic struggle concluded in a way that few of the participants could have imagined, and with very high costs and an outcome that left some victorious but no one truly satisfied. Even today, nearly three decades after the collapse of socialist Yugoslavia, discussions about the legacy of the Yugoslav State Security Service and the lack of an overall confrontation with the past figure regularly in public and political discourse in the former Yugoslavia, perhaps nowhere more frequently and problematically than in contemporary Croatia.

In January 2020, Krešo Beljak, the president of the Croatian Peasant Party (*Hrvatska seljačka stranka*, HSS), provided a very vivid illustration of how politically sensitive the topic of the Udba's assassinations remains today. On 11 January 2020, Beljak on Twitter reacted to a tweet claiming that the Udba had perpetrated over 100 political assassinations outside Yugoslavia between 1945 and 1990. Beljak's responded, 'Over 100?? Obviously not enough. We sow [*sic*] who did the shit and who made all the wars from 91. to 99. Fascist [*sic*] in ex-YU and in other countries who unfortunately escaped UDB-a.'[1] A veritable media frenzy ensued, and Beljak's comment was widely condemned by other Croat politicians and by historians in Croatia for being both inappropriate and disrespectful of the victims of these assassinations.[2] Beljak quickly apologized for his tweet, saying that he was 'sorry that it could be concluded from my announcement that I support political killings, but that, of course, is not true.'[3] Yet while Beljak certainly unacceptably trivialized and justified the Udba's extrajudicial killings, his tweet also touched a very raw nerve precisely because of the deeply entangled, paradoxical and still poorly understood links between Croat émigrés, the Republic of Croatia and the wars of Yugoslav succession in the 1990s.

Unanswered questions and future research directions

Much research remains to be done on the topics dealt with in this book and on related topics, but a lot hinges on how much access researchers will be granted in coming years to relevant archives, particularly those archives in Belgrade which remain largely off-limits. One very interesting area that has hitherto received relatively little attention is the economic activities of the Yugoslav State Security Service during the final decade of Yugoslavia's existence. While it is clear that the Udba had since at least the end of the 1950s viewed commercial activities abroad as a way of gaining cover for operations and also for dabbling in prosperous matters, these activities seem to have grown exponentially in the 1980s. Most relevant for the present topic is the link between the accumulation of hard currency abroad and so-called 'black funds', i.e. slush funds from which covert operations could be financed.[4]

As stated in the introduction, the question of archival access also remains relevant. In Serbia, the archives of the Yugoslav State Security Service remain largely inaccessible with the exception of those documents which can be found scattered around in other related collections, such as that of the federal presidency. The role of the military intelligence and security services in carrying out surveillance and other operations abroad against the Yugoslav emigration remains largely invisible, as it remains virtually impossible to obtain access to the relevant military archives. Moreover, it is evident that the Yugoslav State Security Service on several occasions in its history engaged in purges – sometimes more systematic and sometimes less so – of its archives.[5] Finally, indications abound that substantial portions of the archives of the Yugoslav State Security Service were haphazardly misappropriated during the violent collapse of the Yugoslav state. Both former employees of the Yugoslav State Security Service and their former opponents seem to have extensively misappropriated and pilfered large portions of these documents – particularly but not only in Bosnia and Herzegovina – and to have hamstered these documents away in private homes or offices. The existence of such 'private' archives can easily be confirmed by perusing the footnotes of books published in the past three decades in the former Yugoslavia.

That having been noted, I believe that the likelihood that new archival sources will substantially change or invalidate the analysis in this book is very small. The available documentation repeatedly and conclusively shows that the Yugoslav State Security Service was willing to go to extraordinary lengths to counter radical members of the Yugoslav emigration. There can be no doubt that

Yugoslav state agents on repeated occasions carried out assassinations, and that they did so not as rogue agents but as agents of the state.

To serve, protect and kill

Before describing the strange story of émigrés and the Yugoslav State Security Service during and after the collapse of Yugoslavia, it will be useful to summarize some of the major findings of the previous chapters. First and foremost, there can be no doubt that the Yugoslav State Security Service engaged in a protracted competition with nationalist émigrés and that Yugoslav operatives made use of violent means including abductions and kidnappings in their attempt to disrupt, stop and subdue those émigrés – particularly Croats – who were assessed to be especially extreme and prone to commit violent acts.

Several different terms were used by the Yugoslav State Security Service when its employees expressed the desired outcome of operations aimed at émigrés. Some of these were euphemisms, such as the terms '*paralizacija*' (paralysation) and '*neutralizacija*' (neutralization). Overall, it is probably most accurate to state that the ultimate common goal of all of the Udba's operations against émigrés was their '*pasivizacija*' (pacification). That is, the target of the operation was to cease to engage in any future hostile activities.

Obviously, this outcome could be achieved by killing the target. And the available documentation irrefutably demonstrates that the Yugoslav State Security Service did assassinate émigrés, using until the late 1960s the explicit term '*likvidacija*' (liquidation), which could only mean killing, replacing it later with the euphemism '*izvršenje specijalnog zadatka*' (carrying out a special task). The available state of archival documentation is such that it has hitherto not proven possible to prove that all those émigrés whom the Yugoslav State Security Service allegedly murdered were indeed killed by the Yugoslav state. And we must remain sceptical and leave open the possibility that some émigrés who suffered violent deaths were in fact the victims of tragic accidents or were killed by actors not otherwise connected with the Yugoslav state. However, besides the assassinations which can be demonstrated beyond a reasonable doubt, we also must not lose sight of the fact that certain émigrés in connection with whom the Yugoslav State Security Service used euphemisms such as '*neutralizacija*' were subsequently killed in circumstances pointing indelibly towards the Yugoslav state. Two examples of this are Nikica Martinović and Bruno Bušić. Martinović was a leading figure in the Bleiburg Honour Guard. In the annual work plan of the Slovenian SDV for the period from November 1974 until December 1975 preparations to paralyse Martinović and his colleagues were foreseen.[6] May 1975 was listed as the deadline for these preparations, probably because the thirtieth anniversary of the massacre was to be observed in that month. As it happened, Martinović was killed in February.[7] On the other hand, other persons mentioned as the close collaborators of Martinović were not killed.

As noted earlier, in January 1977 a meeting was held in the Croatian RSUP to discuss the allegedly terrorist activities of Croat émigrés, where Bruno Bušić was the first émigré mentioned. He was assassinated in October 1978. At the same meeting, the case of Franjo Goreta, the assassin of Yugoslav consular officer Sava Milovanović, was discussed. It was agreed that more detailed intelligence would be gathered about Goreta 'and then – if possible – the earlier planned and already approved combination' was to be implemented.[8] On 13 December 1980 Goreta survived an assassination attempt in Saarbrücken in West Germany.[9]

However, it must be emphasized that such killings in most cases only occurred as a last resort measure. The preferred outcome was undoubtedly the pacification of hostile émigré activity because the target himself decided to desist from further such activity. Whether this occurred because the target was dissuaded from such activity because his relatives in Yugoslavia put pressure on him, because he became distracted or disillusioned by infighting in émigré organizations, was arrested by the police in his country of residence, or whether he simply stopped because he had fallen in love, started a family or new job or become otherwise distracted was at the end of the day immaterial for the Yugoslav State Security Service.

The Croatian SDS mentioned the violent deaths of émigré Croats in their internal documentation, both in the Đureković case and elsewhere.[10] As previously noted, the nature of the SDS's interest in these deaths was often terse and uninquisitive, standing in stark contrast to their interest in these persons while they had still been alive, and hinting that the SDS knew quite well who the perpetrators of the killings were. Just as revealingly, the SRH Council for the Protection of the Constitutional Order discussed the violent deaths of several émigrés without the members of the council demonstrating any real interest in the identity of the perpetrators. For example, at the session of 9 December 1981, the council discussed the deaths of Stanko Nižić (killed in Zurich on 24 August 1981), Ante Kostić (killed in Munich on 9 October 1981) and Mate Kolić (killed in Paris on 19 October 1981).[11]

The rumours which regularly blossomed in émigré circles after such murders, attributing them to the Udba, were duly noted in the reports of the SDS but were rarely commented upon and never explicitly confirmed. 'He was killed owing to an internal settling of accounts in émigré circles' was the preferred euphemism that the Udba espoused both in its internal reports and which was adopted also by the Yugoslav and sometimes also the foreign press.

In the nearly three decades since the implosion of Yugoslavia, very few former employees of the Udba have been willing to discuss the assassinations which their organization carried out abroad. Most of those who have spoken have chosen to deny any knowledge of the assassinations.[12] Others have acknowledged the plausibility of Yugoslav state involvement in the killings but have insisted that they only heard 'water cooler gossip' (*kuloarske priče*) and knew nothing specific or verifiable about such operations.

Yet as we have seen, there have been some notable acknowledgements, such as those of Dušan Stupar, the former chief of the SDB Centre in Belgrade. In a Serbian documentary series in 2008, General Aleksandar Vasiljević, a very high-ranking former member of the JNA Security Administration, stated that 'very selective' decisions regarding the assassination of émigrés had taken place at 'the highest level' in Yugoslavia.[13] This confirms the statements elsewhere of Ivan Lasić, who both served as a chief in the Bosnian SDB and later worked in the Second Administration of the SSUP SDB.[14]

The statements of Vasiljević and Lasić also seem logical because of the very strict guidelines that were in place from at least the 1960s regarding the operations of the Yugoslav State Security Service abroad. It beggars belief to think that republican state security services would have undertaken assassinations abroad without express permission from the very top of the SSUP SDB and the party-state. After all, the republican state security services were not even allowed to arrange meetings abroad with previously existing and approved informants without first clearing every such meeting with the SSUP SDB. And as has been repeatedly emphasized, the risks to Yugoslav security and reputation from botched operations abroad, particularly those involving the use of armed force, were immense. From the documentation reviewed here, albeit with very restricted access to whatever archives still exist in Belgrade, it seems readily apparent that republican security services were intimately involved in the planning and implementation of operations abroad but only with the express approval of the centre.

Keeping in mind that we lack access to the most sensitive Yugoslav archives, and also that the very nature of oral decisions is that they leave little or no trace in the archives, it is still possible based on the very large amount of available circumstantial evidence to reach some tentative but highly probable conclusions.

First, as long as Tito lived, it is simply inconceivable that any decisions to undertake assassinations outside of Yugoslavia would have been taken without his express approval. Second, after Tito died, it is highly probable that decisions of this nature were discussed and taken within the Federal Council for the Protection of the Constitutional Order, which was subordinate to the federal presidency. In all likelihood, these decisions were transmitted confidentially to a very small number of relevant officials in the Federal Yugoslav State Security Service and the relevant republican and provincial state security services who were responsible for implementing and operationalizing these decisions.

Why did the West German authorities tolerate the assassinations?

The relatively passive stance of leading Western German officials regarding the prolific and at times violent activities of the Yugoslav State Security Service requires some explanation. Overall, it needs to be remembered that the assassinations of émigrés on West German soil, however irritating and problematic they must have been for the West German authorities, were but one of a whole range of issues which informed the bilateral relationship between Yugoslavia and West Germany. Most importantly, particularly after the 1960s, Yugoslavia came to play a very important role as a mediator or a bridge between West Germany and the East Bloc in the context of Willy Brandt's *Ostpolitik*. Moreover, the irritation caused by the Udba's activities in West Germany was at least to some extent countered by severe annoyance with Croat émigrés in West Germany plotting and carrying out violent attacks against Yugoslav targets.

Gerhart Baum, who served as West German Federal minister of the interior from June 1978 until September 1982, testified in Munich about a meeting with his Yugoslav counterpart Franjo Herljević in Belgrade at the beginning of the 1980s.[15] According to Baum, Herljević referred to the controversial suicides of convicted Red Army Faction terrorists in the Stammheim prison in Stuttgart in 1977 and stated that the Yugoslav authorities would have acted similarly. Baum interpreted this statement to imply that Herljević believed that the West German authorities had murdered the prisoners, and that an implicit parallel was being drawn to the conduct of the Yugoslav State Security Service in West Germany.

From 5 to 8 September 1983, the President of West Germany, Karl Carstens, undertook an official state visit to Yugoslavia. Only approximately six weeks had passed since the assassination of Stjepan Đureković in a garage in Wolfratshausen.

The state visit was discussed at a session of the federal Yugoslav presidency on 16 September 1983.[16] The presidency reviewed a report about the visit dated 12 September 1983 produced by the SSIP.[17] The third point of this report dealt with the activities of the 'anti-Yugoslav hostile emigration'. President Carsten had stated that the Federal Republic of Germany was opposed to all terrorism, regardless of its origins. The report noted that the topic had also been raised in a meeting between the Yugoslav and West German foreign ministers.

> During the one-on-one meeting with federal secretary L. Mojsov, Minister Genscher discretely posed the question of the alleged involvement of our services in émigré circles in the BRD (the case of the murder of S. Đureković). Genscher simultaneously apologized for the very tendentious television programmes which had been broadcast on the same occasion. Federal minister L. Mojsov distanced himself from the topic.[18]

Hence, even at the height of the campaign of Yugoslav state assassinations, when Croat émigrés were being killed every through months in West Germany, top West German officials seemed very reluctant to pursue the matter with Yugoslav officials.

In the Munich trial, there were differing opinions expressed by retired West German officials. One of these, Gerhart Baum, stated that the West German authorities at the time assumed that the Yugoslav authorities were responsible for the killings of émigrés. Baum was particularly critical of the January 1982 murder in Untergruppenbach near Stuttgart of three Kosovo Albanians, Jusuf Gërvalla, Bardhosh Gërvalla and Kadri Zeka, which Baum called 'indisputable state terrorism'.[19] By contrast, Klaus von Dohnanyi, who worked as minister of state in the West German Foreign Ministry from 1976 until 1981, stated that there was only circumstantial information. According to von Dohnanyi, this information did not justify a diplomatic intervention, and West Germany to a considerable extent relied on Yugoslavia as a country that was not a Warsaw Pact member.[20] A note of the meeting between West German Chancellor Helmut Schmidt and the president of the federal Yugoslav government Veselin Đuranović from February 1981 also indicated that the West German authorities cooperated with their Yugoslav colleagues in the suppression of potentially violent émigré activity.[21] Chancellor Schmidt made it clear that there were indications that the Yugoslav authorities seemed to be undertaking activities in West Germany that were not compatible with 'our laws', but simultaneously stated that no one wanted to address this too loudly so as not to endanger the West German-Yugoslav bilateral relationship.

Chancellor Schmidt encouraged his counterpart to ascertain what activities the Yugoslav authorities were involved in on West German territory. Đuranović by contrast expressed dismay that the West German authorities did not grant the requests filed by the Yugoslav state for the extradition of suspected terrorists. More problematically, Đuranović also claimed that as a former member of the Council for the Protection of the Constitutional Order, he had no awareness that orders had been given to the Yugoslav State Security Service to violate the laws of other countries, nor did he know of any case in which the Yugoslav State Security Service had done so. Đuranović further claimed that the party-state had full control of the activities of the Yugoslav State Security Service, which had not been the case until the purge of Ranković in 1966.

Did the assassinations have their desired effect?

The obvious goal of all the work of the Yugoslav State Security Service as regarded the 'hostile emigration' was to discover all of their hostile and in particular violent plans and activities in a timely manner so as to disrupt and prevent these from developing. From a strategic point of view, the ultimate goal – probably unattainable even in ideal circumstances – was to counteract hostilely intentioned émigrés to such an extent that they became 'pacified' and permanently abandoned any attempts to foment or otherwise act against socialist Yugoslavia.

Seen from this perspective, the assassinations had a decidedly mixed record. It is abundantly clear that the very name 'Udba' struck fear into the hearts of nearly all political active émigrés and became a kind of synonym for the power of the Yugoslav party-state. Undoubtedly, many émigrés over the years abandoned political activism and also potential involvement in terrorist activities because they feared becoming the next victims of the Udba. For obvious reasons, it is very difficult to identify positively such causality, but it certainly existed. Thus in February 1979, a few months after the assassination of Bruno Bušić, the informant 'Marko' reported from Paris regarding the 'unparalleled fear and distrust' which dominated among local Croats.[22] Many of them had moved apartments and/or changed telephone numbers since Bušić's murder, and 'Marko' believed that it would take a long time before the émigré groups would be able to recover from this blow. In the meantime, the SDS remained interested in obtaining the telephone number of Ante Lovrić, an émigré who was spreading flyers in which the SDS was identified as being responsible for the murder. The goal was to put him under 'psychological pressure'.[23]

In a time when prominent Croat and other Yugoslav émigrés were dying violent deaths with alarming frequency, the distrust was enormous. Seen from the perspective of the Yugoslav State Security Service, this paranoia had the added possible collateral benefit of provoking further strife and even violent physical altercations in émigré circles. An example of this occurred in Frankfurt in May 1980 between the Croat émigrés Ljubomir Dragoje and Tomislav Mičić. The informant 'Zaviše' reported that Mičić had accused the mistress of Dragoje of being an agent of 'the Udba'.[24] Dragoje countered by accusing Mičić of being the one working for 'the Udba', and further accusing Mičić of being responsible for the death of the émigré Nikola Milićević in Frankfurt in January 1980. In actuality, Tomislav Mičić was under operational processing (OO) by SDB Centre Tuzla, while Ljubomir Dragoje was subject to OO at the hands of SDS Centre Osijek.[25] Later, Dragoje threatened to kill Mičić.[26] In any case, it is clear that the Yugoslav State Security Service regarded such rivalries and episodes of mutual suspicion and paranoia in the emigration as being highly useful.

On the other hand, the violent and highly publicized deaths of prominent Croat émigrés certainly also functioned as a powerful motivator, as a radicalizing force for existing and perhaps previously moderate émigrés, and as a catalyser for the recruitment of new – and in particular young – participants in the struggle for Croatian independence. This latter claim can be more easily demonstrated, and the Yugoslav State Security Service was keenly aware of this unintended consequence of the assassinations, with young émigrés chomping at the bit to carry out reprisal attacks against Yugoslav targets. In this sense, like 'targeted killings' in the Middle East and elsewhere, the assassinations of the Yugoslav State Security Service certainly neutralized some terrorists, intimidated and suppressed others, and thereby averted some future attacks, but the operations also perpetuated a circle of violence and probably also claimed innocent lives.[27] When the intensity and frequency of émigré terrorism began to subside in the early 1980s, this development had several causes, of which the assassinations were only one.

The extreme secrecy surrounding the campaign of assassinations and paucity of archival documentation with explicit mentions of this phenomenon makes it difficult to reach any firm conclusions regarding the opinions of the Yugoslav party-state leadership on the subject. A rare explicit mention of assassinations occurred at a March 1971 meeting of the Executive Bureau of the SKJ Presidency. Stane Dolanc, who headed this body, expressed strong misgivings about 'liquidations', calling the Executive Bureau 'a forum where we can speak about these things, that this will need to be investigated, to see who did that, how and why'.[28] Dolanc referred back to a meeting approximately a year earlier when the Bureau had apparently discussed an attempted assassination of an émigré. According to Dolanc, the Bureau had at that point unanimously decided that Yugoslavia should not be involved in such operations and this was a 'completely faulty policy. However, things continued even after that'.[29] Dolanc referred to the attempted assassination of Ante Vukić in Dortmund in October 1968, where some kind of 'gas bomb' [*plinska bomba*] had been utilized. Dolanc further mentioned tensions with Sweden regarding the assassination in December 1969 of Sava Čubrilović, a Serb émigré living in Sweden. Dolanc noted that he did not know that 'our service' had killed Čubrilović, and continued, 'anyway, comrades, all those things are very difficult to find out, even when you talk to those who work here directly'.[30]

Notwithstanding Dolanc's and his colleagues very serious misgivings in 1970 and 1971, the historical records show that the Yugoslav party-state did not abandon its campaign of assassinations. On the contrary, and undoubtedly further stimulated as discussed by the shocking events in and around Bugojno in the summer of 1972, the practice of assassinations continued unabated throughout the 1970s and into the 1980s, with the last alleged assassinations taking place in 1990 on the eve of Yugoslavia's collapse. Moreover, as we have also seen, Dolanc himself showed no inhibitions, in his later capacity as federal secretary for internal affairs, of presiding over further assassinations, including that of Stjepan Đureković.

Certainly, despite the strong anti-communist predilections of the intelligence and security services of West Germany, the United States, Australia and other Western countries, these services also used the term 'terrorism' in connection with Croat émigrés. As early as 1963, the Australian authorities reported about camps in which Croat émigrés held 'courses for espionage and terrorist-diversionist activities against the SFR of Yugoslavia'.[31] Any hesitation that these services had in doing so vanished once extreme Croats perpetrated armed attacks on the territory of Western states. The increased vigilance of Western intelligence and security services probably contributed as much if not more to the decrease in Croat émigré terrorism than did the state-sanctioned assassination campaign, although this as we have seen continued unabated through the 1980s. In 1988, Vinko Sindičić, who had worked for decades for the Yugoslav State Security Service and has been suspected of involvement in many assassinations, attempted to murder the Croat émigré Nikola Štedul while he was walking his dog in Kirkcaldy, Scotland.[32] Sindičić was caught before he could flee the UK and was convicted of attempted murder.[33] In 1989, the Croat émigré Ante Đapić was murdered in Nuremberg. And as late as 1990, ethnic Albanians in Belgium and Switzerland were assassinated, murders for which Božidar Spasić of the SSUP SDB subsequently claimed responsibility in his memoirs.[34]

There is a trite old phrase about one man's terrorist being another man's freedom fighter. There can be no doubt that a very small but significant portion of Croat émigrés engaged over years and even decades in terrorist activities. Since the independence of the Republic of Croatia in 1991, officials in Croatia have been loath to use the term 'terrorism', but there can be no doubt that this is the correct term to describe the armed and violent attacks perpetrated by the HRB and others against Yugoslav targets both inside Yugoslavia and abroad.[35] Suffice it to say that in present-day Croatia, those Croats who committed violent acts in the name of the Croat nation or Croatian independence are portrayed as noble patriots. In the case of those who died or were imprisoned, e.g. the hijacker and man responsible for the death of a New York City police officer Zvonko Bušić and the Bugojno insurrectionists, they are most often portrayed as martyrs for the cause, and it is considered bad taste or a sign of lacking patriotism to refer to their acts as terrorism.[36] (Zvonko Bušić committed suicide after his return to Croatia.) Some on the political right in Croatia even assert that most of the violent acts committed by Croats between 1945 and 1991 were actually committed by 'the Udba' or at the instigation of its *agents provocateurs*. The Croat émigrés who have appeared on the pages of this book were all undoubtedly possessed and moved by a deep love of the Croat nation and a passionate drive to establish an independent Croatian state. Yet it is also worth considering whether the terrorist attacks committed by the most extreme among them accelerated or delayed the fulfilment of that dream. And even if the Udba spurred them to commit any attacks, it is the perpetrators of these attacks who bear ultimate responsibility for their actions. The historian Tvrtko Jakovina has for example argued that the case for Croatian independence would have benefitted much more from effectively organized lobbying on the part of moderate Croat émigrés, and that the terrorist incidents committed by extremists impacted very negatively on the image of Croats and Croatia.[37] Jakovina notes that the American newsweekly *Time* in 1972 wrote that there was no more dangerous or problematic ethnic minority on the European continent than the Croats. The émigrés, Jakovina notes, appear in some years to have succeeded in their goal of dissuading Western European tourists from travelling to Yugoslavia. However, given that the bulk of this tourism was to

Croatia's Adriatic coast, the economic losses caused by this decrease in tourism disproportionately affected the very Croats in whose name the extremists were allegedly fighting. Moreover, the violent and brazen attacks perpetrated by Croat terrorists in Western countries, particularly in 1970s and 1980s, made it clear that these extremists did not regard the West as solid allies and that Western citizens were acceptable 'collateral damage'. The predictable result was an increasingly hostile stance by otherwise anti-communist governments who began to crack down on extremist elements in the Croat emigration. As Mate Tokić has noted, 'the red line the Croats held to before 1972 had been one the security services of the West tacitly accepted. When the former crossed that line, the latter had no choice but to act.'[38]

After the long war: A new war, a strange ceasefire, strange bedfellows and selective collective memory in independent Croatia

Confronted in the late 1980s by increasing political instability and by the menacing threat of the new leader of Serbia Slobodan Milošević's overtures to Serb nationalists and the centralist and authoritarian enthusiasts within the JNA, the SDS in Croatia began to consider its options. Having enjoyed relatively broad autonomy from Belgrade since the promulgation of the 1974 constitution, the leading cadres in the SDS, and in particular the Croats among them, had little appetite for a return to the old system of centralist authoritarianism that had existed until the purge of Ranković in 1966.

The Udba collapsed alongside Yugoslavia into mutually antagonistic and warring intelligence services, paralleling the dissolution of the state which it had been established to protect. In April 1990, the first free multi-party elections were held in Croatia, resulting in the victory of the Croatian Democratic Union (*Hrvatska demokratska zajednica*, HDZ) led by Franjo Tuđman, who became independent Croatia's first president. A former Yugoslav partisan and general in the JNA, Tuđman became a historian and leader of the Institute for the History of the Workers' Movement of Croatia in Zagreb before his historical revisionism led to his dismissal from both his post and the League of Communists. As we have seen, Tuđman was closely affiliated with Bruno Bušić, one of the most prominent of the Udba's victims. Imprisoned on several occasions for nationalism, Tuđman became a dissident and a *cause célèbre* for Amnesty International as a 'prisoner of conscience'.[39] As a relatively high-ranking former member of the communist regime and as a known nationalist, Tuđman's activities were monitored for decades by the SDS.

During the late 1980s, as Yugoslavia moved uneasily and inconsistently towards multi-party rule, Tuđman and his associates in Croatia began to expand and nurture their contacts to the Croat diaspora. Doing so inevitably brought Tuđman into contact with members of 'the hostile extreme emigration'. Therefore, rather than attempt to neutralize the establishment of the HDZ and its relationship with the Croat emigration, the SDS read the writing on the wall and calculated that it had to adjust to survive in post-communist Croatia. Moreover, the violent events in Romania in December 1989 probably powerfully concentrated the minds of the leadership of the SDS, who wanted to avoid such a scenario in Croatia.[40] In his capacity as the chief of the SDS in 1990, Josip Perković played a key role in providing safe passage to prominent returning émigrés, many of whom he and his subordinates had watched and pursued in previous years.[41] To name but the most famous example, the Bosnian Croat émigré Gojko Šušak, who had left Yugoslavia in 1968, returned to Croatia in January 1990, immediately joined the HDZ and eventually became Croatia's minister of defence.[42] In the words of a person close to Gojko Šušak, 'Perković put himself at the disposal of Croatia, and Šušak was a gracious man with whom you could reach an agreement within three minutes. He brought Perković into the émigré circle and everyone shook his hand. … Besides, everyone was afraid of him.'[43]

Thus, to the astonishment and anger of many of the émigrés who knew that Perković had in the Croatian SDS headed operations aimed against 'the hostile emigration', he was permitted to remain employed even after the victory of the nationalist HDZ in the April 1990 elections. In 1991, Perković transferred to work in the Ministry of Defence of the Republic of Croatia. Although the details of the compromise leading to Perković's continued employment remain murky, it seems clear that Tuđman had concluded that Perković's formidable skills set could now be best applied in the fight against the new enemy – the Croatian Serbs and their supporters in Serbia. So Perković and others played a key role in the arming of the nascent Croatian state. '[44]

In a letter which Josip Perković sent on 17 September 1992 to Croatian President Franjo Tuđman, Perković claimed to have no specific knowledge of liquidations undertaken by the Yugoslav State Security Service.[45] Perković wrote that he regarded such methods as 'not regularly accepted methods' in Croatia and that, insofar as they had been employed, had been done so by individuals and not by the service as a whole. However, this letter has to read in the context of Perković's positioning of himself and his associates for continued service as intelligence and security professionals in the newly independent Republic of Croatia. Despite the decades which Perković had spent pursuing and counteracting Croat émigrés engaged in various forms of anti-Yugoslav activities, and notwithstanding his final post in the Socialist Republic of Croatia as the chief of the SDS, he rather seamlessly managed to occupy several leading positions in first the Croatian Ministry of Internal Affairs and then the Croatian Ministry of Defence until his eventual retirement in 1998.

Hence, the ranks of the Ministry of Internal Affairs and the Ministry of Defence in Croatia in the early 1990s were filled with a strange and volatile mixture of nationalist émigré returnees and long-serving formerly communist Udba employees. One can only surmise that this must have led to any number of awkward and uncomfortable in the corridors of various government buildings.

This situation also required a delicate and not always successful balancing act by Franjo Tuđman, who needed both erstwhile opposing camps to be united in the struggle for Croatian independence. So while coopting much of the SDS, Tuđman simultaneously gave his blessing to an important body mentioned in the introduction, the Council for the Confirmation of Postwar Victims of the Communist System Killed Abroad, which was in turn part of the larger Commission for the Confirmation of Wartime and Postwar Victims. Yet the compromise threatened to go off the rails several times, such as when Blagoje Zelić, a former employee of SDS Centre Split, and Pero Gudelj, a lower-ranking SDS employee, were kidnapped and interrogated for days in December 1991. Persons linked to the Council, including Bože Vukušić, were allegedly involved, and the Council later used the 'evidence' obtained from the illegal interrogations carried out during Zelić's abduction.[46] However, it was the airing in October 1992 on Croatian state television of a documentary film about the life and death of Bruno Bušić which was undoubtedly linked to the fall of Josip Perković. He was formally dismissed as assistant minister of defence on 10 October and forced into retirement, but Minister Šušak retained him as an advisor.[47] The airing of the film only six days later seemed to mark the implicit end of a just as implicit amnesty of similar Udba officials, with investigations and litigation against them increasing thereafter. Two years later, Perković was himself the victim of an unsuccessful assassination attempt.[48]

The details of this period remain shrouded in controversy, although – and perhaps also because – many of the most prominent actors have published their own conflicting versions about this crucial period in Yugoslav and Croatian history.[49] The topic requires much more in-depth treatment than it can receive here, but a few summary observations can be made. Most importantly, surveying the developments of the 1990s and comparing them to the preceding period that has been the subject of this book, it seems clear that an implicit or explicit truce was negotiated between the leadership of the SDS on the one hand and the nationalist-dissident and émigré core of the HDZ on the other. In exchange for putting their considerable institutional, operational and technical knowledge at the disposal of the newly elected leaders of Croatia, Tuđman and his subordinates did not conduct any kind of large-scale purges or pursuing lustration of the state security service. This deal was in some respect perhaps harder for the HDZ to stomach than the SDS, since many émigrés and dissidents were surely chomping at the bit to settle accounts and obtain vengeance for decades of suppression and, not least, the deaths of their émigré colleagues. Yet the HDZ knew that it had embarked upon a difficult path towards the primary goal of Croatian independence, with very strong opposition from the Yugoslav centralists in the Yugoslav People's Army, the increasingly aggressive regime of Milošević and a restive and scared Serb minority in Croatia. Strategically it made eminent sense to strike a deal with at least the ethnic Croats in the SDS, particularly if they proved willing to reconfigure and recalibrate their focus away from Croat émigrés and nationalism and towards the suppression of Yugoslav centralists and Serb nationalists. The HDZ simply did not have the time, resources or personnel to start from scratch in creating a state apparatus – and by extension a state security service – and they could not afford to engage in a frontal confrontation with the likes of Josip Perković and his subordinates. In the words of Marko Melčić, who for a while in the 1990s headed the HDZ in Zagreb, leading figures in the SDS understood very well that they had to change the ethnic composition of the Service to adjust to the times. 'They threw out some Serbs because they spoiled the structure, but Udba – our destiny, in an orderly manner became constitutive [*državotvorna*] of the [new and independent Croatian] state.'[50]

As Croatia armed, declared independence and ultimately fought a protracted war against Yugoslavia/Serbia and the Serb minority in Croatia, an uneasy truce persisted between the HDZ and the SDS, which was rebranded in May 1991 as the Service for the Protection of the Constitutional Order (*Služba za zaštitu ustavnog poretka*, SZUP). When seen from the perspective of the history of the assassinations perpetrated by the Yugoslav State Security Service, the truce was not without its ironies. For example, both Franjo Goreta and one of the men who had plotted to kill him in West Germany in the early 1980s returned to Croatia, and both volunteered to fight in what in Croatia became known as the

Homeland War (*Domovinski rat*).[51] Ilija Stanić, the assassin of Vjekoslav Luburić, joined the Bosnian branch of the HDZ![52] And while the Bosnian Croats in June 1992 established a brigade named after Ante Bruno Bušić, Ludvig Pavlović, the sole survivor of the Bugojno Nineteen, was freed from prison in December 1990 but subsequently died on the battlefield in Bosnia in September 1991.[53] After his death, the Bosnian Croats formed a unit named after him as well.

While some former émigrés such as Gojko Šušak held powerful government posts in Croatia in the early 1990s, others exerted influence in other ways. Vice Vukojević, who would later head the Croatian Supreme Court, and Bože Vukušić became the engine driving the *Sabor*'s commission investigating communist crimes.[54] And Ernest Bauer, whom Manolić identifies as a long-time officer in the West German BND, became an advisor to President Tuđman. Manolić states that he was at times uncertain whom Bauer was actually working for, and claims that the BND was given a copy of almost the entire archive of the SDS.[55]

There are also some very mysterious and still unexplained questions regarding the relationship between the SDS and Željko Ražnatović 'Arkan', probably the single most notorious Serb paramilitary of the wars of Yugoslav succession, and a person frequently mentioned as a contract killer for the Yugoslav State Security Service. It bears noting that on 9 January 1990, the chief of the SDB of the RSUP Serbia wrote to Zdravko Mustač, who by that time was serving as the chief of the SSUP SDB and informed him that Ražnatović had been used operationally by the SDB of the SSUP for several years without the knowledge or consent of the SDB of the RSUP of Serbia.[56] Ražnatović was arrested in Croatia in November 1990 and was convicted at a trial but was then released in 1991, after which he went on to commit a series of atrocities in Croatia and Bosnia and Herzegovina.[57] It is unclear what precisely transpired, but it is evident that former SDS members were involved in developments during his 'sojourn' in Croatia. Manolić plausibly argues that Ražnatović's release was linked to earlier cooperation between the SDS and Ražnatović in covert operations in Western Europe.[58] Particularly interesting is Manolić's use of the term 'old-new service', highlighting the continuity in the Croatian State Security Service after the multi-party elections in April 1990. However, with the Vance Plan and the ceasefire that took effect in early 1992 in Croatia, the greatest threat to Croatia's existence as an independent state passed. From that point on, infighting between hardline nationalists including former émigrés and the veterans of the SDS increased.

One of the central points made in this book is that both the Yugoslav State Security Service and their opponents in the Croat emigration agreed that they were engaged in a 'war' against each other. Indeed, while I was writing this book, the Croatian state television station HRT broadcast a ten-part documentary series called '*Rat prije rata*' (The War before the War). Miljenko Manjkas, a spin doctor for the HDZ, produced the series. Although Tuđman died in 1999, this series faithfully adheres to a major tenet of his worldview, namely his ambition of reconciling the warring communist and fascist camps in twentieth-century Croatian history and hence achieving a unified Croat nation.[59] The series intersperses heavily caricatured dramatizations of real historical events with interviews with numerous key actors from the late 1980s and early 1990s in Croatia and analysis from Croat historians and publicists: the carefully curated collection of interlocutors ensures that newer Croatian history is presented in a patriotic, teleological and relatively uncritical manner in which the oppressed Croat nation – at home and in the diaspora – battles against remarkable odds to attain independence against Yugoslav communists and Great Serb nationalists. Generally speaking, in the series Croats are 'the good guys' and are victims of Yugoslav and Serbian oppression.

Yet among the founding members of the HDZ and various high-ranking Croat military and police officials, one interlocutor in the series stands out: Josip Perković.[60] Almost every episode of the HRT series includes excerpts from a long interview with Perković that was apparently conducted before his extradition to Germany in 2014. Nary a critical word about Perković is uttered by the narrator or the other interlocutors in the series, and both Perković and the others who mention him portray him as a crucial and positive actor in the process of the struggle for Croatian independence. (This contrasts with the brief portrayal in the series of Zdravko Mustač as a meek and servile appeaser of Belgrade's centralists.) In one dramatization in the seventh episode of the series, Perković is shown calming the nerves of Josip Boljkovac, the minister of internal affairs from May 1990 until August 1991, as Boljkovac considers the fraught and dangerous issue of Croatian arms imports from neighbouring Hungary. And, indeed, contemporary actors such as Josip Manolić, Martin Špegelj, Boljkovac himself – not to mention their erstwhile opponent Aleksandar Vasiljević of the JNA – have in their memoirs confirmed that Perković played a very important role and was involved in arms smuggling for the nascent Croatian army.

Paradoxically, however, the very same series also features melodramatic reenactments of the assassinations of Bruno Bušić in Paris in 1978 and of Stjepan Đureković in Wolfratshausen in 1983, and of various SDS operations against other émigrés and against 'internal enemies' such as Tuđman and the Croat nationalist Marko Veselica. And while it is hardly a secret in Croatia that Perković was one of the SDS officials most responsible for counteracting extremists in the Croat emigration in the 1970s and 1980s, a viewer of the HRT series without previous knowledge of this fact would never be able to reach this conclusion based on his portrayal and his own statements. In particular, nothing whatsoever is said or done to draw a connection between Perković and the aforementioned assassinations. Indeed, no mention at all is made in the series of the Munich trial or Perković's conviction! As for Perković himself, he in 2013 told a Croat journalist

> Look, a story has already emerged that we from the Udba [together] with Tuđman made some kind of strategy for the creation of the state, that we even forced him to do so. Someone even said that he had to give in to us because we would otherwise have liquidated him. That is crazy. I will talk about that someday, but not yet.[61]

As of January 2020, Perković is serving his sentence, now in a Croatian prison. Neither he nor Zdravko Mustač has spoken publicly about these matters since their trial began.

The tensions suppressed during the early 1990s still inform many contemporary political conflicts in Croatia. More broadly, the at times quite dysfunctional Croatian political system to this day suffers from politicians, journalists and social media commentators who carelessly but rather pervasively blame 'the Udba' for seemingly everything that afflicts contemporary Croatia. Dejan Jović has thoroughly analysed how Croatian society wrestles with ontological (in)security and conspiracy theories including the allegedly resilient and persistent influence of the Yugoslav State Security Service.[62] In this sense, 'the war' between the émigrés and the Yugoslav State Security Service has, like the often unproductive polemical shouting matches about the Second World War, Jasenovac, Bleiburg and, of course, the wars of Yugoslav succession, become a convenient excuse to not address the underlying problems in contemporary Croatian society.[63]

List of Acronyms

AS	*Arhiv Slovenije* (Archive of the Republic of Slovenia)
ASIO	Australian Security Intelligence Organisation
BKA	*Bundeskriminalamt* (Federal Criminal Police Office)
BND	*Bundesnachrichtendienst* (Federal Intelligence Agency)
CK	*Centralni komitet* (Central Committee)
DSIP	*Državni sekretarijat za inostrane poslove* (State Secretariat for Foreign Affairs)
DSUP	*Državni sekretarijat za unutrašnje poslove* (State Secretariat for Internal Affairs)
HDS	*Hrvatska državotvorna stranka* (Croatian State-Forming Party)
HDZ	*Hrvatska demokratska zajednica* (Croatian Democratic Union)
HNO	*Hrvatski narodni otpor* (Croatian National Resistance)
HNV	*Hrvatsko narodno vijeće* (Croatian National Council)
HOP	*Hrvatski oslobodilački pokret* (Croatian Liberation Movement)
HOS	*Hrvatske oružane snage* (Croatian Armed Forces)
HRB	*Hrvatsko revolucionarno bratstvo* (Croatian Revolutionary Brotherhood)
ICTY	International Criminal Tribunal for the Former Yugoslavia
JNA	*Jugoslovenska narodna armija* (Yugoslav People's Army)
KOS	*Kontraobaveštajna služba* (Counterintelligence Service)
KPJ	*Komunistička partija Jugoslavije* (Communist Party of Yugoslavia)
NAA	National Archives of Australia
OZN-a	*Odeljenje za zaštitu naroda* (Department for the Protection of the People)

POA   *Protuobavještajna agencija* (Counterintelligence Agency)

PSUP   *Pokrajinski sekretarijat za unutrašnje poslove* (Provincial Secretariat for Internal Affairs)

RSUP   *Republički sekretarijat za unutrašnje poslove* (Republican Secretariat for Internal Affairs)

SDB   *Služba državne bezb(j)ednosti* (State Security Service)

SDS   *Služba državne sigurnosti* (State Security Service – Croatia)

SDV   *Služba državne varnost* (State Security Service – Slovenia)

SFRJ   *Socijalistička Federativna Republika Jugoslavija* (Socialist Federal Republic of Yugoslavia)

SID   *Služba za istraživanje i dokumentaciju* (Service for Research and Documentation)

SIV   *Savezno izvršno veće* (Federal Executive Council)

SJB   *Služba javne bezb(j)ednosti* (Public Security Service)

SJS   *Služba javne sigurnosti* (Public Security Service – Croatia)

šk   škatla (Box)

SKH   *Savez komunista Hrvatske* (League of Communists of Croatia)

SKJ   *Savez komunista Jugoslavije* (League of Communists of Yugoslavia)

SRBiH   *Socijalistička Republika Bosna i Hercegovina* (Socialist Republic of Bosnia and Herzegovina)

SRH   *Socijalistička Republika Hrvatska* (Socialist Republic of Croatia)

SRS   *Socijalistična Republika Slovenija* (Socialist Republic of Slovenia)

SSIP   *Savezni sekretarijat za inostrane poslove* (Federal Secretariat for Foreign Affairs)

SSNO   *Savezni sekretarijat za narodnu odbranu* (Federal Secretariat for People's Defence)

SSUP   *Savezni sekretarijat za unutrašnje poslove* (Federal Secretariat for Internal Affairs)

SUP   *Sekretarijat za unutrašnje poslove* (Secretariat for Internal Affairs)

SZUP   *Služba za zaštitu ustavnog poretka* (Service for the Protection of the Constitutional Order)

TO   *Teritorijalna odbrana* (Territorial Defence)

TRUP   *Tajne revolucionarne ustaške postrojbe* (Secret Revolutionary Ustaša Formations)

UB   *Uprava bezbednosti* (Security Administration)

UDB-a   *Uprava državne bezbednosti* (State Security Administration)

UID   *Uprava za istraživanje i dokumentaciju* (Administration for Research and Documentation)

List of Archival Collections Consulted

Archives of the Republic of Slovenia

Fond 1931 Republiški sekretariat za notranje zadeve Socialistične Republike Slovenije (Republican Secretariat for Internal Affairs of the Socialist Republic of Slovenia)

Archive of Yugoslavia

Fond 803 Savezno predsedništvo SFRJ (SFRJ Federal Presidency)

Australian National Archives (online)

Croatian State Archives

Fond 1561 Služba državne sigurnosti Socijalističke Republike Hrvatske (State Security Service of the Socialist Republic of Croatia)

Notes

Introduction

1 One of the more curious features of the German judicial system is that the actual written judgement in criminal cases can be issued months after the trial has ended and the verdict has been pronounced. In the case of the trial of Perković and Mustač, the trial chamber issued its 217-page judgement on 9 March 2017.

2 According to media reports, a report existed in principle at the time of the extradition of Mustač and Perković in 2014 that they would be allowed to serve their sentences in Croatia. The extradition itself was extremely controversial in Croatia and at the time caused a major crisis between Croatia and Germany. The differences in Croatian and German sentencing laws mean that the sentence served in Croatia will likely be at most twenty years. HRT, 'Perković i Mustač u Hrvatskoj će služiti kaznu od 20 godina,' 29 May 2018.

3 Adam Entous and Evan Osnos, 'Qassem Suleimani and How Nations Decide to Kill,' *The New Yorker*, 3 February 2020.

4 'assassination, n.'. OED Online. December 2018. Oxford University Press, http://www.oed.com.ez.statsbiblioteket.dk:2048/view/Entry/11735?redirectedFrom=assassination (accessed 20 December 2019).

5 Zaryab Iqbal and Christopher Zorn, 'Sic Semper Tyrannis? Power, Repression, and Assassination since the Second World War,' *The Journal of Politics*, Vol. 68, No. 3 (August 2006), 489–501.

6 Lindsay Porter, *Assassination: A History of Political Murder* (London: Thames and Hudson, 2010).

7 Avery Plaw, *Targeting Terrorists: A License to Kill?* (London: Routledge, 2008); Nir Gazit and Robert J. Brym, 'State-Directed Political Assassination in Israel: A Political Hypothesis,' *International Sociology*, Vol. 26, No. 6, 862; Steven R. David, 'Fatal Choices: Israel's Policy of Targeted Killings,' *Mideast Security and Policy Studies*, No. 51 (September 2002), http://besacenter.org/wp-content/uploads/2002/09/msps51.pdf (accessed 20 December 2019).

8 David, 'Fatal Choices,' 2.

9 SSUP, 'Material for the White Paper on Terrorist Actions of the Fascist Emigration Originally Stemming from Yugoslavia,' February 1978, ARS. F. 1931, šk. 1156; SSUP, 'Short-Term and Long-Term Programmatic Directions for the Research on Hostile and Other Activities Harmful to Society (Draft),' 19 June 1973, 13, ARS. F. 1931, šk. 3093.

10   Sreten Kovačević, *Hronologija antijugoslovenskog terorizma, 1960–1980* (Belgrade: IŠRO, 1981); Milenko Doder, *Jugoslovenska neprijateljska emigracija* (Zagreb: Centar za Informacije i publicitet, 1989).

11   A posthumously edited collection of Bušić's writings is approximately 700 pages long. Bruno Bušić, *Jedino Hrvatska! Sabrani spisi* (Toronto: ZIRAL, 1983).

12   Stjepan Đureković, *Ja: Josip Broz-Tito* (International Books, 1982); Stjepan Đureković, *Komunizam: velika prevara* (International Books, 1982); Stjepan Đureković, *Sinovi orla* (International Books, 1982); Stjepan Đureković, *Slom ideala (Izpovjed titovog ministra)* (International Books, 1983); Stjepan Đureković, *Crveni manageri* (International Books, 1983). Although International Books was listed as the publisher for all books, and the place of publication as the United States of America, all of the books were, as will be seen subsequently, self-published by Đureković.

13   Hans-Peter Rullmann, *Mordauftrag aus Belgrad: Dokumentation über die Belgrader Mordmaschine* (Hamburg: Ost-Dienst, 1981). Rullmann was arrested and convicted in Yugoslavia on charges of military espionage in the early 1970s. Tito pardoned Rullmann after he had served fifteen months of a six-year sentence, and he was expelled to West Germany. He subsequently founded a German-Croat friendship association and a Croatian-language émigré newspaper. Bernd Robionek notes that prior to the 1970s, Rullmann had actually articulated views which were very critical of Croat émigrés. Bernd Robionek, 'Gutachten zur Strafsache Prates,' Oberlandesgericht München, 20 March 2008, 10–11.

14   A sterling example of this is the pamphlet *Istina o Nezavisnoj državi Hrvatskoj* published by Ivan de Mihalovich-Korvin (a pseudonym) in Buenos Aires in 1991.

15   The Slovene Roman Leljak is perhaps the most egregious such publicist. After initially publishing profusely on the massacres perpetrated by the Yugoslav communists at the end of the Second World War and immediately thereafter, Leljak has more recently turned to publishing books and producing films that explicitly deny the mass atrocities of the Ustaša regime, in particular those committed at the main Ustaša concentration camp at Jasenovac. It must be noted that Leljak testified as a prosecution witness in the trial of Mustač and Perković.

16   The most substantial, but lacking, English-language treatment of this topic is Paul Hockenos, *Homeland Calling: Exile Patriotism and the Balkan Wars* (Ithaca: Cornell University Press, 2003).

17   This topic will be dealt with in the book's final chapter.

18   For an overview of the general state of research on this topic and of Vukušić's publications, see Bernd Robionek, 'Geschichtswissenschaftliches Gutachten im Verfahren 7 St 5/14 (2) vor dem Oberlandesgericht München,' 2015, 3–6.

19   The actual murderer of Tatar was another émigré, Damir Šišnjak, who said that he was acting on the instructions of Vukušić and using a gun provided by him.

Vukušić denied any involvement. Karlsruhe District Court Judgement of Bože Vukušić and Damir Šišnjak, I Ks 12/83, I AK 40/83, 2 January 1985; SDS Centre Split Information No. 521, 1 November 1983; Official Note of SDB Centre Mostar, SDB Detachment Čapljina, 22 June 1984; Official Note of SDS Centre Zenica, 27 June 1984, HDA, F. 1561, Dossier of Bože Vukušić.

20 See, for example, Marko Lopušina, *Ubice u ime države* (Novi Sad: Prometej, 2012), the cover of which features a photograph of Stjepan Đurekovićʼs murdered body. Lopušina seems to have received a considerable amount of his information from employees of the Udba. It is notable that Lopušina in some of his books thanks known former high-ranking officials of the Serbian State Security Service. See the foreword to Marko Lopušina, *Ubij bližnjeg svog: Jugoslovenska tajna policija 1945.-2002.* (Belgrade: Marso, 2014).

21 Petar Dragišić, *Ko je pucao u Jugoslaviju? Jugoslovenska politička emigracija na zapadu 1968-1980.* (Belgrade: Institut za noviju istoriju Srbije, 2019), 13.

22 Mate Nikola Tokić, *For the Homeland Ready! Croat Diaspora Terrorism during the Cold War* (West Lafayette: Purdue University Press, 2020).

23 Alexander Clarkson; *Fragmented Fatherland: Immigration and Cold War Conflict in the Federal Republic of Germany, 1945-80* (New York: Berghahn Books, 2013); Christopher A. Molnar, ʻImagining Yugoslavs: Migration and the Cold War in Postwar West Germany,ʼ *Central European History*, Vol. 47 (2014), 138–69; Christopher A. Molnar, *Memory, Politics and Yugoslav Migrations to Postwar Germany* (Bloomington: Indiana University Press, 2018).

24 Srđan Cvetković, *Između srpa i čekića 3: Oblici otpora komunističkom režimu u Srbiji, 1944. -1991.* (Belgrade: Službeni glasnik, 2013), 233–302.

25 Council for the Confirmation of Postwar Victims of the Communist System Killed Abroad, Republic of Croatia *Sabor*, ʻPostwar Victims of SFRJ State Terror Abroad,ʼ 30 September 1999. The report of the overall commission was not officially accepted by the *Sabor* because of its controversial revisionist findings related to the number of Jewish and Serb victims during the Second World War.

26 Vukojević later also published his own voluminous dossier compiled by the Croatian State Security Service. Vice Vukojević, *Vice Vukojević – Dosje 240271* (Zagreb: Hrvatski križni put, 2015).

27 Council for the Confirmation of Postwar Victims of the Communist System Killed Abroad, Republic of Croatia *Sabor*, ʻPostwar Victims of SFRJ State Terror Abroad,ʼ 30 September 1999, 7.

28 For a critical view of the use of the files of communist security services, see Katherine Verdery, *Secrets and Truths: Ethnography in the Archive of Romaniaʼs Secret Police* (Budapest: Central European University Press, 2013).

29 A list of émigré organizations produced by the State Security Service of the Yugoslav Federal Secretariat for Internal Affairs in 1976 listed 34 known

active Croat émigré organizations, compared to 15 Albanian, 8 Macedonian, 7 Muslim, 22 Slovene and 21 Serb organizations. SSUP SDB, 'Instructions on the Nomenclature from the Domain of State Security with Nomenclatures [*sic*],' April 1976, HDA, F. 1561, šifra 3.

30   Anto Nobilo, *Obrana hrvatskog kontraobavještajca Josipa Perkovića na njemačkom sudu* (Zagreb: VBZ, 2018). As regards the accused, Josip Perković has received immeasurably more media attention in Croatia than Zdravko Mustač, most likely because Perković played a much more important – and controversial – role in Croatia's secession from Yugoslavia and in the subsequent war. For a portrait of Perković, see Orhidea Gaura Hodak, *Tuđman i Perković: Istina o tajnoj vezi koja je formirala Hrvatsku* (Zagreb: Profil, 2014).

31   Christian Axboe Nielsen, 'Leadership Analysis in International Criminal Justice,' in Adejoké Babington-Ashaye, Aimée Comrie and Akingbolahan Adeniran, eds., *International Criminal Investigations: Law and Practice* (The Hague: Eleven International Publishing, 2018), 207–30.

32   Without in any way endorsing their findings, I note several authors in Croatia have probed the motives for the assassination of Đureković. See for example Branko Vukas, *Stjepan Đureković: Što ga je ubilo* (Zagreb: Naklada Pavičić, 2014). I also note that Vukas has chosen to ask *what* – not *who* – killed Đureković.

33   See also the comments on witness testimony versus structural documentation in Nielsen, 'Leadership Analysis in International Criminal Justice.'

34   On the disintegration of the language formerly known as Serbo-Croatian, see Robert D. Greenberg, *Language and Identity in the Balkans* (Oxford: Oxford University Press, 2008).

35   According to Srđan Cvetković, the choice of the term 'service' was supposed to improve the image, suggesting that the 'secret police' were servants of the party-state and the people. Srđan Cvetković. 'Kako je spaljeno pet kilometara dosijea UDB-e,' *Arhiv*, Vol. 9, No. 1–2 (2008), 71f.

Chapter 1

1   For an official summary of the emergence of the Yugoslav security services, see Obren Ž. Đorđević, *Osnovi državne bezbednosti: opšti deo* (Belgrade: VŠUP, 1980), 270–88.

2   The Slovene and Serbo-Croatian transliteration of Russian names is given here. Ljuba Dornik Šubelj, *Oddelek za zaščito naroda za Slovenijo* (Ljubljana: ARS, 1999), 17.

3   Order of Marshal Josip Broz Tito, 13 May 1944, ARS 1931, box 697. It should be noted that the earliest documents refer to the Department *of* the Protection of

the People (*Odjeljenje zaštite naroda*), which later became known officially as the Department for the Protection of the People (*Odjeljenje za zaštitu naroda*).

4   For histories of the Ozna, see Šubelj, *Oddelek za zaščito naroda za Slovenijo*; Ljuba Dornik Šubelj, *Ozna in prevzem oblasti 1944–46* (Ljubljana: Modrijan, 2013); Kosta Nikolić, *Mač revolucije, Ozna u Jugoslaviji* (Belgrade: Službeni glasnik, 2013); Zdenko Radelić, *Obavještajni centri, Ozna i Udba u Hrvatskoj (1942–1954); Obavještajni centri, Ozna i Udba u Hrvatskoj: Kadrovi (1942–1954)* (Zagreb: Hrvatski institut za povijest, 2019).

5   Dispatch of Lieutenant General Aleksandar Ranković, 18 May 1944, ARS, f. 1931, šk. 697.

6   The KNOJ existed until Tito disbanded them in 1953. Nikolić, *Mač revolucije: OZNA u Jugoslaviji*, 48, 51; M.Le., 'Korpus narodne odbrane Jugoslavije (KNOJ),' in *Vojna enciklopedija*, Vol. 4, 628–9.

7   Minutes of the Meeting of the Central Committee of the Communist Party of Croatia, 6 July 1945, cited in Barbara Vojnović, *Zapisnici politbiroa Centralnog komiteta Komunističke partije Hrvatske, 1945–1952* (Zagreb: Hrvatski državni arhiv, 2005), 64.

8   For a (very) empathetic account of Ranković's dismissal, see Svetko Kovač, Bojan Dimitrjević and Irena Popović Grigorov, *Slučaj Ranković* (Belgrade: Medija Centar „Odbrana," 2014); Vojin Lukić, *Brionski plenum: Obračun sa Aleksandrom Rankovićem* (Belgrade: Stručna knjiga, 1990).

9   On the reorganization of the Yugoslav State Security Service after 1966, see Edmund Schweissguth, 'Die Reorganisation des Staatssicherheitsdienstes in der SFR Jugoslawien,' *Jahrbuch für Ostrecht*, Vol. 10, No. 1 (1969), 45–68. Cyril A. Zebot memorably remarked that 'the process of liberalization and decentralization is not politically safeguarded in a framework of democratic alternatives'. Cyril A. Zebot, Review of *Le fédéralisme yougoslave*, *Slavic Review*, Vol. 27, No. 1 (March 1968), 159.

10   SSUP SDB, 'Contribution to Considerations Regarding the Functions of the Federation in the Domain of Internal Affairs,' December 1970, ARS, F. 1931, šk. 2304.

11   SFRJ Constitution, *Službeni list SFRJ*, No. 9/74, 21 February 1974.

12   Preamble of SFRJ Constitution, *Službeni list SFRJ*, No. 9/74, 21 February 1974, 214.

13   SFRJ Constitution, *Službeni list SFRJ*, No. 9/74, 21 February 1974, 252–5.

14   SFRJ Constitution, *Službeni list SFRJ*, No. 9/74, 21 February 1974, 248–52.

15   SFRJ Constitution, *Službeni list SFRJ*, No. 9/74, 21 February 1974, 256–8.

16   Rules of Procedure for the SFRJ Presidency, *Službeni list SFRJ*, No. 30/72, 15 June 1972, 593–600; Rules of Procedure for the SFRJ Presidency, *Službeni list SFRJ*, No. 6/81, 30 January 1981, No. 6/81, 189–200; Decision on the Changes and Amendments to the Rules of Procedure for the SFRJ Presidency, *Službeni list SFRJ*, No. 69/83, 30 December 1983, 1921–4.

17   Decision on the Organization and the Jurisdiction of the Services of the SFRJ
     Presidency, *Službeni list SFRJ*, No. 74/80, 31 December 1980, 2289–94. 31
     December 1980.
18   Transcript of 77th Expanded Session of the Executive Bureau of the SKJ
     Presidency, 23 March 1971, AJ, F. 507, IV, fasc. 139, 9. Stane Dolanc seems himself
     to have been confused about the number of intelligence and security agencies
     operating in Yugoslavia, because the Federal Secretariat for Foreign Affairs in fact
     had only one intelligence agency. In all likelihood, the mention of a second SSIP
     service referred to those in the SSIP who were responsible for diplomatic security.
19   SSIP SID, 'Jurisdiction, Tasks and Programmatic Orientation of the Service for
     Research and Documentation,' 17 May 1983, AJ, F. 803, fasc. 1790, 1.
20   SSIP SID, 'Jurisdiction, Tasks and Programmatic Orientation of the Service
     for Research and Documentation,' 17 May 1983, AJ, F. 803, fasc. 1790, 7.
21   SSIP SID, 'Jurisdiction, Tasks and Programmatic Orientation of the Service for
     Research and Documentation,' 17 May 1983, AJ, F. 803, fasc. 1790, 4.
22   SSIP SID, 'Jurisdiction, Tasks and Programmatic Orientation of the Service
     for Research and Documentation,' 17 May 1983, AJ, F. 803, fasc. 1790, 8.
     Compare however with the searing criticism of the work of the UID/SID – and
     more generally the SSIP – meted out by members of the SKJ Presidency in
     1971. Transcript of 77th Expanded Session of the Executive Bureau of the SKJ
     Presidency, 23 March 1971, AJ, F. 507, IV, fasc. 139, 40, 47, 48.
23   *Vojna bezbednost* (Belgrade: Vojnoizdavački i novinski centar, 1986), S. 103–17;
     Vojnaobaveštajna služba (Belgrade: Vojnoizdavački i novinski centar, 1990). For a
     description of the jurisdiction of the SSNO, see Articles 79–88, Law on All People's
     Defence, *Službeni list SFRJ*, No. 21/82, 23 April 1982, 589–91.
24   'Instructions on the Cooperation, Mutual Relationship and Obligations of the
     State Security Service and the Second Administration of the General Staff of the
     Yugoslav People's Army,' 9 November 1971, 2, ARS, F. 1931, Šk. 1196.
25   SSUP, 'Information on the Cooperation of Federal, Republicans and Provincial
     Administrative Organs in the Realization of the Function of Security,' 22 May 1985,
     S. 16, ARS, F. 1931, šk. 2261.
26   Transcript of 77th Expanded Session of the Executive Bureau of the SKJ
     Presidency, 23 March 1971, AJ, F. 507, IV, fasc. 139, 2, 5.
27   SSUP, SSNO and SSIP, 'Draft Instructions on Mutual Cooperation of Organs
     Responsible for Matters of State Security,' December 1980, ARS, F. 1931, šk. 1196.
     See also SSUP, SSNO and SSIP, 'Uniform Principles of the Application of Measures
     and Methods in the Execution of Matters of the State Security Service,' 4 February
     1975, ARS, F. 1931, šk. 2233.
28   SSUP, SSNO and SSIP, 'Uniform Principles on the Application of Measures and
     Methods in the Execution of Matters of the State Security Service,' 4 February
     1975, ARS, F. 1931, šk. 2233.

29 See, for example: 'Instructions on the Cooperation between the State Secretariat for Foreign Affairs and the State Secretariat for Internal Affairs,' 1 October 1968. ARS, F. 1931, šk. 1196; 'Instructions on the Cooperation, Mutual Relationship and Obligations of the State Security Service and the Respective Organs of the Federal Secretariat for Foreign Affairs,' 9 November 1971, ARS, F. 1931, šk. 1196; 'Instructions on the Cooperation, Mutual Relationship and Obligations of the State Security Service and the Security Organs of the JNA,' 9. November 1971, ARS, F. 1931, šk. 1196.

30 SSUP, Legal Affairs Administration, 'Uniform Principles on the Use of Means and Methods Which the Organs, Which Carry Out Matters of State Security, Use in Their Work – Proposal, 1 September 1984,' ARS, F. 1931, šk. 2258; SFRJ Presidency, 'Decision on the Uniform Principles on the Use of Means and Methods Which the Organs, Which Carry Out Matters of State Security, Use in Their Work,' 17 April 1985, ARS, F. 1931, šk. 2261. See also SSUP, 'Information on the Cooperation of Federal, Republicans and Provincial Administrative Organs in the Realization of the Function of Security,' 22 May 1985, ARS, F. 1931, šk. 2261.

31 On the violence in Yugoslavia during the Second World War and its consequences, see Jozo Tomasevich, *War and Revolution in Yugoslavia, 1941–1945: The Chetniks* (Stanford: Stanford University Press, 1975); Tomislav Dulić, *Utopias of Nation: Local Mass Killing in Bosnia and Herzegovina, 1941–1942* (Stockholm: Elanders Gotab, 2005); Marko Attila Hoare, *Genocide and Resistance in Hitler's Bosnia: The Partisans and the Chetniks* (Oxford: Oxford University Press, 2006); Max Bergholz, *Violence as a Generative Force: Identity, Nationalism, and Memory in a Balkan Community* (Ithaca: Cornell University Press, 2016).

32 Ivo Banac, *With Stalin against Tito: Cominformist Splits in Yugoslav Communism* (Ithaca: Cornell University Press, 1988); Martin Previšić, *Povijest Golog otoka* (Zagreb: Fraktura, 2019).

33 See, for example, Ondřej Vojtěchovský, *Iz Praga protiv Tita! Jugoslavenska informbiroovska emigracija u Čehoslovačkoj* (Zagreb: Srednja Europa, 2016).

34 Tvrtko Jakovina, *Treća strana hladnog rata* (Zagreb: Fraktura, 2011).

35 Christian Axboe Nielsen, 'Never-Ending Vigilance: The Yugoslav State Security Service and Cominform Supporters after Goli Otok,' in Tvrtko Jakovina and Martin Previšić, eds., *The Tito-Stalin Split 70 Years After* (Zagreb and Ljubljana: Sveučilište u Zagreb, Univerza v Ljubljani, 2019), 109–20.

36 SFRJ Constitution, *Službeni list SFRJ*, No. 9/74, 21 February 1974, Article 281, point 8.

37 SFRJ Constitution, *Službeni list SFRJ*, No. 9/74, 21 February 1974, Article 313.

38 SFRJ Constitution, *Službeni list SFRJ*, No. 9/74, 21 February 1974, Article 281.

39 Law on Federal Councils, *Službeni list SFRJ*, No. 66/74, 27 December 1974, 2002–4; Law on the Changes and Amendments to the Law on Federal Councils, *Službeni list SFRJ*, 17/78, 7 April 1978, 1833; Law on the Changes in the Law on Federal Councils, *Službeni list SFRJ*, 40/78, 14 July 1978, 1834; Law on the Federal Council

for the Protection of the Constitutional Order, *Službeni list SFRJ*, No. 57/83, 4 November 1983, 1581–2.

40 Article 17, Law on Federal Councils, *Službeni list SFRJ*, No. 66/74, 27 December 1974, 2003.

41 Article 20, Law on Federal Councils, *Službeni list SFRJ*, No. 66/74, 27 December 1974, 2003. Cf. Article 8, Law on the Foundations of the System of State Security, *Službeni list SFRJ*, No. 1/74, 3 January 1974, 2.

42 Decision on the Nomination of the President and Members of the Federal Council for the Protection of the Constitutional Order, *Službeni list SFRJ*, No. 8/75, 10 January 1975.

43 Decision on the Nomination of the President and Members of the Federal Council for the Protection of the Constitutional Order, *Službeni list SFRJ*, No. 55/82, 17 September 1982, 1373.

44 SFRJ Constitution, *Službeni list SFRJ*, No. 9/74, 21 February 1974, 258.

45 SFRJ Constitution, *Službeni list SFRJ*, No. 9/74, 21 February 1974, 258.

46 Law on the Organization and the Jurisdiction of Federal Administrative Organs and Federal Organizations, *Službeni list SFRJ*, 28 April 1978, No. 22/78, 753–8; Decision on the Measures for the Implementation of Articles 47–55 of the Law on the Organization and Jurisdiction of Federal Administrative Organs and Federal Organizations, *Službeni list SFRJ*, 5 May 1978, No. 24/78, 971–2.

47 Article 8, Law on the Foundations of the System of State Security, *Službeni list SFRJ*, No. 1/74, 3 January 1974, 2.

48 Josip Perković and Jan Gabriš, 'Služba državne sigurnosti republičkog sekretarijata za unutarnje poslove SR Hrvatske u vremenu 1980. – 30. svibnja 1990. godine,' Zagreb, June 1997, unpublished internal paper, 34, 40.

49 Letter of Stane Dolanc, Secretary of the Executive Council of the Presidency of the SKJ SFRJ Central Committee to the Presidents of the Central Committees of the Republics and Autonomous Provinces, 2 July 1975, ARS, F. 1931, šk. 1202.

50 This list is based on various sources, including official gazettes and official internal journals of the SSUP.

51 Articles 21–22, Law on the Foundations of the System of State Security, *Službeni list SFRJ*, No. 1/74, 3 January 1974, 449; Article 16, Law on the Performance of Internal Affairs from the Jurisdiction of Federal Administrative Organs, *Službeni list SFRJ*, No. 7/85, 15 February 1985. See also SSUP, 'Report on the Results and Some Experiences with Routine and Complete Inspection of the SDB SSUP in the State Security Services of the RSUPs and PSUPs,' October 1987, 1, ARS, F. 1931, šk. 2271.

52 SSUP, 'Report on the Results and Some Experiences with Routine and Complete Inspection of the SDB SSUP in the State Security Services of the RSUPs and PSUPs,' October 1987, 4, ARS, F. 1931, šk. 2271.

53 Josip Perković and Jan Gabriš, 'Služba državne sigurnosti republičkog sekretarijata za unutarnje poslove SR Hrvatske u vremenu 1980. – 30. svibnja 1990. godine,' Zagreb, June 1997, unpublished internal paper, 32.

54 Josip Perković and Jan Gabriš, 'Služba državne sigurnosti republičkog sekretarijata za unutarnje poslove SR Hrvatske u vremenu 1980. – 30. svibnja 1990. godine,' Zagreb, June 1997, unpublished internal paper, 163.

55 Josip Perković and Jan Gabriš, 'Služba državne sigurnosti republičkog sekretarijata za unutarnje poslove SR Hrvatske u vremenu 1980. – 30. svibnja 1990. godine,' Zagreb, June 1997, unpublished internal paper, 1.

56 Josip Perković and Jan Gabriš, 'Služba državne sigurnosti republičkog sekretarijata za unutarnje poslove SR Hrvatske u vremenu 1980. – 30. svibnja 1990. godine,' Zagreb, June 1997, unpublished internal paper, 33.

57 Basic Law on Internal Affairs, *Službeni list SFRJ*, No. 49/66, December 1966.

58 Law on the Performance of Internal Affairs from the Jurisdiction of the Federal Administrative Organs, *Službeni list SFRJ*, Nr. 60/71, 30 December 1971; Law on the Amendment of the Law on the Performance of Internal Affairs from the Jurisdiction of the Federal Administrative Organs, *Službeni list*, No. 32/75, 27 June 1975; Law on the Changes and Amendments to the Law on the Performance of Internal Affairs from the Jurisdiction of the Federal Administrative Organs, *Službeni list*, No. 25/81, 24 April 1981; Law on the Performance of Internal Affairs from the Jurisdiction of the Federal Administrative Organs, *Službeni list*, No. 7/85, 15 February 1985.

59 Law on the Foundations of the System of State Security, *Službeni list SFRJ*, No. 1/74, 3 January 1974; Law on the Foundations of the System of State Security, *Službeni list SFRJ*, No. 15/84, 30 March 1984.

60 Article 7, Law on the Foundations of the System of State Security, *Službeni list SFRJ*, No. 1/74, 3 January 1974, 1–2.

61 CIA, 'Jewel Purchases Allegedly Being Made in the Name of Alexander Rankovic,' 1 September 1949; CIA, 'Yugoslavia – The Fall of Rankovic,' 5 July 1966.

62 Josip Perković and Jan Gabriš, 'Služba državne sigurnosti republičkog sekretarijata za unutarnje poslove SR Hrvatske u vremenu 1980. – 30. svibnja 1990. godine,' Zagreb, June 1997, unpublished internal paper, 32.

63 SSUP, 'The Tasks of the Organs of Internal Affairs in the Implementation of the Directives of the President of the Republic,' 7 August 1972, 19–20, ARS, F. 1931, šk. 1362; SSUP SDB, 'Collection of Material: The Views and Conclusions of the 56th Session of the Executive Office of the SKJ Presidency Regarding Current Security Problems,' September 1973, S. 76, ARS, F. 1931, šk. 1362.

64 SSUP, Centre for Professional Training, 'Operational Processing – Materials – Part Two,' 1974, ARS, F. 1931, šk. 2308, 12.

65 Article 397, Constitution of the Socialist Republic of Croatia, *Narodne novine*, No. 8/74, 22 February 1974, 150–4; Law on the Organization and Jurisdiction of Administrative

Organs and Republican Organizations, *Narodne novine*, No. 44/79, 23.Oktober 1979, 663; Law on the Changes and Amendments to the Law on the Organization and Jurisdiction of Administrative Organs and Republican Organizations, *Narodne novine*, No. 18/82, 29 April 1982, 354–5; Law on the Changes and Amendments to the Law on the Organization and Jurisdiction of Administrative Organs and Republican Organizations, *Narodne novine*, No. 33/83, 9 August 1982, 562–3.

66 Article 33, Law on the Organs of Internal Affairs, *Narodne novine*, No. 44/79, 23 October 1979, 674. This law was amended in 1981, 1985 and 1989.

67 Law on Internal Affairs, *Narodne novine*, 21 March 1977, No. 11/77, 152–65.

68 Law on Internal Affairs, *Narodne novine*, No. 44/79, 23 October 1979, 671. Cf. Article 9 of the Law on the Organization and Jurisdiction of Administrative Organs and Republican Organizations, *Narodne novine*, No. 44/79, 23 October 1979., 664; cf. Article 332, Paragraph 5 of the Constitution of the Socialist Republic of Croatia, *Narodne novine*, No. 8/74, 22 February 1974, 148.

69 Article 30, Law on the Organs of Internal Affairs (Corrected Text), *Narodne novine*, No. 44/79, 23 October 1979, 674.

70 SRH RSUP, Rulebook (Consolidated Text) on the Internal Organization and the Manner of Work of the State Security Service, 2 June 1981, 6.

71 Article 46, Law on the Organization and Jurisdiction of Administrative Organs and Republican Organizations, *Narodne novine*, No. 44/79, 23 October 1979, 668.

72 Article 47, Law on the Organization and Jurisdiction of Administrative Organs and Republican Organizations, *Narodne novine*, No. 44/79, 23 October 1979, 668.

73 Josip Perković and Jan Gabriš, 'Služba državne sigurnosti republičkog sekretarijata za unutarnje poslove SR Hrvatske u vremenu 1980. – 30. svibnja 1990. godine,' 1997, Zagreb, June 1997, unpublished internal paper, 7.

74 Josip Perković and Jan Gabriš, 'Služba državne sigurnosti republičkog sekretarijata za unutarnje poslove SR Hrvatske u vremenu 1980. – 30. svibnja 1990. godine,' Zagreb, June 1997, unpublished internal paper, 50.

75 Article 32, Law on the Organs of Internal Affairs (Corrected Text), *Narodne novine*, No. 44/79, 23 October 1979, 674.

76 Article 31, Law on the Organs of Internal Affairs (Corrected Text), *Narodne novine*, No. 44/79, 23 October 1979, 674.

77 Articles 30 and 33, Law on the Organs of Internal Affairs (Corrected Text), *Narodne novine*, No. 44/79, 23 October 1979, 674.

78 Article 32, Law on the Organs of Internal Affairs (Corrected Text), *Narodne novine*, No. 44/79, 23 October 1979, 674.

79 This section was abolished prior to 1980.

80 POA, 'Rekonstrukcija rada i aktivnosti SDS,' April 2006, 6.

81 SDV, 'Proposal for Changes to the Systematization of the Administration of the State Security Service,' 11 February 1975, ARS, F. 1931, šk. 2233.

82   Josip Perković and Jan Gabriš, 'Služba državne sigurnosti republičkog sekretarijata za unutarnje poslove SR Hrvatske u vremenu 1980. – 30. svibnja 1990. godine,' Zagreb, June 1997, unpublished internal paper, 8.

83   SRH Presidency, Decision on the Establishment of the Council for the Protection of the Constitutional Order and Its Tasks and Areas of Competence, Article 5, 28 May 1980; Minutes of the Session of the SDS Council, 4 June 1985. The Council was preceded by a short-lived Commission for State Security, which met on 27 June 1974, 12 December 1974 and 17 January 1975. See handwritten information at the beginning of HDA, F. 1561, 10.2_69-1.

84   SRH Presidency, Decision on the Establishment of the Council for the Protection of the Constitutional Order and Its Tasks and Areas of Competence, Article 7, 28 May 1980.

85   SRH Council for the Protection of the Constitutional Order, Minutes of the 1st Session, 10 July 1975; HDA, F. 1561, 10.2_69-1, 2.

86   SRH Council for the Protection of the Constitutional Order, Minutes of the 1st Session, 10 July 1975; HDA, F. 1561, 10.2_69-1, 3, 7–8.

87   SRH Presidency, Decision on the Establishment of the Council for the Protection of the Constitutional Order and Its Tasks and Areas of Competence, Article 5, 28 May 1980. For the legal basis of the republican councils in the SRH, see the Law on Republican Councils, *Narodne novine*, No. 12/75, 139–41; Law on the Changes and Amendments to the Law on Republican Councils, *Narodne novine*, No. 17/78, 29 April 1978, 390–1.

88   SRH Presidency, Decision on the Establishment of the Council for the Protection of the Constitutional Order and Its Tasks and Areas of Competence, Article 8, 28 May 1980; Article 60, Rulebook on the Organization and Work of the SRH Presidency, *Narodne novine*, No. 5/82, 2 February 1982, 89.

89   SRH Presidency, Invitation to 1st Session of the Council for the Protection of the Constitutional Order on 1 July 1975, 27 June 1975, HDA, F. 1561, 10.2_69-1.

90   SRH Council for the Protection of the Constitutional Order, Minutes of the 1st Session, 10 July 1975; HDA, F. 1561, 10.2_69-1, 10.

91   Decision on the Nomination of the President and Members of the SRH Council for the Protection of the Constitutional Order, 16 July 1980, 4.

92   Decision on the Nomination of the President and Members of the SRH Council for the Protection of the Constitutional Order, 17 July 1982, 1.

93   Overview of the Sessions of the SRH Council for the Protection of the Constitutional Order, 351–3.

94   Minutes of the 1st Session of the SRH Council for the Protection of the Constitutional Order, 9 July 1982, 2.

95   On occasion, the meetings of the Council were held in the offices of the SDS, for example, on 22 October 1980. Transcript of Tape Recording of the 1st Session

of the SRH Council for the Protection of the Constitutional Order, 22 October 1980, 4.

96 Transcript of Tape Recording of the 1st Session of the SRH Council for the Protection of the Constitutional Order, 3 April 1980, 11.

97 Josip Perković and Jan Gabriš, 'Služba državne sigurnosti republičkog sekretarijata za unutarnje poslove SR Hrvatske u vremenu 1980. – 30. svibnja 1990. godine,' Zagreb, June 1997, unpublished internal paper, 16.

98 For an explanation of the significance of these topics, see Tomislav Dulić and Roland Kostić, 'Yugoslavs in Arms: Guerrilla Tradition, Total Defence and the Ethnic Security Dilemma,' *Europe-Asia Studies*, Vol. 62, No. 7 (2010), 1051–72.

99 Transcript of Tape Recording of the Session of the SRH Council for the Protection of the Constitutional Order, 3 April 1980, 11.

100 Transcript of Tape Recording of the Session of the SRH Council for the Protection of the Constitutional Order, 3 April 1980, 13.

101 Transcript of Tape Recording of the Session of the SRH Council for the Protection of the Constitutional Order, 3 April 1980, 70.

102 Article 64, Law on the Organs of Internal Affairs, *Narodne novine*, No. 44/79, 23 October 1979, 677; Josip Perković and Jan Gabriš, 'Služba državne sigurnosti republičkog sekretarijata za unutarnje poslove SR Hrvatske u vremenu 1980. – 30. svibnja 1990. godine,' 1997, S. 7.

103 Josip Perković and Jan Gabriš, 'Služba državne sigurnosti republičkog sekretarijata za unutarnje poslove SR Hrvatske u vremenu 1980. – 30. svibnja 1990. godine,' Zagreb, June 1997, unpublished internal paper, 105.

104 Josip Perković And Jan Gabriš, 'Služba državne sigurnosti republičkog sekretarijata za unutarnje poslove SR Hrvatske u vremenu 1980. – 30. svibnja 1990. godine,' Zagreb, June 1997, unpublished internal paper, 50, 58; Letter of Josip Perković to President Franjo Tuđman, 17 September 1992.

105 Josip Perković and Jan Gabriš, 'Služba državne sigurnosti republičkog sekretarijata za unutarnje poslove SR Hrvatske u vremenu 1980. – 30. svibnja 1990. godine,' Zagreb, June 1997, unpublished internal paper, 105.

106 Josip Perković and Jan Gabriš, 'Služba državne sigurnosti republičkog sekretarijata za unutarnje poslove SR Hrvatske u vremenu 1980. – 30. svibnja 1990. godine,' Zagreb, June 1997, unpublished internal paper, 22.

107 Goran Petrović, *Vesela Udba*, 2nd Edition (Valjevo: Topalović, 2016), 78.

108 Bojan Dimitrijević, 'Odjek Brionskog plenuma na službu unutrašnjih poslova,' *Istorija 20. veka*, No. 2 (2001), 83f; Srđan Cvetković. 'Kako je spaljeno pet kilometara dosijea UDB-e,' *Arhiv*, Vol. 9, No. 1–2 (2008), 71–84; Srđan Cvetković, *Između srpa i čekića 2: Politička represija u Srbiji, 1953–1985* (Belgrade: Službeni glasnik, 2011), 11f.

109 See the forewords to Goran Miloradović and Aleksej Timofejev, *Između dve otadžbine: Jugoslovenski politički emigranti u Sovjetskom Savezu 1948–1956*

(Belgrade: Arhiv Srbije, 2016) and Dragoslav Mihailović et al., *Zatočenici Golog otoka: Registar lica osuđivanih zbog Informbiroa* (Belgrade: Arhiv Srbije, 2016).

110 Christian Axboe Nielsen, Review of Josip Manolić, *Politika i domovina: Moja borba za suverenu i socijalnu Hrvatsku, Southeastern Europe*, Vol. 41, No. 2 (2017), 231–3.

111 SSUP, Centre for Professional Training, 'Operational Processing – Materials – Part Two,' 1974, ARS, F. 1931, šk. 2308.

112 SSUP, Centre for Professional Training, 'Operational Processing – Materials – Part Two,' 1974, ARS, F. 1931, šk. 2308.

113 SSUP, Centre for Professional Training, 'Operational Processing – Materials – Part Two,' 1974, ARS, F. 1931, šk. 2308, 9.

114 SDS Centre Split, Proposal for Dossier for Franjo Goreta, January 1976, HDA, F. 1561, Dossier of Franjo Goreta.

115 SSUP, Centre for Professional Training, 'Operational Processing – Materials – Part Two,' 1974, ARS, F. 1931, šk. 2308, 3.

116 SSUP, Centre for Professional Training, 'Operational Processing – Materials – Part Two,' 1974, ARS, F. 1931, šk. 2308, 3–4.

117 SSUP, Centre for Professional Training, 'Operational Processing – Materials – Part Two,' 1974, ARS, F. 1931, šk. 2308, 19.

118 SSUP, Centre for Professional Training, 'Operational Processing – Materials – Part Two,' 1974, ARS, F. 1931, šk. 2308, 4–7.

119 SSUP, Centre for Professional Training, 'Operational Processing – Materials – Part Two,' 1974, ARS, F. 1931, šk. 2308, 19–21.

120 Article 48 in August 1975 Rulebook, ARS, F. 1931, šk. 2233. In the available copy of this document, there is no Article 49, but the relevant language may stem from both articles.

121 SSUP, Centre for Professional Training, 'Operational Processing – Materials – Part Two,' 1974, ARS, F. 1931, šk. 2308, 22.

122 SSUP, Centre for Professional Training, 'Operational Processing – Materials – Part Two,' 1974, ARS, F. 1931, šk. 2308, 23.

123 SSUP, Centre for Professional Training, 'Operational Processing – Materials – Part Two,' 1974, ARS, F. 1931, šk. 2308, 23.

124 SSUP, Centre for Professional Training, 'Operational Processing – Materials – Part Two,' 1974, ARS, F. 1931, šk. 2308, 9, 25–6.

125 SSUP, Centre for Professional Training, 'Operational Processing – Materials – Part Two,' 1974, ARS, F. 1931, šk. 2308, 10.

126 On double agents, see SSUP, Centre for Professional Training, 'Operational Processing – Materials – Part Two,' 1974, ARS, F. 1931, šk. 2308, 34–7; Article 54 in August 1975 Rulebook, ARS, F. 1931, šk. 2233. Interestingly, triple and even quadruple agents also existed. For a mention of a quadruple agent, see Transcript of 77th Expanded Session of the Executive Bureau of the SKJ Presidency, 23 March 1971, AJ, F. 507, IV, fasc. 139, 11.

127 SSUP, Centre for Professional Training, 'Operational Processing – Materials – Part Two,' 1974, ARS, F. 1931, šk. 2308, 26.

128 SSUP, Centre for Professional Training, 'Operational Processing – Materials – Part Two,' 1974, ARS, F. 1931, šk. 2308, 27.

129 Article 48, SSUP SDB, 'Rulebook on the Work of the State Security Service,' August 1975, ARS, F. 1931, šk. 2233.

130 SSUP, Centre for Professional Training, 'Operational Processing – Materials – Part Two,' 1974, ARS, F. 1931, šk. 2308, 28.

131 SSUP, Centre for Professional Training, 'Operational Processing – Materials – Part Two,' 1974, ARS, F. 1931, šk. 2308, 76.

132 Josip Perković and Jan Gabriš, 'Služba državne sigurnosti republičkog sekretarijata za unutarnje poslove SR Hrvatske u vremenu 1980. – 30. svibnja 1990. godine,' Zagreb, June 1997, unpublished internal paper, 23.

133 SSUP, Centre for Professional Training, 'Operational Processing – Materials – Part Two,' 1974, ARS, F. 1931, šk. 2308, 29.

134 SSUP, Centre for Professional Training, 'Operational Processing – Materials – Part Two,' 1974, ARS, F. 1931, šk. 2308, 81.

135 SSUP, Centre for Professional Training, 'Operational Processing – Materials – Part Two,' 1974, ARS, F. 1931, šk. 2308, 83.

136 SSUP SDB, 'Instructions with Classification Schemes for the Classification of Data in the Realm of State Security,' 4 November 1975, 13, ARS, F. 1931, šk. 2234.

137 SSUP, Centre for Professional Training, 'Operational Processing – Materials – Part Two,' 1974, S. 83, ARS, F. 1931, šk. 2308.

138 SSUP, Centre for Professional Training, 'Operational Processing – Materials – Part Two,' 1974, ARS, F. 1931, šk. 2308, 3.

139 SSUP, Centre for Professional Training, 'Operational Processing – Materials – Part Two,' 1974, ARS, F. 1931, šk. 2308, 62.

140 SSUP, Centre for Professional Training, 'Operational Processing – Materials – Part Two,' 1974, ARS, F. 1931, šk. 2308, 63.

141 SSUP, Centre for Professional Training, 'Operational Processing – Materials – Part Two,' 1974, ARS, F. 1931, šk. 2308, 71.

142 Article 51 in August 1975 Rulebook, ARS, F. 1931, šk. 2233.

143 Remaining 'in touch with us' [*vezano za nas*] of course also presumed the maintenance of loyalty. SSUP, Centre for Professional Training, 'Operational Processing – Materials – Part Two,' 1974, ARS, F. 1931, šk. 2308, 16.

144 Goran Petrović, who began working in the Serbian State Security Service in the 1980s and much later served briefly as the head of the Service, wrote that 'an operational position is some kind of informal term for connections with informants, operations, friends and acquaintances which the operatives of the DB had. What is the difference? Fuck it, I don't know either.' Goran Petrović, *Vesela Udba*, 2nd Edition (Valjevo: Topalović, 2016), 52.

145 Articles 41–46 in August 1975 Rulebook, ARS, F. 1931, šk. 2233.

146 Article 47 in August 1975 SDB Rulebook, ARS, F. 1931, šk. 2233. It should be noted that the usage of the term '*rezidentura*' deviates from the (Soviet) Russian usage, where the term referred to a KGB 'station' situated within a Soviet embassy, and employed only professional agents.

147 SSUP, Centre for Professional Training, 'Operational Processing – Materials – Part Two,' 1974, ARS, F. 1931, šk. 2308, 39. See also Articles 76–8 in the August 1975 Rulebook, ARS, F. 1931, šk. 2233.

148 SSUP, Centre for Professional Training, 'Operational Processing – Materials – Part Two,' 1974, ARS, F. 1931, šk. 2308, 45.

149 SSUP, Centre for Professional Training, 'Operational Processing – Materials – Part Two,' 1974, ARS, F. 1931, šk. 2308, 49. It was also mentioned that the Law on Amnesty from 1962 had the effect of dissuading many émigrés from continuing with or initiating hostile activities. Ibid., 51.

150 SSUP, Centre for Professional Training, 'Operational Processing – Materials – Part Two,' 1974, ARS, F. 1931, šk. 2308, 49–50.

151 SSUP, Centre for Professional Training, 'Operational Processing – Materials – Part Two,' 1974, ARS, F. 1931, šk. 2308, 50.

152 SSUP, Centre for Professional Training, 'Operational Processing – Materials – Part Two,' 1974, ARS, F. 1931, šk. 2308, 53.

153 Đorđević, *Osnovi državne bezbednosti*, 103.

154 Instructions on the Counterintelligence Work of the SDB Abroad, 2.

155 Instructions on the Counterintelligence Work of the SDB Abroad, 4–5.

156 SDB SSUP, Third Sector, 'Information on the Establishment of a Special Work Unit of the State Security Service for Surveillance Activities Abroad,' 15 March 1968. Reproduced in: Roman Leljak, *Tajni pravilniki UDBE za likvidacije* (Kapelski vrh: Društvo za raziskovanje polpretekle zgodovine, 2014), 56–68.

157 SDB SSUP, Third Sector, 'Information on the Establishment of a Special Work Unit of the State Security Service for Surveillance Activities Abroad,' 15 March 1968, 2.

158 SDB SSUP, Third Sector, 'Information on the Establishment of a Special Work Unit of the State Security Service for Surveillance Activities Abroad,' 15 March 1968, 2.

159 SDB SSUP, Third Sector, 'Information on the Establishment of a Special Work Unit of the State Security Service for Surveillance Activities Abroad,' 15 March 1968, 2.

160 SDB SSUP, Third Sector, 'Information on the Establishment of a Special Work Unit of the State Security Service for Surveillance Activities Abroad,' 15 March 1968, 3.

161 SDB SSUP, Third Sector, 'Information on the Establishment of a Special Work Unit of the State Security Service for Surveillance Activities Abroad,' 15 March 1968, 2. Regarding surveillance and observation, see 'Operational Processing – Materials – Part Two,' 1974, 2–3.

162 Josip Perković and Jan Gabriš, 'Služba državne sigurnosti republičkog sekretarijata za unutarnje poslove SR Hrvatske u vremenu 1980. – 30. svibnja 1990. godine,' 1997, S. 105.

163 Božidar Spasić, *Lasica koja govori: Osnovne pretpostavke borbe protiv terorizma*, 3rd Edition (Belgrade: Knjiga komerc, 2000).

164 SSUP SDB, 'Affairs and Functions of the State Security Service of the SSUP,' 25 December 1971, ARS, F. 1931, šk. 2304, 7.

165 SSUP SDB, 'Affairs and Functions of the State Security Service of the SSUP,' 7.

166 SSUP SDB, 'Affairs and Functions of the State Security Service of the SSUP,' 10.

167 SSUP SDB, 'Affairs and Functions of the State Security Service of the SSUP,' 11.

168 SSUP SDB, 'Affairs and Functions of the State Security Service of the SSUP,' 11.

169 ARS, F. 1931, šk. 2233. This document can also be found at ARS, F. 1931, šk. 1189. Compare with the instructions of the SSUP SDB from January 1967 and from January 1989. From January 1967: ARS, F. 1931, šk. 2226; from January 1989: ARS, F. 1931, šk. 1189.

170 Article 53 in August 1975 Rulebook, ARS, F. 1931, šk. 2233.

171 Article 72 in August 1975 Rulebook, ARS, F. 1931, šk. 2233.

172 See, for example, SDS Zagreb, Second Section, Operational Diary for Vjekoslav 'Maks' Luburić, commenced 10 March 1967. The first entry states 'Luburić is placed under operational processing as a separate subject because of the danger which his activity presents for our country.'

173 See, for example, the dossier for the operation 'Mura' conducted by the SDS in the late 1960s. HDA, F. 1561, šifra 1, 10.0/13, 1.

174 SSUP SDB, 'Instructions on the Work of the State Security Service Abroad,' 28 December 1979, ARS, F. 1931, šk. 2233.

175 SSUP SDB, 'Instructions on the Work of the State Security Service Abroad,' 28 December 1979, Point 5, ARS, F. 1931, šk. 2233.

176 See, for example, the SDV's *registrirana tekoča zadeva* (registered current affair, i.e. operation), *Dizel* (Diesel), which encompassed a very large number of West German scholarly institutions and associations working on Yugoslavia and the Balkans from October 1972 onwards. ARS, F. 1931, RTZ-247 Dizel.

177 SSUP SDB, 'Instructions on the Work of the State Security Service Abroad,' 28 December 1979, Point 20, ARS, F. 1931, šk. 2233.

178 SSUP SDB, 'Instructions on the Work of the State Security Service Abroad,' 28 December 1979, Point 20, ARS, F. 1931, šk. 2233.

179 The Council for the Confirmation of Postwar Victims of the Communist System Killed Abroad also cites the term 'offensive actions' (*ofanzivne akcije*). Without providing a source, the Council also claimed that Federal Secretary for Internal Affairs Franjo Herljević proposed the establishment of a 'Section for Offensive Actions' within the Second Administration of the SSUP SDB. Council for the Confirmation of Postwar Victims of the Communist System Killed Abroad,

Republic of Croatia *Sabor*, 'Postwar Victims of SFRJ State Terror Abroad,' 30 September 1999, 9–10.

180 The Seventh Sector (or Administration) of the SSUP SDB produced provided fake passports and other fake documentation for agents traveling abroad. Instructions on the Counterintelligence Work of the SDB Abroad, 17.

181 See, for example, the mention of the radio communications system known as 'System 1100'. SDV, Official Note, 17. March 1969, ARS, F. 1931, šk. 2414, 37; SSUP SDB Dispatch to the SDV, Sector I, 11 February 1969, šk. 2414, 36.

182 Bernd Robionek, 'Gutachten zur Strafsache Prates,' Oberlandesgericht München, 20 March 2008, 12. See also the case of Franjo Goreta in Chapter X.

183 SSUP SDB, 'Instructions on the Work of the State Security Service Abroad,' 28 December 1979, Point 5, ARS, F. 1931, šk. 2233.

184 SSUP SDB, 'Instructions on the Counterintelligence Work of the SDB Abroad,' 16–17.

185 'Institut bezbednosti je rezultat opštih napora naše zajednice na izgradnji i jačanju bezbednosti i društvene samozaštite,' *13. maj*, November–December 1976; Marko Lopušina, 'Tajne sobe eksperata BIA,' 11 October 2008, *Novosti* (Belgrade); Report of Dragan Mojsovski, 'The Work and Successes of the Institute of Security,' in SSUP SDB, 'Collection of the Consultations on the Work of Counterintelligence and Intelligence of the SDB and Other Services Which Execute Tasks of State Security,' July 1988, 473, ARS, F. 1931, šk. 2311.

186 SDV, 'Special Weapons and Means for Fine Acts of Sabotage [*fina diverzija*],' undated, ARS, F. 1931, šk. 2234; SDV, 'Operational-Technical Means for Sabotge,' undated, ARS, F. 1931, šk. 2235.

187 BKA, 'Terroristische Gewaltkriminalität durch Jugoslawen: Politisch motivierte Gewaltkriminalität durch Jugoslawen in der Bundesrepublik Deutschland,' Juni 1984, vierte Fortschreibung des Berichtes vom Juni 1977, 83–6.

Chapter 2

1   Martina Grahek Ravančić, *Bleiburg i križni put 1945. Historiografija, publicistika i memoarska literatura*, 2. izmijenjeno i dopunjeno izdanje (Zagreb: Hrvatski institut za povijest, 2015); Pål Kostø. 'Bleiburg: The Creation of a National Martyrology,' *Europe-Asia Studies*, Vol. 62, No. 7 (September 2010), 1153–74; Vladimir Geiger, 'Human Losses of the Croats in World War II and the Immediate Post-War Period Caused by the Chetniks (Yugoslav Army in the Fatherland) and the Partisans (People's Liberation Army and the Partisan Detachments of Yugoslavia/Yugoslav Army) and the Yugoslav Communist Authorities Numerical Indicators,' *Review of Croatian History*, Vol. 8, No. 1 (2012), 77–121; see also the special issue of *Politička misao* on transnational approaches to remembering Bleiburg, *Politička misao*, Vol. 55, No. 2 (2018).

2   On the crimes of the NDH, see Alexander Korb, 'Understanding Ustaša Violence,' *Journal of Genocide Research*, Vol. 12, Nos. 1–2 (2010), 1–18; Rory Yeomans, *Visions of Annihilation: The Ustaša Regime and the Cultural Politics of Fascism, 1941–1945* (Pittsburgh, PA: University of Pittsburgh Press, 2013; Tomislav Dulić, *Utopias of Nation: Local Mass Killing in Bosnia and Herzegovina, 1941–1942* (Stockholm: Elanders Gotab, 2005); Mark Biondich, 'Religion and Nation in Wartime Croatia: Reflections on the Ustaša Policy of Forced Religious Conversions,' *The Slavonic and East European Review*, Vol. 83, No. 1 (2005), 71–116; Ivo Goldstein, *Jasenovac* (Zagreb: Fraktura, 2018); Sabrina Ramet, 'The NDH – An Introduction,' *Totalitarian Movements and Political Religions*, Vol. 7, No. 4 (2006), 399–408.

3   Josip Broz Tito cited in Kosta Nikolić, *Ozna*, 169.

4   Zdenko Radelić, *Križari gerila u Hrvatskoj, 1945–1950* (Zagreb: Dom i Svijet, 2002); Tomislav Jonjić, 'Organised Resistance to the Yugoslav Communist Regime in Croatia in 1945–1953,' *Review of Croatian History*, Vol. 3, No. 1 (February 2007), 109–45; Ivica Lučić, 'Hrvatska protukomunistička gerila u Bosni i Hercegovini od 1945. do 1951.,' *Časopis za suvremenu povijest*, Vol. 42, No. 3 (2010), 631–70.

5   OZNA FNRJ, 'Register of Prominent Figures of the Yugoslav Political Emigration as of 1 March 1946,' 1 March 1946, ARS, F. 1931, šk. 1168.

6   Josip Jurčević in Bože Vukušić, *Tajni rat UDBE protiv hrvatskoga iseljeništva*, 3rd Expanded Edition (Zagreb: Klub hrvatskih povratnika iz iseljeništva, 2002, 9.

7   I disagree with the term 'proxy war'; however, since the agents of the Yugoslav State Security Service on the one hand and Croat émigrés on the other hand were not acting as proxies, but rather directly to further their own interests. Alexander Clarkson, *Fragmented Fatherland: Immigration and Cold War Conflict in the Federal Republic of Germany, 1945–80* (New York: Berghahn Books, 2013), 6.

8   It should be noted that people emigrated both eastwards and westwards from Yugoslavia for political reasons. Particularly after the 1948 split between Tito and Stalin, a large number of Yugoslavs who agreed with the Cominform Resolution emigrated to (or decided to stay in) the East Bloc countries. However, the subject of this book is the émigrés who went to the West. Perković and Gabriš claim that the term 'fascist emigration' was used until 1985. There are some indications that it persisted even before then, but the terms 'hostile emigration' or 'hostile portion of the emigration' can also be found already from the end of the 1950s. Josip Perković and Jan Gabriš, 'Služba državne sigurnosti republičkog sekretarijata za unutarnje poslove SR Hrvatske u vremenu 1980. – 30. svibnja 1990. godine,' 1997, S. 61, 106.

9   Obren Ž. Đorđević, *Osnovi državne bezbednosti: opšti deo* (Belgrade: VŠUP, 1980), 152–3. For a recent attempt at defining 'Croat political migration,' see Jakov Žižić, 'Što je hrvatska politička emigracija?,' *Političke analize* (December 2013), 61–4.

10   Đorđević, *Osnovi državne bezbednosti*, 163.

11   Mate Nikola Tokić, *For the Homeland Ready! Croat Diaspora Terrorism during the Cold War* (West Lafayette: Purdue University Press, 2020). 2.

12   Ivo Goldstein, *Hrvatska, 1918–2008* (Zagreb: EPH Liber, 2008), 384.

13   Vladimir Žerjavić, 'Kretanja stanovništva i demografski gubici Republike Hrvatske u razdoblju od 1900. do 1991.', *ČSP*, 2–3, 1993, 78–9. See also Ivica Nejašmić, 'Iseljavanje iz Hrvatske. Brojčani aspekt stoljetnog procesa', in Ivan Crkvenčić, ed., *Političko-geografska i demografska pitanja Hrvatske* (Zagreb: Savez geografskih društava Hrvatske, 1991), 61–82.

14   Tokić, *For the Homeland Ready!*, 25.

15   Clarkson, *Fragmented Fatherland*, 59. According to the Yugoslav State Commission for the Determination of Crimes of the Occupiers and their Collaborators, in a summary report from September 1947, the Commission had identified 64,969 war criminals, of whom 49,245 were Yugoslav nationals and 15,724 were foreign (mainly German and Italian) nationals. The same report claimed that 'the larger part of the confirmed war criminals has been brought before our people's courts'. These figures were compiled on the basis of reports submitted by the republican Commissions. Personal communication from Mark Biondich, 1 August 2019.

16   In the official view, these opponents predominantly included 'members of the quisling apparatus … members of bourgeois society … soldiers, non-commissioned officers, officers and generals of the former Yugoslav army … prisoners of war who under the influence of anti-communist propaganda refused to return to Yugoslavia … renegades, members of illegal organizations, convicted of war crimes'. Đorđević, *Osnovi državne bezbednosti*, 152.

17   A number of historians believe that the Yugoslav communist regime undertook the prosecution and conviction of Alojzije Stepinac, the archbishop of Zagreb partly because Ante Pavelić had successfully escaped and could not be prosecuted. In addition, Stepinac's trial provided a useful counterpoint in the name of brotherhood and unity to the trial of the Serb Chetnik leader, Dragoljub 'Draža' Mihailović.

18   As of July 1948, the British government alone had received 1,800 such requests, but had only agreed to extradite fifty-eight persons. Stephen Clissold, 'Croat Separatism: Nationalism, Dissidence and Terrorism', *Conflict Studies*, No. 103 (January 1979).

19   I am indebted to Mark Biondich for this point. Artuković was convicted and sentenced to death. He died of natural causes in a Yugoslav prison in January 1988. On anti-communism and US unwillingness to prosecute or extradite Eastern Europeans suspected of war crimes during the Second World War, see Judy Feigin, 'The Office of Special Investigations: Striving for Accountability in the Aftermath of the Holocaust', US Department of Justice, December 2006.

20   Edmund Schweissguth, 'Die Reorganisation des Staatssicherheitsdienstes in der SFR Jugoslawien', *Jahrbuch für Ostrecht*, Vol. 10, No. 1 (1969), 55–6.

21   Schweissguth, 'Die Reorganisation des Staatssicherheitsdienstes in der SFR Jugoslawien,' 59.

22   Lest it go unremarked, denialism among Croat political émigrés includes the denial that the NDH was an inherently fascist construction. See, for example, Kazimir Katalinić, *Od poraza do pobjede: Povijest hrvatske političke emigracije, 1945.–1990.*, Vol. 1 (Zagreb: Naklada Trpimir, 2017–18), 23–4.

23   Radelić, *Križari gerila u Hrvatskoj, 1945–1950.*

24   Radelić, *Križari gerila u Hrvatskoj, 1945–1950.*

25   Tokić, *For the Homeland Ready!*, 26.

26   Tokić, *For the Homeland Ready!*, 41f.

27   Tokić, *For the Homeland Ready!*, 43f. Allegations exist that the Yugoslav State Security Service was involved in the Pavelić-Stojadinović rapprochement. Kazimir Katalinić, Vol. 1, 227–9.

28   Clissold, 'Croat Separatism,' 6.

29   Library and Archives of Canada, RG 25, Vol. 9361, File 20-18-1-5, Part 15, Doc: 'The Chicago Danica (Morning Star): Executive Committee of the Croatian National Council.' (April 9, 1975), 11, cited in Tokić, Introduction.

30   On the flight of Pavelić and his postwar movements, see Ante Delić, 'Djelovanje Ante Pavelića 1945.–1953. godine,' doctoral dissertation, University of Zadar, 2016; Ante Delić, 'On the Concealment of Ante Pavelić in Austria in 1945–1946,' *Review of Croatian History*, Vol. 7, No. 1 (2011), 293–313.

31   Clissold, 'Croat Separatism,' 6.

32   Tokić, *For the Homeland Ready!*, 39.

33   Quoted in Tokić, *For the Homeland Ready!*, 40.

34   Vukušić, *Tajni rat UDBE protiv hrvatskoga iseljeništva*, 42–3.

35   Vladimir Ivanović, *Geburtstag pišeš normalno: Jugoslavenski gastarbajteri u Austriji i SR Nemačkoj* (Belgrade: ISI, 2012); Brigitte Le Normand, 'The *Gastarbajteri* as a Transnational Working Class,' in Rory Archer, Igor Duda and Paul Stubbs, eds., *Social Inequalities and Discontent in Yugoslav Socialism* (London: Routledge, 2016), 38–57; Christopher A. Molnar, *Memory, Politics and Yugoslav Migrations to Postwar Germany* (Bloomington: Indiana University Press, 2018).

36   Ante Batović, *The Croatian Spring: Nationalism, Repression and Foreign Policy under Tito* (London: I.B. Tauris, 2017), 17–18.

37   SSIP, 'Minutes of Consultation about Problems of Employment and the Residency of Yugoslav Workers Abroad, Held in Krapinske Toplice,' 29 July 1971, ARS, F. 1931, šk. 385, DSC_0019. Christopher A. Molnar, 'Imagining Yugoslavs: Migration and the Cold War in Postwar West Germany,' *Central European History* Vol. 47 (2014), 138–69.

38   William Zimmerman, *Open Borders, Nonalignment, and the Political Evolution of Yugoslavia* (Princeton: Princeton University Press, 1987), 106.

39 Clarkson, *Fragmented Fatherland*, 61.

40 Molnar, 'Imagining Yugoslavs: Migration and the Cold War in Postwar West Germany', 146.

41 Vukušić, *Tajni rat UDBE protiv hrvatskoga iseljeništva*, 15.

42 For one example, see Ivo Omrčanin's pamphlet 'Seed of Blood', published in Sydney in July 1961. A copy exists in the NAA dossier of Srećko Rover, A 6119, 2737.

43 Josip Jurčević Josip in Vukušić, *Tajni rat UDBE protiv hrvatskoga iseljeništva*, 10.

44 SSUP SDB, 'The Security Situation and the Implementation of the Directive of the President of the Republic', 16 September 1972, 25, ARS, F. 1931, šk. 1362.

45 West German and other officials conducted such debriefings not only to collect intelligence on Yugoslavia but also in order to try to detect Yugoslav communists who might try to infiltrate Western Europe. On the Zirndorf camp, see Molnar, *Memory, Politics, and Yugoslav Migrations to Postwar Germany*, 66–7, 102, 104; SDS Centre Zagreb, Information No. 44, 21 January 1970, HDA, F. 1561, SDS Centre Zagreb, Folder 78.

46 Tokić, *For the Homeland Ready!*, 67; SDS Centre Zagreb, Information No. 323, 30 April 1968, HDA, F. 1561, SDS Centre Osijek, Folder 77; SDS Centre Osijek, Information No. 1, 8 January 1972, HDA, F. 1561, SDS Centre Osijek, Folder 19.

47 Mate Nikola Tokić, 'Landscapes of Conflict: Unity and Disunity in Post-Second World War Croatian Émigré Separatism', *European Review of History*, Vol. 16, No. 5 (2009), 744.

48 Molnar, 'Imagining Yugoslavs', 150.

49 SSIP, 'Minutes of Consultation about Problems of Employment and the Residency of Yugoslav Workers Abroad, Held in Krapinske Toplice', 29 July 1971, ARS, F. 1931, šk. 385.

50 Zdenko Radelić, 'Ozna/Udba: Popisi neprijatelja i njihova kategorizacija (1940-ih i 1950-ih)', *Časopis za suvremenu povijest*, Vol. 49 (2017), 70–1. Radelić correctly observes that as regards the 1955 instructions and instructions, rules and regulations of the Yugoslav State Security Service more generally speaking, it is often difficult to figure out whether these documents were issued for the first time, as amendments to previous similar documents or whether these documents were a bureaucratic expression of the need for constant repetition and reminders.

51 See, for example, the letter of the Federal Undersecretary Đuro Stanković to the Slovenian Undersecretary Bogomir Peršič, 19 March 1957, 1, ARS, F. 1931, šk. 1189.

52 On Cominform émigrés and Cominformists in Yugoslavia, see Christian Axboe Nielsen, 'Never-ending Vigilance: The Yugoslav State Security Service and Cominform Supporters after Goli Otok', in Tvrtko Jakovina and Martin Previšić, eds., The Tito-Stalin Split 70 Years After (Zagreb and Ljubljana: Sveučilište u Zagreb, Univerza v Ljubljani, 2019), 109–20.

53 SSUP, Centre for Professional Training, 'Operational Processing – Materials – Part Two', 51, 1974, ARS, F. 1931, šk. 2308; Aleksandar Ranković, 'On the Law of

Amnesty, *New Yugoslav Law*, Vol. 13, No. 1–2 (January–June 1962), 3–11; 'The
Law of Amnesty, *New Yugoslav Law*, Vol. 13, No. 1–2 (January–June 1962), 66–7.

54   In practice the application of the amnesty was not wholly consistent. On the
     amnesty, see the speech of Aleksandar Ranković, 'Človek in njegova svoboda v
     svobodni domovini sta največji vrednoti,' *Dolenjski list*, 22 March 1962, 3.

55   DSUP NR Slovenia, Letter, 6 April 1962, ARS, F. 1931, šk. 1192.

56   SSUP, 'Instructions for the Creation and Maintenance of Dossiers of Yugoslav
     Émigrés and for the Establishment in the Organs of Internal Affairs of a
     Centralized Documentation of the Yugoslav Emigration,' 1962, ARS, F. 1931, šk.
     1192. See also DSUP, 'Technical Instructions for the Completion of Questionnaires
     on Yugoslav Émigrés,' March 1962, ARS, F. 1931, šk. 1192.

57   DSUP Form JEM – 1, 'Questionnaire on Yugoslav Émigré.' See example from June
     1963 in the dossier of Ernest Bauer, HDA, F. 1561.

58   DSUP NR Slovenia, letter, 6 April 1962, ARS, F. 1931, šk. 1192; DSUP NR Slovenia,
     letter, 16 April 1962, ARS, F. 1931, šk. 1192

59   Republican Secretariat for Internal Affairs of the Socialist Republic of Slovenia,
     'Handbook on Some Problems Which Are of Significance for State Security, and
     Tasks Related to Their Solution,' May 1970, 50, ARS, F. 1931, šk. 1195.

60   Republican Secretariat for Internal Affairs of the Socialist Republic of Slovenia,
     'Handbook on Some Problems Which Are of Significance for State Security, and
     Tasks Related to Their Solution,' May 1970, 50, ARS, F. 1931, šk. 1195.

61   SSUP SDB, 'Operation "Raduša", 4 May 1973, 3, ARS, F. 1931, šk. 1160.

62   Report of Vice Sopta, UDB Mostar Department, 30 August 1961, in Vice
     Vukojević, *Dosje 240271* (Zagreb: Udruga Hrvatski križni put, 2015), 165.

63   Transcript of 77th Expanded Session of the Executive Bureau of the SKJ
     Presidency, 23 March 1971, AJ, F. 507 IV, fasc. 139, 33.

64   SFRJ Presidency, 'Conclusions Regarding Defence and Security Aspects of the
     Employment of Our Citizens Abroad,' 5 February 1973, ARS. F. 1931, šk. 385.

65   Ibid.

66   Ibid.; see also SSUP to RSNZ Slovenia, 4 May 1973, ARS. F. 1931, šk. 385; SSUP
     SDB, 'Security Aspects of the Employment of Yugoslav Workers Abroad,' April
     1973, šk. 385.

67   Decades later, Blagoje Jovović, a Serb émigré in Argentina, claimed responsibility
     for the assassination. Given the paucity of reliable information regarding the
     shooting of Pavelić, it is useless to attempt here to identify whether Jovović was
     in fact the assailant and whether or not he was acting on behalf of the Yugoslav
     State Security Service. However, there can be no doubt that Yugoslav State Security
     Service was interested in either kidnapping or killing Pavelić. Moreover, and
     perhaps equally importantly, most Croat émigrés were convinced that the Yugoslav
     state was behind the attack on Pavelić. Tihomir-Tiho Burzanović, *Knjiga o Blagoju
     Jovoviću – Dva metka za Pavelića* (Self-published).

68 Tokić, *For the Homeland Ready!*, 55.

69 Cited in Vukušić, *Tajni rat UDBE protiv hrvatskoga iseljeništva*, 17; Clissold, 'Croat Separatism', 7.

70 Vukušić, *Tajni rat UDBE protiv hrvatskoga iseljeništva*, 16–17; CIA, 'Current Activities of Ante Pavelić', 25 April 1951.

71 For an example of early Cold War CIA monitoring of the activities of Pavelić and his associates, see CIA, 'Ustaša Activity Abroad', 2 October 1951.

72 Vukušić, *Tajni rat UDBE protiv hrvatskoga iseljeništva*, 18.

73 Bože Vukušić, *HRB – Hrvatsko revolucionarno bratstvo: Rat prije rata*, 2nd Edition (Zagreb: Klub hrvatskih povratnika iz iseljeništva, 2012), 81.

74 Tokić, *For the Homeland Ready!*, 47.

75 See definition of 'semi-émigrés' in Tokić, *For the Homeland Ready!*, 16f.

76 Vukušić, *HRB – Hrvatsko revolucionarno bratstvo*, 25.

77 Vukušić, *HRB – Hrvatsko revolucionarno bratstvo*, 88–90.

78 SUP Kotara Osijek, State Security, Eighth Sector, 15 January 1961, HDA, F. 1561, Dossier of Geza Pašti.

79 The information summarized here comes from a summary of intelligence reports about Pašti contained in his dossier and dated 12 October 1966. HDA, F. 1561, Dossier of Geza Pašti.

80 Tokić, *For the Homeland Ready!*, 74.

81 Vukušić, *HRB – Hrvatsko revolucionarno bratstvo*, 26, 32.

82 Quoted in Vukušić, *HRB – Hrvatsko revolucionarno bratstvo*, 30.

83 Vukušić, *HRB – Hrvatsko revolucionarno bratstvo*, 32, 41.

84 See, for example, SSUP SDB, 'Overview of the Members and Connections of the HRB in Western European Countries', 2 July 1973, ARS, F. 1931, šk. 1207.

85 The information summarized here comes from a summary of intelligence reports about Pašti contained in his dossier and dated 12 October 1966. HDA, F. 1561, Dossier of Geza Pašti.

86 SDB Croatia, Note of 7 March 1966, HDA, F. 1561, Dossier of Vjekoslav Luburić.

87 SDB Official Note, undated, HDA, F. 1561, Dossier of Geza Pašti. See also the Operational Diary of SDB Osijek initiated on 2 February 1962, especially the entries for 4 and 7 November 1964.

88 Vukušić, *Tajni rat Udbe*, 208. On Ćurak see information in JPZM Documentation.

89 SDB Osijek, Operational Diary for Geza Pašti. Cf. SUP Osijek, State Security, 3 August 1966 and SUP Split, State Security, undated note and criminal complaint dated 21 September 1965, regarding Tomislav Krolo. These documents were provided to the German authorities by Bože Vukušić. It is evident from the operational diary that the SDB had in March 1963 proposed that Pašti should cease to be a person of interest. Emphasizing the confusion among Western agencies regarding which émigrés were active on which side, the German police apparently arrested and sought to deport Pašti on suspicion of being the 'Udba agent' who had betrayed the nine HRB members.

90 SDB Osijek, Operational Diary for Geza Pašti, 15 January 1965. For a similar
    formulation for the TRUP member Tomislav Krolo in the documentation of SDB
    Split, see Vukušić, *HRB – Hrvatsko revolucionarno bratstvo*, 89.

91 Summary of informant's report in summary of intelligence reports about Pašti
    dated 12 October 1966. HDA, F. 1561, Dossier of Geza Pašti. On Pašti, Škrinjarić,
    and Pavičić, see also SDV, 'Overview of the Extreme Political Emigration in
    Europe,' 25 September 1965, ARS, F. 1931, šk. 1168.

92 Serbo-Croatian translation of West German Federal Criminal Office report,
    15 February 1967, HDA, F. 1961, Dossier of Geza Pašti.

93 SDB Osijek, Operational Diary for Geza Pašti, 3 August 1966. It is however not
    clear why the SDB would have waited until 3 August 1966 to compose a 'plan for
    processing in 1966'. In the document, there are no entries between 15 January 1965
    and 3 August 1966.

94 SUP Osijek, State Security, 3 August 1966 HDA, F. 1961, Dossier of Geza Pašti.

95 SUP Osijek, State Security, 3 August 1966 HDA, F. 1961, Dossier of Geza Pašti.

96 SDB Osijek, Operational Diary for Geza Pašti, 12 October 1966 HDA, F. 1961,
    Dossier of Geza Pašti.

97 SDB Osijek, Operational Diary for Geza Pašti, 13 October 1966; see also SDS
    Centre Osijek, Geza Pašti, Proposal to Strike from Operational Processing,
    11 April 1967.

98 Excerpt from translated list of HRB members composed by the West German
    criminal police, Group E III in Bad Godesberg, 8 March 1967, HDA, F. 1961,
    Dossier of Geza Pašti.

99 Note of Commissioner of Police, Canberra, Australia, 4 July 1973 and (Police?)
    Note for File Regarding Joseph Senic [Josip Senić], 1967, National Archives of
    Australia, A6980, S203534. Senić claimed to have seen Pašti as late as August 1965.
    Senić was himself killed in Heidelberg in March 1972.

100 Letter to Commonwealth Migration Officer, 14 July 1964; Australian Department
    of External Affairs to Australian Embassy in Paris, 15 October 1964, National
    Archives of Australia, A6980, S203534.

101 Canadian Department of External Affairs to Australian High Commission in
    Ottawa, 15 January 1964, National Archives of Australia, A6980, S203534.

102 Cited in Letter to Secretary, Department of Immigration, Canberra, August
    1964; Letter to minister regarding 'Josif [*sic*] (Joseph) SENIC – Aged 28 Years
    Application for Passport,' 1964, National Archives of Australia, in Josip Senić file.

103 ASIO Director-General C.C.F. Spry to the Secretary, Department of Immigration,
    8 January 1969, in Josip Senić file.

104 SDS Osijek, 1971, overview of Josip Senić.

105 The application of Josip Senić for Australian Naturalization lists 22 February 1959
    as the date of his arrival. In Josip Senić file.

106 SDS Osijek, 1971, overview of Josip Senić.

107 Letter of Jack M. Davis, Acting Commissioner of the Commonwealth Police, to the Secretary, Department of Immigration, Canberra, August 1964, National Archives of Australia, in Josip Senić file.

108 Letter of New South Wales Senior Constable R.J. Parsons, 27 August 1964, National Archives of Australia, in Josip Senić file.

109 Letter of Josip Senić to the Secretary of the Immigration Department, 16 September 1964, in Josip Senić file.

110 Letter of Jack M. Davis, Acting Commissioner of the Commonwealth Police, to the Secretary, Department of Immigration, Canberra, 12 October 1964, National Archives of Australia, in Josip Senić file.

111 Letter of Josip Senić to the Secretary of the Immigration Department, 28 October 1964, in Josip Senić file.

112 Letter received by Australian Embassy, Bonn, 28 July 1965, in Josip Senić file. It is plausible that the postcard was sent by an informant working for the Yugoslav State Security Service.

113 Letter of Secretary P.R. Hayden to the Minister, 16 September 1965, NAA, Dossier of Srećko Rover, A6980, S201953, Part 1, 10.

114 Attempts by the Yugoslav State Security Service to convince Senić's father to help to 'pacify' Senić were in the meantime abandoned. SDS Osijek, 1971, overview of Josip Senić.

115 Note to the Acting Australian Minister [probably of Migration], 1968, in Josip Senić file.

116 This summary of the case of Goreta stems from the Bavarian Provincial High Court's judgement in the trial of Mustač and Perković, citing the judgement of the Provincial Court in Saarbrücken of 23 July 1981 (Js 54/80). Bavarian Provincial High Court, Judgment in the Case against Zdravko Mustač and Josip Perković (7 St 5/14(2)), 72. On the relationship between Senić and Goreta, see Vukušić, *HRB – Hrvatsko revolucionarno bratstvo*, 113.

117 Excerpt from translation of report of BKA office in Bad Godesberg of 15 February 1967, HDA, F. 1561, Dossier of Franjo Goreta.

118 Excerpt from translation of report of BKA office in Bad Godesberg of 15 February 1967, HDA, F. 1561, Dossier of Franjo Goreta.

119 Excerpt from translation of report of BKA office in Bad Godesberg of 15 February 1967, HDA, F. 1561, Dossier of Franjo Goreta.

120 Note on Franjo Goreta, 1975, HDA, F. 1561, Dossier of Franjo Goreta.

121 Somewhat incongruously, the file also stated that Goreta 'had the task of liquidating Senić'. SDS Osijek, 1971, overview of Josip Senić.

122 DSIP SID to SSUP SDB, First Administration, 26 May 1966, in SDS Senić dossier.

123 Official Note justifying contact with Franjo Goreta, 27 May 1966, in SDS Senić dossier.

124 Yugoslav Consulate in Stuttgart to DSIP, Chief of Consular Affairs, 5 June 1966, in SDS Senić dossier.

125 SDS Centre Osijek, Operational Sector, 25 April 1967, in SDS Senić dossier.

126 Letter of the Commonwealth Police to the Secretary of Immigration, 5 October 1966, in Josip Senić file.

127 Letter of B.L. Murray, Senior Migration Officer, Australian Embassy, Stockholm, 3 January 1967, in Josip Senić file. Senić was keen that the flights bringing him back to Australia should not connect through Belgrade, as he obviously feared arrest if he transited through there. During his stay in Sweden, Senić had worked on strengthening the HRB there. SDS Osijek, 1971, overview of Josip Senić.

128 Letter to Commonwealth Director of Migration, 25 September 1967, in Josip Senić file. Senić reacted by claiming that he felt discriminated against compared to Australian Serbs and Jews, many of the latter having fought in Israel. Department of Immigration, Note for File, 18 March 1968.

129 Note to the Acting Australian Minister [probably of Migration], July 1968, in Josip Senić file.

130 Letter to the Acting Australian Minister [probably of Migration], 1968, in Josip Senić file.

131 Letter of the Acting Secretary to the Acting Minister, May 1970, in Josip Senić file. The Yugoslav authorities were also convinced that Senić had been involved in the attack on the consulate in Sydney. SDS Osijek, 1971, overview of Josip Senić.

132 Quoted in letter of ASIO Director-General C.C.F. Spry to the Secretary, Department of Immigration, 8 January 1969, in Josip Senić file.

133 Centre SDS information dated 29 September 1970 cited in SDS Osijek, 1971, overview of Josip Senić.

134 SDS Operational Diary for Josip Senić, HDA, F. 1561, Dossier of Josip Senić.

135 SDS Osijek, 1971, overview of Josip Senić.

136 SDS Operational Diary for Josip Senić.

137 SDS Operational Diary for Josip Senić.

138 Official Note, 16 June 1967, in SDS Senić dossier.

139 SDS Centre Osijek, Operational Plan for Josip Senić for 1970, 17 April 1970, in SDS Senić dossier.

140 SDS Centre Osijek, Operational Plan for Josip Senić for 1971, 2 March 1970, in SDS Senić dossier.

141 The SDS cited information in November 1970 according to which Senić had left Australia for Europe. SDS Osijek, 1971, overview of Josip Senić.

142 SDS Operational Diary for Josip Senić, 22 March 1971.

143 SDS Centre Split, Excerpt from Informational Report, 19 August 1971, in SDS Senić dossier.

144 SDS Centre Split, Informational Report, 8 September 1971, in SDS Senić dossier.

145 SDS Centre Split, Informational Report, 7 September 1971; SDS Centre Split, Informational Report, 28 September 1971, in SDS Senić dossier.

146 SDS Centre Rijeka, Informational Report, 19 October 1971, in SDS Senić dossier.

147 For the more specific alleged details surrounding Senić's assassination, see Vukušić, *Rat prije rata*, 138–41.

148 SDS Centre Osijek, Official Note, 18 April 1972.

149 SDS Centre Osijek, Information Sheet for Josip Senić, dated 2 December 1967. The list of approval for operational processing is listed as 8 June 1966.

150 'Umoren Josip Senić,' *Pregled*, March 1972, HDA, F. 1561, Dossier of Drago Jilek.

151 SDB Croatia, Note of 7 March 1966, HDA, F. 1561, Dossier of Vjekoslav Luburić.

152 See undated (1972) fragment of letter from L.S.J. Harper, Acting Commissioner in NAA, Dossier of Srećko Rover, A6980, S201953, Part 1, 8.

153 This section summarizes Vukušić, *HRB – Hrvatsko revolucionarno bratstvo*, 95–100.

154 Vukušić, *HRB – Hrvatsko revolucionarno bratstvo*, 96. The tape recording was subsequently aired in 2012 in the HRT documentary series, *Jugoslavenske tajne službe* (Yugoslav Secret Services).

155 CIA, 'Croatian Emigre Activity,' 15 September 1972, 3.

156 CIA, 'Croatian Emigre Activity,' 15 September 1972, 5.

157 Vukušić, *HRB – Hrvatsko revolucionarno bratstvo*, 90–1.

158 Brajković chose to remain in prison, but Barešić received political asylum in Spain before emigrating to Paraguay, where he worked as a presidential bodyguard. He was later extradited to the United States and then finally back to Sweden, where he remained in prison until 1987 before returning to Paraguay. In July 1991, Barešić came back to Croatia and immediately established a paramilitary unit. He was killed in combat only three weeks later. Tvrtko Jakovina, 'Hrvatski politički emigranti: Teroristi ili domoljubi?,' *Globus*, 25 July 2008, 42–8.

159 CIA, 'Croatian Emigre Activity,' 15 September 1972, 2.

160 Tokić, *For the Homeland Ready!*, 49.

Chapter 3

1 SSUP SDB, 'Instructions on Counterintelligence Work of the SDB Abroad,' undated.

2 SSUP SDB, 'Instructions on Counterintelligence Work of the SDB Abroad,' undated, 2–3.

3 SSUP SDB, 'Instructions on Counterintelligence Work of the SDB Abroad,' undated, 2–3.

4 SSUP SDB, 'Instructions on Counterintelligence Work of the SDB Abroad,' undated, 18–19.

5   SSUP SDB, 'Instructions on Counterintelligence Work of the SDB Abroad,' undated, 18–19.

6   SSUP SDB, 'Instructions on Counterintelligence Work of the SDB Abroad,' undated, 4–5.

7   SSUP SDB, 'Instructions on Counterintelligence Work of the SDB Abroad,' undated, 18–19.

8   SSUP SDB, 'Instructions on Counterintelligence Work of the SDB Abroad,' undated, 16–17.

9   SSUP SDB, 'Instructions on Counterintelligence Work of the SDB Abroad,' undated, 4–5.

10   SDS Centre Zagreb, Second Department, Special Information No. 46, 31 January 1967, HDA, F. 1561, SDS Centre Zagreb, Folder 76.

11   See for example SDS Centre Zagreb, Information No. 172, 24 August 1972, HDA, F. 1561, SDS Centre Zagreb, Folder 80.

12   SSUP SDB, 'Instructions on Counterintelligence Work of the SDB Abroad,' undated, 12–13.

13   SSUP SDB, 'Instructions on Counterintelligence Work of the SDB Abroad,' undated, 4–5.

14   SSUP SDB, 'Instructions on Counterintelligence Work of the SDB Abroad,' undated, 4–5.

15   SSUP SDB, 'Instructions on Counterintelligence Work of the SDB Abroad,' undated, 12–13.

16   SSUP SDB, 'Instructions on Counterintelligence Work of the SDB Abroad,' undated, 16.

17   SSUP SDB, 'Instructions on Counterintelligence Work of the SDB Abroad,' undated, 16.

18   SSUP SDB, 'Instructions on Counterintelligence Work of the SDB Abroad,' undated, 17. An example of this is the code name 'Leopard,' which was used abroad as an 'operational-technical means.' SRBiH RSUP, 'Combatting the Activity of Foreign Intelligence Services and the Hostile Emigration,' April 1987, 444.

19   For a more realistic view, but where financial questions nonetheless figure in Israeli intelligence operations and assassinations abroad, see Ronen Bergman, *Rise and Kill First: The Secret History of Israel's Targeted Assassinations* (London: John Murray, 2018).

20   SDS Centre Zagreb, Information No. 942, 26 October 1967, HDA, F. 1561, SDS Centre Zagreb, Folder 76.

21   SSUP SDB, 'Instructions on the Use of Means for Special Expenditures of the SDB in the SSUP,' 23 April 1976.

22   SSUP SDB, 'Instructions on the Use of Means for Special Expenditures of the SDB in the SSUP,' 23 April 1976, 1–2.

23 SSUP SDB, 'Instructions on the Use of Means for Special Expenditures of the SDB in the SSUP,' 23 April 1976, 1–2.

24 SSUP SDB, 'Instructions on the Use of Means for Special Expenditures of the SDB in the SSUP,' 23 April 1976, 5.

25 Second Department of the SDV, 4 February 1975.

26 'Instructions on the Use of Means for Special Expenditures of the SDB in the SSUP,' 23 April 1976, 3.

27 For a summary in his own words of Krunoslav Draganović's return to Yugoslavia, see the long excerpt from *Sjećanja dr. Krunoslava Stjepana Draganovića* cited in Bože Vukušić, *HRB – Hrvatsko revolucionarno bratstvo: Rat prije rata*, 2nd Edition (Zagreb: Klub hrvatskih povratnika iz iseljeništva, 2012), 71–8. See also Miroslav Akmadža, *Krunoslav Draganović, Iskazi komunističkim istražiteljima* (Zagreb: Hrvatski institut za povijest, 2010), 27–80.

28 Igor Omerza, *88 Stopnic do pekla* (Celovec: Mohorjeva družba, 2013).

29 SDS Centre Zagreb, Official Note, 20 July 1982. Regarding the case of Todorović, see SSUP, 'Information on the Hostile Activity Which Aims at Undermining the Economic Foundation of Society and about the Tasks of the Organs of Internal Affairs – Especially the SDB – to Suppress This Activity,' August 1974, ARS, F. 1931, šk. 1404 (Microfilm).

30 Transcription of the Tape Recording of the Session of the Executive Office of the SKJ Presidency, 16 and 17 April 1974, 110, ARS, F. 1931, šk. 1404 (Microfilm).

31 SDV, Official Note, June 1970, 6, ARS, F. 1931, šk. 1404.

32 Omerza, *88 Stopnic do pekla*, 35; Report on the Meeting of the SDV and the SSUP SDB, 26 December 1972, ARS, F. 1931, šk. 1404; Goran Petrović, *Vesela Udba*, 2nd Edition (Valjevo: Topalović, 2016), 107.

33 GSUP Belgrade, 'Information on the Criminal and Other Activities of Slobodan – Bata Todorović,' 12 December 1972, ARS, F. 1931, šk. 1404. Quoted in Omerza, *88 Stopnic do pekla*, 48.

34 RSUP SR Serbia, Official Note, 10 April 1973, ARS, F. 1931, šk. 1404. Quoted in Omerza, *88 Stopnic do pekla*, 53; SDB Belgrade Department, Overview of the Measures Undertaken against Slobodan Bata Todorović and His Connections, 13 June 1974, ARS, F. 1931, šk. 1404.

35 SDB Belgrade Department, Overview of the Measures Undertaken against Slobodan Bata Todorović and His Connections, 13 June 1974, 2, ARS, F. 1931, šk. 1404.

36 SDB Belgrade Department, Overview of the Measures Undertaken against Slobodan Bata Todorović and His Connections, 13 June 1974, 4–6, ARS, F. 1931, šk. 1404.

37 SDB Belgrade Department, Overview of the Measures Undertaken against Slobodan Bata Todorović and His Connections, 13 June 1974, 9, ARS, F. 1931, šk. 1404

38 Transcription of the Tape Recording of the Session of the Executive Office of the SKJ Presidency, 16 and 17 April 1974, 37, ARS, F. 1931, šk. 1404 (Microfilm).

39 Transcription of the Tape Recording of the Session of the Executive Office of the SKJ Presidency, 16 and 17 April 1974, 132, ARS, F. 1931, šk. 1404 (Microfilm).

40 Transcription of the Tape Recording of the Session of the Executive Office of the SKJ Presidency, 16 and 17 April 1974, 36, ARS, F. 1931, šk. 1404 (Microfilm).

41 Official Note on the Meeting of the Republican Secretaries for Internal Affairs and the Chiefs of the State Security Services, 15. Mai 1974, ARS, F. 1931, šk. 1404 (Mikrofilm).

42 SDV, Minutes of the Meeting Regarding the Operation '*Magistrala*', 29 May 1974, ARS, F. 1931, šk. 1404 (Mikrofilm); Omerza, *88 Stopnic do pekla*, 138–9, 148.

43 Omerza, *88 Stopnic do pekla*, 26.

44 SDV, List of Participants in the Operation '*Jadran*', ARS, F. 1931, šk. 1404 (Mikrofilm).

45 SSUP, Decision of the Federal Secretary, 3. March 1975, ARS, F. 1931, šk. 1404 (Mikrofilm).

46 Omerza, *88 Stopnic do pekla*, 166.

47 Omerza, *88 Stopnic do pekla*, 214–21.

48 SSUP SDB, 'Proposal for Carrying Out the Operation "Tiper"', 10 December 1974, HDA, F. 1561, 202.2_81, Predmet 21.1.

49 Igor Alborghetti, 'UDBA 1975. – kako je spektakularno propala otmica agenta BND-a', *Express.hr*, undated.

50 SSUP SDB, 'Operation "*Tiper*"', 20 June 1975, 1; Official Note on Meeting in SDS First Sector, 21 March 1975, HDA, F. 1561, 202.2_81, Predmet 21.1.

51 SSUP SDB, First Administration, 'Proposal for Carrying Out the Operation "Tiper"', 10 December 1974; SSUP SDB, First Administration, 'Operation "*Tiper*"', 8 April 1975, HDA, F. 1561, 202.2_81, Predmet 21.1.

52 SSUP SDB, 'Operation "*Tiper*,"' 20 June 1975, 1–2.

53 SSUP SDB, 'Operation "*Tiper*,"' 20 June 1975, 1; SSUP SDB, First Administration, 'Preparations for the Realization of the Operation "Tiper,"' 9 June 1975, HDA, F. 1561, 202.2_81, Predmet 21.1.

54 Official Note on Meeting in SDS First Sector, 21 March 1975; Official Note on Meetings on Operation Tiper, 3, 4 and 7 April 1975, HDA, F. 1561, 202.2_81, Predmet 21.1.

55 For 'Lukrecija's' status as a double agent see SSUP SDB, First Administration, 'Operation "Argus" – Plan for Realization', 25 September 1975, HDA, F. 1561, 202.2_81, Predmet 21.1.

56 Draft of Official Note on Meeting on Operation Tiper, 3 July 1975, HDA, F. 1561, 202.2_81, Predmet 21.1. This draft also notes some involvement of the Bosnian SDB.

57 SSUP SDB, Tenth Administration, First Department, Report on Official Trip in 'Trsteno' in Relation to Operation 'Tiper', 26 July 1975, HDA, F. 1561, 202.2_81, Predmet 21.1.

58 SSUP SDB, First Administration, 'Preparations for the Realization of the Operation *"Tiper"*,' 9 June 1975, 4.

59 SSUP SDB, 'Operation *"Tiper"*,' 20 June 1975, 2.

60 SSUP SDB, First Administration, 'Operation "Argus" – Plan for Realization,' 25 September 1975, HDA, F. 1561, 202.2_81, Predmet 21.1.

61 SSUP SDB, 'Operation *"Argus,"*' 27 June 1975.

62 Official Note on Meeting with 'Žiško', 30 July 1975, HDA, F. 1561, 202.2_81, Predmet 21.1.

63 SSUP SB, First Administration, 'Operation *"Tiper"*,' 25 March 1975, HDA, F. 1561, 202.2_81, Predmet 21.1.

64 SSUP SDB, First Administration, 'Preparations for the Realization of the Operation *"Tiper"*,' 9 June 1975, HDA, F. 1561, 202.2_81, Predmet 21.1.

65 SSUP SDB, First Administration, 'Preparations for the Realization of the Operation *"Tiper"*,' 9 June 1975, 2–3.

66 SSUP SDB, First Administration, 'Preparations for the Realization of the Operation *"Tiper"*,' 9 June 1975, 3.

67 SSUP SDB, First Administration, 'Preparations for the Realization of the Operation *"Tiper"*,' 9 June 1975, 3–4.

68 SSUP SDB, First Administration, 'Operational Sketch for the Realization of the Operation *"Tiper"*,' 17 July 1975.

69 SSUP SDB, First Administration, 'Preparations for the Realization of the Operation *"Tiper"*,' 9 June 1975, 6.

70 SRBiH SDB, 'Security Indicators', Remarks of the Federal Secretary for Internal Affairs Franjo Herljević, 80.

71 SSUP SDB, First Administration, 'Preparations for the Realization of the Operation *"Tiper"*,' 9 June 1975, 5.

72 SSUP SDB, First Administration, 'Preparations for the Realization of the Operation *"Tiper"*,' 9 June 1975, 4–5. See also SDS, 'Anaesthetics', 25 March 1975; SDS, 'Enquiry for the Preparation of Anaesthesia', 1 April 1975; SSUP SDB, First Administration, SSUP SDB, SSUP SDB, First Administration, 'Operational Sketch for the Realization of the Operation *"Tiper"*,' 17 July 1975.

73 SDS First Sector to SSUP SDB First Administration, 11 August 1975, HDA, F. 1561, 202.2_81, Predmet 21.1.

74 SDV to SSUP SDB First Administration, 12 September 1975, HDA, F. 1561, 202.2_81, Predmet 21.1.

75 SDS Centre Rijeka to SSUP SDB and SDS, 31 August 1975, HDA, F. 1561, 202.2_81, Predmet 21.1.

76 SDS Centre Rijeka to SSUP SDB and SDS, 3 September 1975, HDA, F. 1561, 202.2_81, Predmet 21.1.

77 SSUP SDB, First Administration, 'Operation "Argus" – Plan for Realization,' 25 September 1975, HDA, F. 1561, 202.2_81, Predmet 21.1.

78 RSUP SRS SDV, Informational Report, 20 January 1976, 4.

79 RSUP SRH SDS Third Section, 9 November 1982.

80 SSUP SDB, Rulebook for the Work of the State Security Service, 1 August 1975, 23.

81 Christopher Molnar, 'Imagining Yugoslavs: Migration and the Cold War in Postwar West Germany,' *Central European History*, Vol. 47 (2014), 148.

82 On diplomatic relations between West Germany and Yugoslavia, see Vladimir Ivanović, 'Obnavljanje diplomatskih odnosa između Socijalističke Federativne Republike Jugoslavije i Savezne Republike Nemačke,' *Istorija 20. veka*, No. 2 (2005), 129–45.

83 Going further back in Yugoslav history, it is worth recalling, for example, that after the assassination of King Aleksandar Karađorđević in Marseille in October 1934, Italy and Hungary severely curtailed their support for the Ustaša movement.

84 Yugoslavia and West Germany severed diplomatic relations in 1957 after Yugoslavia recognized East Germany. Diplomatic relations were not reestablished until 1968, but in the meantime the trade mission 'functioned as Yugoslavia's de facto embassy'. Mate Nikola Tokić, *For the Homeland Ready! Croat Diaspora Terrorism during the Cold War* (West Lafayette: Purdue University Press, 2020), 95.

85 Tokić, *For the Homeland Ready*, 95.

86 On *Ostpolitik*, see Molnar, 'Imagining Yugoslavs,' 158–69.

87 Bernd Robionek, 'Geschichtswissenschaftliches Gutachten im Verfahren 7 St 5/14 (2) vor dem Oberlandesgericht München,' 2015, 7.

88 SDS Centre Zagreb, 'Minutes of the Meeting with Federal Secretary for Internal Affairs Franjo Herljević,' 21 December 1977.

89 SDS Centre Zagreb, 'Minutes of the Meeting with Federal Secretary for Internal Affairs Franjo Herljević,' 21 December 1977, 39.

90 SDS Centre Zagreb, 'Minutes of the Meeting with Federal Secretary for Internal Affairs Franjo Herljević,' 21 December 1977, 39.

91 SDS Centre Zagreb, 'Minutes of the Meeting with Federal Secretary for Internal Affairs Franjo Herljević,' 21 December 1977, 42.

92 SDS Centre Zagreb, 'Minutes of the Meeting with Federal Secretary for Internal Affairs Franjo Herljević,' 21 December 1977, 42.

93 SDS Centre Zagreb, 'Minutes of the Meeting with Federal Secretary for Internal Affairs Franjo Herljević,' 21 December 1977, 41.

94 SDS Centre Zagreb, 'Minutes of the Meeting with Federal Secretary for Internal Affairs Franjo Herljević,' 21 December 1977, 41.

95 SDS Centre Zagreb, 'Minutes of the Meeting with Federal Secretary for Internal Affairs Franjo Herljević,' 21 December 1977, 44.

Chapter 4

1 SSUP SDB, 'Action Plan of the Security Services for the Confrontation with Sabotage and Terrorist Activities of the Hostile Portion of the Emigration,' 16 February 1972, ARS, F. 1931, šk. 387.

2 SSUP SDB, 'Action Plan of the Security Services for the Confrontation with Sabotage and Terrorist Activities of the Hostile Portion of the Emigration,' 16 February 1972, 8, ARS, F. 1931, šk. 387.

3 SSUP SDB, 'Theses for the Long-Term Programme of Activities of the Security Services and Other Societal Factors with Respect to the Hostile Emigration,' 16 March 1972, ARS, F. 1931, šk. 387.

4 Ante Batović, *The Croatian Spring: Nationalism, Repression and Foreign Policy under Tito* (London: I.B. Tauris, 2017).

5 In the six months from 1 December 1971 until 1 May 1972, 1,160 criminal complaints and 1,816 misdemeanor complaints were filed in Croatia for 'counterrevolutionary attacks on the sociopolitical system.' SSUP, 'The Security Situation and the Implementation of the Directive of the President of the Republic,' 16 September 1972, 26, ARS, F. 1931, šk. 1404.

6 SSUP, 'The Security Situation and the Implementation of the Directive of the President of the Republic,' 16 September 1972, 1, ARS, F. 1931, šk. 1404.

7 For a detailed summary of the uprising from the point of view of the Yugoslav authorities, see SSUP SDB, 'Operation "Raduša",' 4 May 1973, ARS, F. 1931, šk. 1160.

8 Bože Vukušić provides a very detailed – but largely uncritical – account of the uprising. Bože Vukušić, *HRB – Hrvatsko revolucionarno bratstvo: Rat prije rata*, 2. izdanje (Zagreb: Klub hrvatskih povratnika iz iseljeništva, 2012), 149–335. A somewhat more considered view is offered by Igor Omerza, *HRB, Fenix i Udba: Slučaj Stjepana Crnogorca* (Radenci: Društvo za raziskovanje polpretekle zgovodine, 2014). This section draws on both books.

9 Omerza, *HRB*, 92–3.

10 Omerza, *HRB*, 51–2.

11 Omerza, *HRB*, 95; Vukušić, *HRB*, 187–9.

12 Annex to SSUP SDB, 'Operation "Raduša",' 4 May 1973, 4, ARS, F. 1931, šk. 1160.

13 Annex to SSUP SDB, 'Operation "Raduša",' 4 May 1973, 5, ARS, F. 1931, šk. 1160.

14 Annex to SSUP SDB, 'Operation "Raduša",' 4 May 1973, 7, ARS, F. 1931, šk. 1160.

15 Annex to SSUP SDB, 'Operation "Raduša",' 4 May 1973, 8, ARS, F. 1931, šk. 1160.

16 As seen in Chapter 2, Josip Senić, the successor to Geza Pašti, was assassinated near Heidelberg on 9 March 1972. However, Senić was in any case not slated to have participated in the HRB's planned major operation. Omerza, *HRB*, 101.

17 Omerza, *HRB*, 108–9.

usicl\nal Notes*

18 A list of the nineteen with brief biographies appears in Vukušić, *HRB*, 163–5. See also SSUP SDB, 'Brief Information about Members and Links of Ustaša Organizations in Australia,' 27 July 1972, ARS, F. 1931, šk. 386; SSUP SDB, 'Overview of Members and Connections of the HRB in Western European Countries,' 2 July 1973, ARS, F. 1931, šk. 1207; SSUP SDB, 'Monography on the Yugoslav Hostile Emigration in Australia,' October 1975, ARS, F. 1931, šk. 385.

19 Vukušić, *HRB*, 152.

20 JNA report cited in Vukušić, *HRB*, 210.

21 Srđan Cvetković, *Između srpa i čekića 3: Oblici otpora komunističkom režimu u Srbiji, 1944–1991*. (Belgrade: Službeni glasnik, 2013), 278.

22 Omerza, *HRB*, 133.

23 Omerza, *HRB*, 139–45.

24 Excerpt from tape recording of SFRJ Presidency Session of 19 September 1972 in Omerza, *HRB*, 143. The original is located in Arhiv Jugoslavije. Immediately after the quoted excerpt, Tito mentioned that he had recently met in Yugoslavia with Austrian President Franz Jonas, who had been very concerned about the bilateral Austro-Yugoslav relationship.

25 Ludvig Pavlović was released from prison in December 1990. Less than a year later, in September 1991, he died in an armed altercation with JNA troops in Bosnia and Herzegovina.

26 On the relationship between Croat émigrés and Australian politics, see Mate Nikola Tokić, 'Party Politics, National Security, and Émigré Political Violence in Australia, 1949–1973,' in Wilhelm Heitmeyer et al., eds., *Control of Violence: Historical and International Perspectives on Violence in Modern Societies* (New York: Springer, 2011), 395–414.

27 Mate Nikola Tokić, *For the Homeland Ready! Croat Diaspora Terrorism during the Cold War* (West Lafayette: Purdue University Press, 2020), 140f.

28 Tvrtko Jakovina, 'Hrvatski politički emigranti: Teroristi ili domoljubi?' *Globus*, 25 July 2008, 42–8.

29 From the point of view of contemporary international legal standards, the most objectionable aspect of the behaviour of the Yugoslav security forces was the apparent extrajudicial executions of some of those members of the Bugojno group who were captured or surrendered.

30 Tito Directive, 21 July 1972, ARS, F. 1931, šk. 1404.

31 For a presentation of the term 'special war,' see *Vojna bezbednost* (Belgrade: Vojnoizdavački i novinski centar, 1986), 140–4, 197–200; Milivoje Levkov, 'Evolucija savremenog obaveštajno-subverzivnog delovanja i neki bitni elementi pojma "specijalnog rata"', *13. maj*, Vol. 24, No. 4 (April 1971), 13–25. Levkov listed unconventional, antiguerrilla and counterinsurgency operations as well as psychological operations as the most important constituent elements of what he also

stated could be called 'secret', 'underground', 'political-intelligence' or 'subversive' operations – revealing the origins in the US military term 'special warfare'.

32 SSUP SDB, 'Operation "Raduša"', 4 May 1973, 123–4, ARS, F. 1931, šk. 1160.

33 SSUP SDB, 'Operation "Raduša"', 4 May 1973, 124, ARS, F. 1931, šk. 1160.

34 SSUP SDB, 'Assessment of the Announcements of Sabotage and Terror Operations of the Hostile Emigration and the Conclusions Regarding the Measures of the Security Services', 18 March 1973, ARS, F. 1931, šk. 387.

35 SSUP SDB, 'Tasks of the Organs of Internal Affairs Regarding the Implementation of the Conclusions of the Presidency of the Executive Committee of the League of Communists on the Current Questions of the Strengthening of Security and the Self-Defence of the Self-Managing Society', 1 October 1973, ARS, F. 1931, šk. 1151.

36 SSUP SDB, 'Tasks of the Organs of Internal Affairs Regarding the Implementation of the Conclusions of the Presidency of the Executive Committee of the League of Communists on the Current Questions of the Strengthening of Security and the Self-Defence of the Self-Managing Society', 25, 1 October 1973, ARS, F. 1931, šk. 1151. The Yugoslav State Security Service had also earlier acted offensively against the hostile emigration. SSUP SDB, 'Implementation of the Law on Internal Affairs and the State of Affairs in the State Security Service', 4 November 1967, 19–20, ARS, F. 1931, šk. 2304.

37 SSUP SDB, 'Tasks of the Organs of Internal Affairs Regarding the Implementation of the Conclusions of the Presidency of the Executive Committee of the League of Communists on the Current Questions of the Strengthening of Security and the Self-Defence of the Self-Managing Society', 5, 1 October 1973, ARS, F. 1931, šk. 1151.

38 SSUP SDB, 'Tasks of the Organs of Internal Affairs Regarding the Implementation of the Conclusions of the Presidency of the Executive Committee of the League of Communists on the Current Questions of the Strengthening of Security and the Self-Defence of the Self-Managing Society', 5, 1 October 1973, ARS, F. 1931, šk. 1151.

39 SSUP SDB, 'Security Aspects of the Employment of Yugoslav Workers Abroad', 3, April 1973, F. 1931, šk. 385.

40 SSUP SDB, 'Collection of Materials: The Views and Conclusions of the 56th Session of the Executive Committee of the Presidency of the SKJ Regarding Current Security Problems', September 1973, 11, ARS, F. 1931, šk. 1362.

41 Josip Perković and Jan Gabriš, 'Služba državne sigurnosti republičkog sekretarijata za unutarnje poslove SR Hrvatske u vremenu 1980. – 30. svibnja 1990. godine', 1997, 105.

42 SSUP SDB, 'Tasks of the Organs of Internal Affairs Regarding the Implementation of the Conclusions of the Presidency of the Executive Committee of the League of Communists on the Current Questions of the Strengthening of Security and the Self-Defence of the Self-Managing Society', 19, 1 October 1973, ARS, F. 1931, šk. 1151.

43 SSUP SDB, 'Tasks of the Organs of Internal Affairs Regarding the Implementation of the Conclusions of the Presidency of the Executive Committee of the League of Communists on the Current Questions of the Strengthening of Security and the Self-Defence of the Self-Managing Society', 25, 1 October 1973, ARS, F. 1931, šk. 1151.

44 SSUP SDB, 'Tasks of the Organs of Internal Affairs Regarding the Implementation of the Conclusions of the Presidency of the Executive Committee of the League of Communists on the Current Questions of the Strengthening of Security and the Self-Defence of the Self-Managing Society', 25, 1 October 1973, ARS, F. 1931, šk. 1151.

45 SSUP SDB, 'Tasks of the Organs of Internal Affairs Regarding the Implementation of the Conclusions of the Presidency of the Executive Committee of the League of Communists on the Current Questions of the Strengthening of Security and the Self-Defence of the Self-Managing Society', 26, 1 October 1973, ARS, F. 1931, šk. 1151.

46 SSUP SDB, 'Tasks of the Organs of Internal Affairs Regarding the Implementation of the Conclusions of the Presidency of the Executive Committee of the League of Communists on the Current Questions of the Strengthening of Security and the Self-Defence of the Self-Managing Society', 20, 1 October 1973, ARS, F. 1931, šk. 1151.

47 SSUP, Centre for Professional Training, 'Operational Processing – Materials – Part Two', 9, 1974, ARS, F. 1931, šk. 2308.

48 Earlier 'white books' had dealt with topics such as the 'aggression' of the USSR and the Warsaw Pact countries against Yugoslavia, with Albanian-Yugoslav relations and with Yugoslavia's relations with the Vatican.

49 The feature series was published in the first half of 1979 as 'Terrorists from the "Sixth Column"' and was written by Dragan Ganović. This series was also published as a book. Dragan Ganović, *Teroristi iz 'Šeste kolone': Dokumentarna hronika o terorističkoj aktivnosti protiv Jugoslavije* (Belgrade: Borba, 1979).

50 See, for example, Sreten Kovačević, *Hronologija antijugoslovenskog terorizma, 1960–1980* (Belgrade: IŠRO, 1981).

51 Kovačević, *Hronologija antijugoslovenskog terorizma, 1960–1980*, 3.

52 Omerza, *HRB*, 151.

53 Vukušić, *HRB*, 161–2.

54 SDV to SSUP SDB, Second Administration, 3 July 1972, ARS, F. 1931, šk. 1162. See also dispatch of SSUP SDB, Second Administration to SDV, 4 July 1972, ARS, F. 1931, šk. 1162. According to Omerza, 'Duet' was the code name assigned to the operation targeting Stjepan Crnogorac.

55 SSUP SDB Dispatch of 30 June 1972, ARS, F. 1931, šk. 1162, quoted in Omerza, *HRB*, 156–7.

56 SSUP SDB Dispatch of 30 June 1972, ARS, F. 1931, šk. 1162, quoted in Omerza, *HRB*, 156–7.

57 Vukušić, *HRB*, 327.

58 See also the summary of the Crnogorac case in Alfred Elste, Wilhelm Wadl, Hanzi Filipič und Josef Lausegger, *Titos langer Schatten: Bomben- und Geheimdienstterror im Kärnten der 1970er Jahre, 2. korrigierte Auflage* (Klagenfurt: Kärntner Landesarchiv, 2015), 614–21.

59 Omerza, *HRB*, 180–2, 190–1.

60 Omerza summarizes Crnogorac's account. Omerza, *HRB*, 182–4.

61 A document of the Bosnian State Security Service indicates that a member of that service interrogated Crnogorac in Ljubljana on 19 July 1972. Omerza, *HRB*,199.

62 Omerza, *HRB*, 222–4.

63 SDS Centre Zagreb, Information No. 304, 22 October 1973, HDA, F. 1561, Dossier of Marko Logarušić.

64 Omerza cites a SSUP SDB document dated 2 July 1973 from ARS, F. 1931, šk. 1177. Omerza, *HRB*, 214.

65 Elste et al., *Titos langer Schatten*, 614–15.

66 Vukušić, *HRB*, 315–26.

67 Tokić, *For the Homeland Ready!*, 65f.

68 Cited in Tokić, *For the Homeland Ready!*, 199n92.

69 SFRY Presidency, Council for Matters of State Security, Transcript of Meeting Held on 21 March 1972, 45.

70 See, for example, Claus Bienfalt, 'Belgrads langer Arm,' *Die Zeit*, No. 19, 7 May 1982, 33.

71 Numerous dossiers on émigré Croats in the Australian National Archives contain newspaper clippings regarding parliamentary questions on émigré issues. Occasionally such clippings are also found in the archives of the SDS.

72 SSIP, 'Minutes of Consultation about Problems of Employment and the Residency of Yugoslav Workers Abroad, Held in Krapinske Toplice,' 29 July 1971, ARS, F. 1931, šk. 385. DSC_0011, DSC_0012

73 Omerza, *HRB*, 159.

74 Džemal Bijedić quoted in Elste et al., *Titos langer Schatten*, 615.

75 Omerza, *HRB*, 202.

76 See, for example, SRH RSUP SDS, Information No. 9, 'Preparations of the Extreme Emigration for the Staging of Sabotage-Terrorist Operations in Zagreb,' 16 November 1974; HDA, F. 1561, Dossier of Milan Štimac.

77 SSNO, Security Administration – Training Centre for Security, 'Some Manifestations of the Special War against Yugoslavia,' 1974. ARS, F. 1931, šk. 2232.

78 SDS Centre Split, Information No. 237, 24 May 1977.

79 See, for example, the mention of the Social Democrat Willy Brandt and the conservative Christian Socialist Franz Josef Strauss in SSUP SDB, Third Sector, Note from Meeting Held on 3 March 1970, 4.

80 Vukušić, *HRB*, 466.

81   DSIP, SID, Letter, 23 March 1967; SDS Centre Split, Information Nos. 312 and 382, 20 November and 21 December 1967; SDS Centre Zagreb, Proposal for Dossier, 10 May 1968; SSUP SDB to SDS, 1st Sector, 13 August 1968. All documents from HDA, F. 1561, Dossier of Dane Šarac. Several hundred pages seem to have been removed from this dossier.

82   SSUP SDB to SDS, 1st Sector, 13 August 1968, HDA, F. 1561, Dossier of Dane Šarac.

83   On TRUP, Kulenović and Rukavina, see SDV, 'Overview of the Extreme Political Emigration in Europe,' 25 September 1965, ARS, F. 1931, šk. 1168.

84   SDS Centre Zagreb, Information No. 29, 27 January 1969, HDA F. 1561, SDS Centre Zagreb, Folder 77. This report was filed in the context of the operation 'Drina,' which focused on extreme émigrés in West Germany from 1967 to 1970.

85   SSUP, Centre for Professional Training, 'Operational Processing – Materials – Part Two,' 1974, ARS, F. 1931, šk. 2308, 50.

86   See dossier of Milan Dorič 'Hanzi,' ARS, F. 1931, šk. 2414. The dossier includes a receipt for three pistols dated 30 November 1968.

87   Report of Informant 'Muki,' 17 November 1964, HDA, F. 1561, Dossier of Nahid Kulenović.

88   Summary Report on Nahid Kulenović, 31 March 1969, HDA, F. 1561, Dossier of Nahid Kulenović.

89   Dossier Information Sheet, initiated 20 November 1967, HDA, F. 1561, Dossier of Nahid Kulenović.

90   SDS, First Sector to all SDS Sectors, 11 July 1969, HDA, F. 1561, Dossier of Nahid Kulenović.

91   SDB Centre Doboj, 18 April 1972, HDA, F. 1561, Dossier of Nahid Kulenović.

92   SDS Centre Zagreb, Report of Informant of SDS Zenica 'Franjo,' 18 October 1968, HDA, F. 1561, Dossier of Dane Šarac; Vukušić, *HRB*, 467.

93   SDS Centre Bjelovar, Excerpt from Information No. 6, 16 January 1973, HDA, F. 1561, Dossier of Dane Šarac.

94   SDS, 1st Sector to all SDS Centres and the SJS, 9 July 1973, HDA, F. 1561, Dossier of Dane Šarac.

95   SDS, First Sector to all SDS Centres, 8 August 1973, HDA, F. 1561, Dossier of Dane Šarac.

96   SDS, First Sector to SSUP SDB, Second Administration, 30 January 1974, HDA, F. 1561, Dossier of Dane Šarac.

97   See in particular SDS Centre Split, Official Note, 1 July 1975, HDA, F. 1561, Dossier of Dane Šarac. This is the last document in the dossier that predates the assassination attempt against Šarac.

98   Vukušić claims that a decision had already been taken to assassinate Šarac before he was sentenced to prison in West Germany, and that this decision was renewed

after Šarac was released. Vukušić, *HRB*, 466–8; on Šarac's responsibility for the assassination, see minutes of meeting of President Tito and secretaries for internal affairs, 31 August 1975, 13, AJ, F. 803, fasc. 1780. There are indications that the original plan was to kidnap the deputy consul and to use him as a bargaining chip to obtain the release of imprisoned Croats in Yugoslavia. However, this plan was apparently shelved for want of a location in which the kidnapped man could be securely held. SDS Centre Split, Official Note, 13 January 1976, HDA, F. 1561, Dossier of Dane Šarac.

99   Vukušić, *HRB*, 468–9.

100   Minutes of meeting of President Tito and secretaries for internal affairs, 31 August 1975, 11, AJ, F. 803, fasc. 1780.

101   Minutes of meeting of President Tito and secretaries for internal affairs, 31 August 1975, 12, AJ, F. 803, fasc. 1780.

102   Minutes of meeting of President Tito and secretaries for internal affairs, 31 August 1975, 14, AJ, F. 803, fasc. 1780.

103   Speech of the President of the Republic and of Comrade Stane Dolanc, the Secretary of the Executive Committee of the CK SKJ Presidency, 31 August 1975, 1. Emphasis in original.

104   Speech of the President of the Republic and of Comrade Stane Dolanc, the Secretary of the Executive Committee of the CK SKJ Presidency, 31 August 1975, 5.

105   It is worth noting that at a later point in the same meeting, expressing truculent frustration at the persistence of various internal enemies of the Yugoslav state, Tito briefly ruminated about reopening the notorious prison island Goli Otok. Speech of the President of the Republic and of Comrade Stane Dolanc, the Secretary of the Executive Committee of the CK SKJ Presidency, 31 August 1975, 2.

106   SDS, First Sector to SDS Centre Split, 9 August 1975, HDA, F. 1561, Dossier of Dane Šarac.

107   SSUP SDB to SDS, First Section and SRBiH SDB, Fourth Sector, 6 February 1976, HDA, F. 1561, Dossier of Dane Šarac.

108   SSIP SID to SSUP SDB, Second Administration, 14 June 1983, HDA, F. 1561, Dossier of Dane Šarac. Another unsuccessful attempt on Šarac's life apparently took place in January 1984. There may have been more attempts than that one. SSIP SID to SSUP SDB, 17 September 1982 and 12 March 1984, HDA, F. 1561, Dossier of Dane Šarac.

109   Bušić's writings were published in Bruno Bušić, *Jedino Hrvatska! Sabrani spisi* (Toronto: Ziral, 1983).

110   Anđelko Mijatović, *Bruno Bušić: Prilog istraživanju života i djelovanja* (Zagreb: Školska knjiga, 2010), 26.

111 Among the written material provided by the Croatian authorities to the German authorities in connection with the case against Josip Perković and Zdravko Mustač was a collection of forty SDS reports pertinent for the SDS's interest in Bruno Bušić. These reports covered the period from 1967 until April 1980. Among these SDS reports is an excerpt from one dated 8 January 1970 concluding with the remark 'File information in the dossier of Bruno Bušić.' It is possible that the Croatian authorities have not transferred the dossier to the Croatian State Archives (HDA). Staff at the archive informed me in December 2019 that the HDA did not possess a dossier on Bušić, nor did they know where it might be located.

112 Mijatović, *Bruno Bušić*, 31, 41.

113 Mijatović, *Bruno Bušić*, 58f.

114 Mijatović, *Bruno Bušić*, 63.

115 Mijatović, *Bruno Bušić*, 75–7.

116 Mijatović, *Bruno Bušić*, 84.

117 RSUP SRH, 'Conclusions of the Operational Meeting Held in the RSUP SRH, and in Connection with Some Newer Terrorist Operations on the Part of the Ustaša Emigration,' January 1977, 2.

118 SDS Centre Split, Information Reports, 9 and 15 April 1970; SDS Centre Split, Information, 25 April 1970.

119 SDS Centre Split, Information, 9 April 1970.

120 Mijatović, *Bruno Bušić*, 115–17.

121 Mijatović, *Bruno Bušić*, 118; SDS Centre Zagreb Information No. 194, 6 July 1971; SDS Centre Split, Information No. 285, 18 August 1971. On *Matica hrvatska*, see Batović, *The Croatian Spring*, 70–9.

122 Mijatović, *Bruno Bušić*, 134–5, 140.

123 Mijatović, *Bruno Bušić*, 152, 157.

124 Mijatović, *Bruno Bušić*, 196, 198.

125 RSUP SRH, 'Conclusions of the Operational Meeting Held in the RSUP SRH, and in Connection with Some Newer Terrorist Operations on the Part of the Ustaša Emigration,' January 1977, 3. On the hijacking, see the SDS operation '*Let*' (Flight), HDA, F. 1561, šifra 1, 10.04, 14. According to SDS source 'Oskar,' several émigrés in November 1976 were certain that Bruno Bušić had been involved with the hijacking operation and that he had met with Zvonko Bušić. SDS, First Section to SSUP SDB, Second Administration, 2 November 1976. Bruno Bušić also later apparently became involved in preparing the legal defence of Zvonko Bušić. SDS Centre Split, Information No. 237, 24 May 1977.

126 RSUP SRH, 'Conclusions of the Operational Meeting Held in the RSUP SRH, and in Connection with Some Newer Terrorist Operations on the Part of the Ustaša Emigration,' January 1977, 4.

127 SDS Report on Source 'Oskar,' to SSUP SDB, 6 January 1977.

128 SDS Report on Source 'Oskar,' to SSUP SDB, 6 January 1977, 2.

129 A similar but slightly different proposal was voiced with respect to the HRB group around Butković, which appeared second on the list. RSUP SRH, 'Conclusions from the Operational Meeting Held in the RSUP SRH, and in Connection with Some Newer Indications of Terrorist Operations by the Ustaša Emigration,' 11 January 1977, 1, 7–8.

130 SSUP SDB, Second Administration, 'Current Tasks of the SDB for the Further Prevention and Disabling of the Hostile Activity of the Fascist Emigration,' 31 August 1977. This document is also notable for a rare mention of codenames for two 'operational offensive actions': '*Kozjak*' and '*Udar*' (Strike).

131 On the assassination of Bušić, see Mijatović, *Bruno Bušić*, 210–18.

132 SSUP SDB to SRBiH SDB, Fourth Sector, 30 October 1978.

133 SSUP SDB to SRBiH SDB, Fourth Sector, 30 October 1978. Compare report of SDS Centre Rijeka, 23 May 1969, regarding the consequences of the killing of Mile Rukavina and other Croat émigrés. The reactions of the 'internal enemy' to the assassinations of émigrés were of course carefully noted. See also SDS Centre Zagreb, Information No. ???, 1 November 1978.

134 SSUP SDB to SRBiH SDB, Fourth Sector, 30 October 1978. Stjepan Radić was the most important Croat politicians in interwar Yugoslavia. He was shot and wounded on the floor of the Yugoslav parliament in June 1928, and he died of his wounds in August 1928.

135 SDS Centre Split, Information No. 262, 26 February 1969.

136 SDS Second Section to SSUP SDB Second Section, 3 December 1979.

137 SDS Centre Split, Information No. 262, 26 February 1969.

138 HRT, 'Bruno Bušić – Život, djelo, smrt'. Nikola Babić directed the film, which was produced by Uraniafilm.

139 SSUP SDB, 'Information about Sabotage-Terrorist Activity against the SFRJ with Emphasis on the Most Recent Events,' 11 July 1972, 37, ARS, F. 1931, šk. 1160.

140 Bernd Robionek, 'Geschichtswissenschaftliches Gutachten im Verfahren 7 St 5/14 (2) vor dem Oberlandesgericht München,' 2015, 18.

141 SSUP SDB, 'Information: Review of the Newest Indications of Possible Sabotage-Terrorist Operations of the Extreme Portion of the Emigration and Our Measures,' 18 September 1972, 2, ARS, F. 1931, šk. 1404.

142 SSUP SDB, 'Information: Review of the Newest Indications of Possible Sabotage-Terrorist Operations of the Extreme Portion of the Emigration and Our Measures,' 18 September 1972, 9, ARS, F. 1931, šk. 1404. See also the reference to 'special operations' in SSUP SDB, 'Tasks of the Organs of Internal Affairs in the Implementation of the Conclusions of the Executive Committee of the SKJ Presidency about Current Questions of the Strengthening of Security and the Self-Protection of the Self-Managing Society,' 1 October 1973, 25, ARS, F. 1931, šk. 1151.

Chapter 5

1   INA, 'Povijest', https://www.ina.hr/o-kompaniji/povijest/24 (accessed 20 December 2019).

2   Susan Woodward, *Socialist Unemployment: The Political Economy of Yugoslavia, 1945–1990* (Princeton: Princeton University Press, 1969).

3   Hrvoje Klasić, *Mika Špiljak: revolucionar i državnik* (Zagreb: Ljevak, 2019), 166f.

4   SRH GSUP Zagreb, Operational Report 02-SP-'O'-14/82, 10 June 1982; SDS Centre Zagreb, 'Operation "Brk," – Summary of Findings,' 2 September 1982. Unless otherwise noted in this chapter, archival documents cited stem from the SDS Dossier of Stjepan Đureković and from documents disclosed to the parties to the trial of Zdravko Mustač and Josip Perković.

5   SRH GSUP Zagreb, Operational Report 02-SP-'O'-14/82, 10 June 1982.

6   Asylum Application of Stjepan Đureković, 1 June 1982.

7   Munich Judgement, August 2016, 33. A dismaying feature of the Munich judgement is that, unlike the judgements of the trial chambers of the International Criminal Tribunal for the Former Yugoslavia which feature extensive footnotes, the Munich judgement does not provide any footnotes to demonstrate the detailed basis of its reasoning. The criminal procedure in the Munich trial also did not provide for courtroom transcripts. For this reason, my account of the Đureković case is based predominantly on my own review of documentation made available to me as an expert witness in this trial and on my own written notes of the testimony of various witnesses, particularly those who worked for the SDS. I was not present in the courtroom for all witness testimony.

8   SDS, Second Section, Report of 'Stiv,' 25 June 1982 (two reports); SDS Centre Zagreb, Official Note, 2 July 1982.

9   Prates arrived in West Germany in December 1971. He apparently first became a person of note for the Yugoslav authorities after giving a speech about the Croatian Spring at an anniversary celebration of the NDH on 10 May 1972 in Munich. Telegraph of SFRJ General Consulate in Munich, 18 April 1972, HDA, F. 1561, Dossier of Krunoslav Prates.

10 Munich Judgement, August 2016, 42. The SDS's interest in Prates, who was well-connected in émigré networks, went back to at least 1974. SDS Centre Zagreb, Information No. 43, 20 February 1974, HDA, F. 1561, SDS Centre Zagreb, Folder 81. Prates worked for Jelić and was apparently dissatisfied for several reasons, and feared prosecution back in Yugoslavia, all of which could have been used to motivate him to become an informant for the SDS. SDS Centre Osijek, Information No. 120, 19 May 1975, HDA, F. 1561, SDS Centre Osijek, Folder 20.

11 Oberlandesgericht München, Judgment against Krunoslav Prates, 6 St 005/05 (2), confirmed 11 February 2009.

12 SDS, Second Section, Letter with Information on Stjepan Đureković, 28 June 1982, Omot 4.1, S. 15.

13 Munich judgement, 126–7.

14 SDS Centre Zagreb, Official Note, 30 June 1982, Omot 4.1, 16.

15 Josip Perković and Jan Gabriš, 'Služba državne sigurnosti republičkog sekretarijata za unutarnje poslove SR Hrvatske u vremenu 1980. – 30. svibnja 1990. godine,' Zagreb, June 1997, unpublished internal paper, 95.

16 SDS Centre Zagreb, Official Note, 2 July 1982. On 13 November the INA sent a list of the topics that Đureković had worked on. INA to GSUP Zagreb, 13 July 1982.

17 SDS Centre Zagreb, Official Note, 2 July 1982.

18 SDS Centre Zagreb, 'Stjepan Đureković – Findings,' 2 July 1982.

19 SDS Centre Zagreb, Information No. 766, 2 July 1982.

20 SDS Centre Zagreb, Second Section, 7 July 1982. Compare with SDS Centre Split, 30 May 1983; Proposal for the Operational Processing of Milan Buškain, 30 May 1983.

21 The SRH Council for the Protection of the Constitutional Order approved the nomination of Franjo Vugrinec as chief of SDS Centre Zagreb in July 1982 based on the recommendation of Zdravko Mustač. Abridged Minutes of the 1st Session of the SRH Council for the Protection of the Constitutional Order, 9 July 1982.

22 SDS Centre Zagreb, Information No. 833, 2 August 1982.

23 See, for example, SDS Centre Zagreb, Information No. 766, 2 July 1982.

24 SDS, Special Information No. 8 about Stjepan Đureković, 9 September 1982; SDS, Special Information No. 8 about INA-Commerce, 24 September 1983; SDS, Special Information No. 11 about the Books of Stjepan Đureković, 11 October 1982; SDS, Special Information No. 15 about INA-Commerce, 29 October 1982; SDS, Special Information No. 16 about Stjepan Đureković, 4 November 1982; SDS, Special Information No. 21 about Stjepan Đureković, 26 November 1982. See also 'Overview of the Information Reports of the SRH RSUP in Which the SOUR INA – Zagreb Is Mentioned,' undated (1983?). In this document, the Special Information No. 23 of 28 December 1982 as well as Information Nos. 32 and 38 (no dates specified). 'In 1983 no information has been provided about this issue either in information or special information reports.'

25 Transcript of the Tape Recording of the Session of the SRH Council for the Protection of the Constitutional Order, 3 April 1980, 11. As regards the distribution list, see Abridged Minutes of the 2nd Session of the SRH Council for the Protection of the Constitutional Order, 20 July 1982, 3.

26 SDS Centre Zagreb, 'Operation "Brk," – Summary of Findings,' 2 September 1982. The SDS in January 1984 prepared another summary of the measures implemented against Đureković up until that point. SDS, 'An Overview and Some Evaluations of the Activities of Organs and Individuals Which Have Been Encompassed in the Procedure against Individual Persons from the SOUR INA Zagreb,' 23 January

1984. Cf., SDS, 'Special Security Findings: Overview of Indicative Findings about the Links and Contacts of Stjepan Đureković with Individual Persons in the Country,' 13 January 1984.

27 In a later report, an informant claimed that Stjepan and Damir Đureković had gone to Brazil. This proved to be incorrect. SDS Centre Zagreb, Information No. 993, 30 September 1982.

28 SDS Centre Zagreb, 'An Overview of Findings Regarding the Hostile Activity of Stjepan Đureković,' 6 September 1982.

29 SDS Centre Zagreb, Information No. 977, 27 September 1982.

30 Munich Judgement, August 2016, 122.

31 Munich Judgement, August 2016, 33.

32 Julie A. Mertus, *Kosovo: How Myths and Truths Started a War* (Berkeley: University of California Press, 1999).

33 Munich Judgement, August 2016, 33.

34 Munich Judgement, August 2016, 34.

35 SDS, Informational Report, 11 October 1982.

36 Note that this report mentions *Promašaj samoupravljanja*.

37 SDS, Informational Report, 26 November 1982.

38 SDS, Minutes of the 28 September 1982 Session of the Expanded Steering Council, Composed on 5 October 1982, 2–3.

39 SDS, Minutes of the 28 September 1982 Session of the Expanded Steering Council, Composed on 5 October 1982, 7.

40 SDS, Minutes of the 28 September 1982 Session of the Expanded Steering Council, Composed on 5 October 1982, 8.

41 Abridged Minutes of the 3rd Session of the SRH Council for the Protection of the Constitutional Order, 1 October 1982, 1. See also SRH Presidency, Council for the Protection of the Constitutional Order, 'Chronological Overview of the Activity of the Council for the Protection of the Constitutional Order Related to Security Questions in the SOUR INA-Zagreb,' undated (composed between 21 October 1982 and 15 June 1983).

42 Abridged Minutes of the 3rd Session of the SRH Council for the Protection of the Constitutional Order, 12 October 1982, 2.

43 Abridged Minutes of the 3rd Session of the SRH Council for the Protection of the Constitutional Order, 12 October 1982, 2.

44 Abridged Minutes of the 3rd Session of the SRH Council for the Protection of the Constitutional Order, 12 October 1982, 3.

45 Letter from I. Broz, Deputy Manager of INA-Commerce, to the President of the SRH Council for the Protection of the Constitutional Order, 29 October 1982; Deputy Manager of INA-Commerce to the President of the SRH Council for the Protection of the Constitutional Order, 25 January 1983.

46 Abridged Minutes of the 4th Session of the SRH Council for the Protection of the Constitutional Order, 1 November 1982.

47 SDS, Special Information No. 15 on INA-Commerce, 29 October 1982.

48 Abridged Minutes of the 4th Session of the SRH Council for the Protection of the Constitutional Order, 1 November 1982, 1.

49 Abridged Minutes of the 4th Session of the SRH Council for the Protection of the Constitutional Order, 1 November 1982, 2. Geneks (sometimes spelled Genex) was the abbreviated name of *Generaleksport*, the leader export company in Yugoslavia. Its headquarters were in Belgrade. The company was closely connected to the Federal State Security Service. Minutes from Conversation with Comrade Edo Brajnik, 5 April 1974, 5, ARS, F. 1931, šk. 1404. See also Srđan Cvetković, *Između srpa i čekića 2: Politička represija u Srbiji 1953–1985.* (Belgrade: Službeni glasnik, 2011), 121.

50 Abridged Minutes of the 4th Session of the SRH Council for the Protection of the Constitutional Order, 1 November 1982, 3.

51 Abridged Minutes of the 4th Session of the SRH Council for the Protection of the Constitutional Order, 1 November 1982, 4.

52 SSUP SDB to the Second Section of the SDS, 9 November 1982. The information stemmed from SDB Montenegro.

53 Abridged Minutes of the 5th Session of the SRH Council for the Protection of the Constitutional Order, 10 November 1982, 3.

54 SDS Centre Zagreb, 'Đureković Stjepan – Summary of the Findings Hitherto Regarding Hostile Work and Criminal Activity; Operations and Measures Undertaken,' 10 December 1982.

55 SDS Centre Zagreb, 'Results of the Undertaken Measures and Operations in the Operation "Brk",' 17 March 1983.

56 Abridged Minutes of the 6th Session of the SRH Council for the Protection of the Constitutional Order, 14 December 1982, 4.

57 Abridged Minutes of the 6th Session of the SRH Council for the Protection of the Constitutional Order, 14 December 1982, 4.

58 SRH Social Accounting Service, Criminal Complaint, 27 December 1982.

59 'Official Note from the 1st Session of the Council of the SRH Presidency for the Protection of the Constitutional Order Regarding the Determination of the Approach of the Organs of Internal Affairs of the SRH and Other Judicial Inspection Organs Engaged with the SOUR INA Case,' 10 February 1983.

60 SRH Council for the Protection of the Constitutional Order, 'Chronological Overview of the Activity of the Council Related to Current Security Questions in SOUR INA-Zagreb,' undated (treats the period from 21 October 1982 until 15 June 1983).

61 SDS Centre Zagreb to Zagreb District State Prosecutor and Zagreb District Court, Investigative Department, 15 or 16 February 1983.

62 Excerpt from SDS Centre Zagreb, Information No. 346, 16 March 1983.

63 Statement of Snježana Jakšić, 24 August 1982.

64 SDS Centre Zagreb, Information No. 1161, 9 November 1982.

65 SDS Centre Zagreb, Official Note, 3 March 1983. See also SDS Centre Zagreb, Information No. 284, 4 March 1983.

66 SDS Centre Zagreb, Official Note, 3 March 1983.

67 SSUP, Administration for Research, Analysis and Information, 'The Writings of the Ustaša Emigration,' 27 June 1983, 11, ARS, F. 1931, šk. 3093.

68 Munich Judgement, August 2016, para X, 32.

69 SDS Centre Zagreb, Excerpt from Information No. 549, 22 April 1983; SDS Centre Zagreb, Excerpt from Information No. 546, 22 April 1983; SDS Centre Zagreb, Information No. 559, 26 April 1983; SDS Centre Bjelovar, Information No. 87, 5 May 1983.

70 See also the draft of Đureković, 'Why I Am Running for the HNV,' undated; SDS Centre Rijeka, Information No. 289, 28 April 1983.

71 SSUP, Administration for Research, Analysis and Information, 'The Writings of the Ustaša Emigration,' 27 June 1983, 11, ARS, F. 1931, šk. 3093.

72 Klasić, *Mika Špiljak*.

73 Transcript of the Tape Recording of the 8th Session of the Council for the Protection of the Constitutional Order, 15 April 1983, 1.

74 Transcript of the Tape Recording of the 8th Session of the Council for the Protection of the Constitutional Order, 15 April 1983, 2.

75 Transcript of the Tape Recording of the 8th Session of the Council for the Protection of the Constitutional Order, 15 April 1983, 5.

76 Transcript of the Tape Recording of the 8th Session of the Council for the Protection of the Constitutional Order, 15 April 1983, 6.

77 Transcript of the Tape Recording of the 8th Session of the Council for the Protection of the Constitutional Order, 15 April 1983, 7.

78 Transcript of the Tape Recording of the 8th Session of the Council for the Protection of the Constitutional Order, 15 April 1983, 8.

79 Transcript of the Tape Recording of the 8th Session of the Council for the Protection of the Constitutional Order, 15 April 1983, 8.

80 Transcript of the Tape Recording of the 8th Session of the Council for the Protection of the Constitutional Order, 15 April 1983, 11.

81 Transcript of the Tape Recording of the 8th Session of the Council for the Protection of the Constitutional Order, 15 April 1983, 34.

82 Transcript of the Tape Recording of the 8th Session of the Council for the Protection of the Constitutional Order, 15 April 1983, 34–5.

83 Transcript of the Tape Recording of the 8th Session of the Council for the Protection of the Constitutional Order, 15 April 1983, 36.

84 Transcript of the Tape Recording of the 8th Session of the Council for the Protection of the Constitutional Order, 15 April 1983, 36.

85 Transcript of the Tape Recording of the 8th Session of the Council for the Protection of the Constitutional Order, 15 April 1983, 36.

86 Transcript of the Tape Recording of the 8th Session of the Council for the Protection of the Constitutional Order, 15 April 1983, 37. The other members of the council explicitly asked Mustač, who was in his capacity as undersecretary directly responsible for the SDS, whether specific employees [of?] were active as informants for the SDS. Transcript of the Tape Recording of the 8th Session of the Council for the Protection of the Constitutional Order, 15 April 1983, 39–40.

87 Transcript of the Tape Recording of the 8th Session of the Council for the Protection of the Constitutional Order, 15 April 1983, 46.

88 Transcript of the Tape Recording of the 8th Session of the Council for the Protection of the Constitutional Order, 15 April 1983, 46.

89 Transcript of the Tape Recording of the 9th Session of the Council for the Protection of the Constitutional Order, 1 June 1983, 1. The INA affair was also discussed at the SRH Presidency session of 15 June 1983, where the president of the Council for the Protection of the Constitutional Order reported about this matter. The presidency demanded that the council should deal more extensively with this affair. Abridged Minutes of the 35th Session of the SRH Presidency, 15 June 1983, 1–2.

90 Abridged minutes of the 9th Session of the Council for the Protection of the Constitutional Order, 1 June 1983, 4.

91 Abridged minutes of the 10th Session of the Council for the Protection of the Constitutional Order, 9 September 1983. In the meantime, according to these minutes, four sessions of the SRH Presidency and the Presidency of the SKH CK had been held at which the 'unacceptable behaviour' of Pavle Gaži had been discussed.

92 SDS Centre Zagreb, Second Section, Report, 9 June 1983.

93 SDS Centre Split, Information No. 309, 29 June 1983.

94 The SDB in Montenegro reported in February 1983 about an informant, 'Fistik,' who was keeping an eye on émigré extremists. 'Fistik' delivered precise intelligence regarding Ivan Jelić, Krunoslav Prates and Stjepan Đureković and in particular about the printing shop of Jelić. SDB Montenegro, Informant Report, 10 February 1983.

95 Munich judgement, 107.

96 Božidar Spasić, *Lasica koja govori: Osnovne pretpostavke borbe protiv terorizma*, 3rd Edition (Belgrade: Knjiga komerc, 2000), 55.

97 Munich judgement, 78.

98 Spasić, *Lasica*, 82.

99 On Operation Danube, which aimed to discredit Đureković, see Božidar Spasić, *Lasica koja govori: Osnovne pretpostavke borbe protiv terorizma*, 3rd Edition (Belgrade: Knjiga komerc, 2000), 77f. Spasić's credibility is very problematic.

100 Munich judgement, 39.

101 Spasić, *Lasica*, 81–2.
102 Munich judgement, 109.
103 Spasić, *Lasica*, 83–5.
104 See relevant section of Vukas, *Stjepan Đureković: Što ga je ubilo* (Zagreb: Naklada Pavičić, 2014).
105 The following reconstruction of the murder of Đureković is based on the Munich judgement, 49–52. See also the summary of an interview and the testimony of Branko Traživuk, who worked under Josip Perković, Munich judgement, 129–33.
106 Munich judgement, 146–8.
107 Munich judgement, 172–5.
108 Draft article of Stjepan Đureković, undated (July 1983), 25.
109 In émigré circles it is widely believed that Damir Đureković was killed by the Udba. His mother, Gizela Đureković, also believes this. Boris Orešković, 'Perkoviću će suditi za ubojstvo mog muža, a mene zanima tko mi je ubio sina,' *Jutarnji list*, 2 February 2014. See also Orhidea Gaura Hodak, *Tuđman i Perković: Istina o tajnoj vezi koja je formirala Hrvatsku* (Zagreb: Profil, 2014), 89–95.
110 Munich Judgement, 177, 184.
111 Munich Judgement, 190.
112 Munich Judgement, 188.
113 Interview with Dušan Stupar, B92, 'Službena tajna,' Episode 1, 2 October 2008, https://www.youtube.com/watch?v=959H7fL1VYA (accessed 20 December 2019).
114 Interview with Dušan Stupar, Happy televizija, 'Ćirilica,' 14 December 2011, https://www.youtube.com/watch?v=O3mPLyr8bBE (accessed 20 December 2019).
115 Testimony of Dušan Stupar, 12 May 2016; Munich judgement, 203.
116 On the earlier criminal background of Ražnatović, see letter to Federal Secretariat for People's Defence, Third Administration, 19 July 1982, and Report of Republican SUP of Serbia, Administration of the State Security Service, 7 January 1991. Both documents are in the possession of the United Nations' International Criminal Tribunal for the Former Yugoslavia. Ražnatović was killed in Belgrade in January 2000; Božović was killed already in 1991 during the war in Croatia.
117 Stupar further indicated that he had heard that Đureković had resisted. He had in the course of a struggle been injured, allegedly leading the hit team to kill him instead of kidnapping him. However, the court in Munich found no signs of struggle in the garage, and the fact that the first wound which Đureković suffered was a gunshot from behind argued against a botched kidnapping attempt. Munich judgement, 186.
118 Report on Meeting with Dorič, 17 April 1984.
119 Josip Manolić, *Politika i domovina: Moja borba za suverenu i socijalnu Hrvatsku* (Zagreb: Golden Marketing, 2015), 227–31.
120 Munich judgement, 191–2.
121 Munich judgement, 54, 193.

122 'Operation "Brk", undated.
123 See also SDS Centre Zagreb, Information No. 1059, 15 September 1983.
124 SDS Centre Zagreb, Information No. 932, 1 August 1983. See also SDS Centre Zagreb, Information No. 973, August 1983.
125 Acting Republican Secretary for Internal Affairs Zdravko Mustač to the Chief of SDS Centre Zagreb Franjo Vugrinec, 2 September 1983.
126 SDS Centre Zagreb, 'Meeting of the Informant "Viktor" with the BND Agent Neumann, on 19 and 20 September 1983 in Graz', 28 September 1983.
127 SDS Centre Zagreb, 'Meeting of the Informant "Viktor" with the BND Agent Neumann, on 19 and 20 September 1983 in Graz', 28 September 1983, 8.
128 Munich judgement, 56, 205. Several witnesses claimed that Perković had been so angry after the assassination that he had written a letter to the SSUP SDB.
129 SDS Centre Zagreb, Information No. 948, 3 August 1983. See also SDS, Special Information No. 16 about Đureković, 13 September 1983; SDS Centre Zagreb, Information No. 980, 17 August 1983.
130 Zagreb District Prosecutor to SDS Centre Zagreb, 2 September 1983.
131 SDS Centre Zagreb, 'Stjepan Đureković – Summary of Findings and Plan for Further Measures and Actions', 13 March 1984; see also Zagreb District Prosecutor to SRH Presidency, 'Information on the Treatment of Stjepan Đureković', 14 March 1984.
132 Agenda for the 15th Session of the Council for the Protection of the Constitutional Order.
133 The special information report bore the number 1 but is not present in the available documentation. Abridged minutes of the 15th Session of the Council for the Protection of the Constitutional Order, 3.
134 The special information report bore the number 1. Abridged minutes of the 15th Session of the Council for the Protection of the Constitutional Order, 3.
135 Note regarding meeting held in INA, 12 March 1985, 1.
136 Note regarding meeting held in INA, 12 March 1985, 8.
137 Witness Statement of Božidar Spasić, OLG Munich, 21 October 2015; Vukas, *Stjepan Đureković: Što ga je ubilo*, 2014.
138 SDS Centre Zagreb, Second Section, 7 July 1982.

Conclusion

1 Tweet of Beljak, 11 January 2020, 'Beljak o udbaškim ubojstvima: "Preko sto? Očito nedovoljno"', Index.hr, 12 January 2020.
2 'O izjavi predsjednika HSS-a Kreše Beljaka o Udbi', Historiografija.hr, 14 January 2020.

3   'Krešo Beljak se ispričao zbog objave na Twitteru,' *Jutarnji list*, 13 January 2020.

4   See Rado Pezdir's comments in HRT, 'Rat prije rata,' HRT1, 17 September 2018.

5   On the destruction of documentation, see Zdenko Radelić, 'Ozna/Udba: Popisi neprijatelja i njihova kategorizacija (1940-ih i 1950-ih),' *Časopis za suvremenu povijest*, Vol. 49 (2017), 61*n*2; Srđan Cvetković, *Između srpa i čekića 2: Politička represija u Srbiji 1953–1985*. (Belgrad: Službeni glasnik, 2011), 11f.

6   SDV, 'Work Plan of the Organs of Internal Affairs of SR Slovenia for the Protection of the Constitutional Order (November 1974–December 1975),' November 1974, 282.

7   For a summary of the Martinović case, see Alfred Elste, Wilhelm Wadl, Hanzi Filipič und Josef Lausegger, *Titos langer Schatten: Bomben- und Geheimdienstterror im Kärnten der 1970er Jahre, 2. korrigierte Auflage* (Klagenfurt: Kärntner Landesarchiv, 2015), 621–41.

8   RSUP SRH, 'Conclusions from the Operational Meeting Held in the RSUP SRH, and in Connection with Some Newer Indications of Terrorist Operations by the Ustaša Emigration,' 11 January 1977, 7.

9   Three people, Dragan Barač, Georg Huber and Adam Lapčević, were tried and convicted in 1981 for the attempted murder of Goreta. Bože Vukušić, *HRB – Hrvatsko revolucionarno bratstvo: Rat prije rata*, 2nd Edition (Zagreb: Klub hrvatskih povratnika iz iseljeništva, 2012), 449–53.

10   For an example in the case of Nikola Štedul, see SDS, Second Section to all SDS Centres, 28 October 1988; SSUP SDB Second Administration, 3 November 1988; SDS Centre Zagreb, Information Report No. 18, 4 January 1989. Cf. SDS Centre Split, Information Report No. 324, 12 September 1972.

11   Transcript of the Tape Recording of the 11th Session of the SRH Council for the Protection of the Constitutional Order, 9 December 1981. Stanko Nižić was also discussed at the 5th session of the council. Transcript of the Tape Recording of the 5th Session of the SRH Council for the Protection of the Constitutional Order, 6 May 1981.

12   For an overview of the testimony of former Yugoslav State Security officials who testified in the Munich trial of Perković and Mustač, see Munich judgement, 78–90.

13   Interview of Aleksandar Vasiljević, B92, 'Službena tajna,' Episode 1, 2 October 2008, https://www.youtube.com/watch?v=959H7fL1VYA (accessed 20 December 2019). Cf. Report of the Council for the Confirmation of Postwar Victims of the Communist System Killed Abroad, 9. In a book published in 2012 Aleksandar Vasiljević wrote that he already became acquainted with Josip Perković when he was working in Osijek, and that they cooperated in several operations. Aleksandar Vasiljević, *Štit: Akcija vojne bezbednosti* (Belgrade: IGAM, 2012), 25.

14   Transcript of a Videotaped Statement of Ivan Lasić, 13–15.

15   Munich judgement, 61.

16 List of Documentation for the 201st Session of the SFRJ Federal Presidency, AJ, F. 803, fasc. 159.

17 SSIP, 'Report on the Official Visit of the President of the Federal Republic of Germany Karl Carstens in Yugoslavia, from 5 to 8 September 1983,' AJ, F. 803, fasc. 159.

18 SSIP, 'Report on the Official Visit of the President of the Federal Republic of Germany Karl Carstens in Yugoslavia, from 5 to 8 September 1983,' AJ, F. 803, fasc. 159.

19 Munich judgement, 68.

20 Munich judgement, 67–8.

21 Munich judgement, 69–70.

22 SDS Centre Split to RSUP SRH, First Section, 26 February 1979.

23 SDS Centre Split to RSUP SRH, First Section, 26 February 1979, 6. See also SDV, Second Section, 4 February 1975. 'The dispute which has erupted between the president of the UHN [the United Croats of Germany] Vukić and the deceased saboteur Prpić, is the consequence of the sabotage, which has been carried out by the federal SDV [SSUP SDB] against this group. This has been done with the goal of removing Vukić from his position and to stoke suspicion against him within this circle.'

24 Report of SDB Centre Tuzla, 20 June 1980.

25 Report of SDB Centre Tuzla, 20 June 1980, 3. The SDS claimed that Mičić had planned the murder of the Croat émigré Jozo Miloš. RSUP SDB, 'Findings of the State Security Service Regarding the Activity of the Enemy in 1979,' 131.Report of SDB Centre Tuzla, 20 June 1980.

26 Report of SDB Centre Tuzla, 20 June 1980.

27 Ronen Bergman. *Rise and Kill First: The Secret History of Israel's Targeted Assassinations* (London: John Murray, 2018).

28 Transcript of 77th Expanded Session of the Executive Bureau of the SKJ Presidency, 23 March 1971, AJ, F. 507 IV, fasc. 139, 54.

29 Transcript of 77th Expanded Session of the Executive Bureau of the SKJ Presidency, 23 March 1971, AJ, F. 507 IV, fasc. 139, 55.

30 Transcript of 77th Expanded Session of the Executive Bureau of the SKJ Presidency, 23 March 1971, AJ, F. 507 IV, fasc. 139, 55.

31 NARA. RG 59, Box 4151 (1963), Folder: Pol 25 Demonstrations, Protests, Riots (2/1/63), Doc: 'Activities of the Ustashi Terrorist Organizations,' 10, quoted in Mate Nikola Tokić, *For the Homeland Ready! Croat Diaspora Terrorism during the Cold War* (West Lafayette: Purdue University Press, 2020), 67. Very unhelpfully from the perspective of Croat nationalists, the CIA in a 1972 brief also claimed – incorrectly – that 'ustashi' [*sic*] was the Croatian word for 'terrorist'. CIA, 'Croatian Emigre Activity,' 15 September 1972, 1.

32 In line with previous Udba assassinations, the Udba instructed its network of agents and informants to gather information regarding both investigations into the attempted assassination and rumours among émigrés about the incident. SDS, Second Section to all SDS Centres, 28 October 1988, HDA, F. 1561, Dossier of Vinko Sindičić; Official Note of SDB SSUP, Second Administration, 3 November 1988, HDA, F. 1561, Dossier of Vinko Sindičić. The bulk of the documentation contained in Sindičić's dossier pertains to civil litigation in which Sindičić was involved in the 1980s. Not surprisingly, there is no information in his dossier regarding his alleged work as an assassin for the Udba. Yet in an interview conducted by the German police in 2008, Sindičić displayed a watch which he claimed to have received in 1975 as a gift from Federal Secretary for Internal Affairs Franjo Herljević. On Sindičić, see Bernd Robionek, 'Gutachten zur Strafsache Prates,' Oberlandesgericht München, 20 March 2008, 14–16.

33 Sindičić was suspected of being the perpetrator in several other assassinations as well. See SDS Centre Zagreb, Information No. 18, 4 January 1989, HDA, F. 1561, Dossier of Vinko Sindičić.

34 Božidar Spasić, *Lasica koja govori: Osnovne pretpostavke borbe protiv terorizma*, 3rd Edition (Belgrade: Knjiga komerc, 2000). Spasić later denied responsibility for the killings, referring to his own book as a 'romanticized fairy tale', and specifying that when he said that he been the one deciding about such operations, 'I' in fact referred to the state security service. KRIK, 'Ponavlja se suđenje za ubistvo Envera Hadrija,' 20 February 2017.

35 In the tenth episode of the HRT series *Jugoslavenske tajne službe*, the narrator when talking about HRB member Dane Šarac refers to how he continued with 'revolutionary work – or terrorism'.

36 Tomislav Klauški, 'Kako se terorista Bušića opet predstavlja kao heroja i uzora,' *24 Sata*, 7 March 2018.

37 Tvrtko Jakovina, 'Hrvatski politički emigranti: Teroristi ili domoljubi?,' *Globus*, 25 July 2008, 42–8.

38 Tokić, *For the Homeland Ready!*, 142.

39 See SSUP SDB, Administration for Research, Analysis and Information, 'The Anti-Yugoslav Activity of "Amnesty International",' 26 July 1982, ARS, F. 1931, šk. 2325.

40 Orhidea Gaura Hodak, *Tuđman i Perković: Istina o tajnoj vezi koja je formirala Hrvatsku* (Zagreb: Profil, 2014), 131.

41 On this matter and on the SDS's relationship with the nascent future ruling party, the HDZ, see Gaura Hodak, *Tuđman i Perković: Istina o tajnoj vezi koja je formirala Hrvatsku*, 96–182.

42 'Gojko Šušak,' *Večernji list*, 1 December 2016. See also Gaura Hodak, *Tuđman i Perković*, 136–43.

43 Anonymous close associate of the Šušak family quoted in Gaura Hodak, *Tuđman i Perković*, 263–4.

44   Marko Melčić quoted in Gaura Hodak, *Tuđman i Perković*, 171.

45   Munich judgement, 90. Letter of Josip Perković to President Franjo Tuđman, 17 September 1992.

46   Gaura Hodak, *Tuđman i Perković*, 268–71.

47   Gaura Hodak, *Tuđman i Perković*, 275–6.

48   Gaura Hodak, *Tuđman i Perković*, 285.

49   Select works include Josip Boljkovac, *Istina mora izaći van: sjećanja i zapisi prvog ministra unutarnjih poslova neovisne Hrvatske* (Zagreb: Golden Marketing, 2009); Josip Manolić, *Politika i domovina: Moja borba za suverenu i socijalnu Hrvatsku* (Zagreb: Golden Marketing, 2015); Josip Manolić, *Špijuni i domovina: Moja borba za suverenu i socijalnu Hrvatsku* (Zagreb: Golden Marketing, 2016); Martin Špegelj, *Sjećanja vojnika* (Zagreb: Znanje, 2001); Vladimir Šeks, *1991: Moja Sjećanja na stvaranje Hrvatske* (Zagreb: Večernji list, 2015); Vladimir Šeks, *Državni udar: Kako su Manolić i Mesić rušili Tuđmana i hrvatska politika prema BiH*, 2 Volumes (Zagreb: 24 Sata, 2017). Intriguingly, although the SDS dossier of Vladimir Šeks dossier exists in the HDA, it is one of the very few that is not available for public perusal. Manolić and Boljkovac, who were, respectively, the second prime minister and the first minister of internal affairs in independent Croatia, had very little to state in their memoirs about the period prior to 1990 despite having been politically active in socialist Yugoslavia.

50   Gaura Hodak, *Tuđman i Perković*, 171.

51   Vukušić, *HRB – Hrvatsko revolucionarno bratstvo: Rat prije rata*, 2nd Edition, 453.

52   Vukušić, *HRB – Hrvatsko revolucionarno bratstvo*, 100.

53   Hercegovina.info, '17. obljetnica 1. gardijske brigade HVO-a "Bruno Bušić", 8 June 2011; Braniteljski portal, 'Tko je bio Ludvig Pavlović?,' 21 September 2018.

54   The journalist Guara Hodak argues that Vukušić should have continued to serve his German prison sentence after his extradition to Croatia, but that he was instead upon his arrival employed by Vukojević. Gaura Hodak, *Tuđman i Perković*, 267.

55   Josip Manolić, *Politika i domovina: Moja borba za suverenu i socijalnu Hrvatsku* (Zagreb; Golden Marketing, 2015), 357–64.

56   Letter of Chief of the SDB of the RSUP of Serbia, Zoran Janaćković, 9 January 1990. This document is in the possession of the United Nations' International Criminal Tribunal for the Former Yugoslavia (ICTY).

57   Željko Ražnatović was indicted under seal by the ICTY on 23 September 1997 for war crimes and crimes against humanity and would most likely have been put on trial had he not been assassinated in January 2000. The indictment was unsealed after his death. ICTY, *Prosecutor v. Željko Ražnatović* (IT-97-27).

58   Manolić, *Politika i domovina*, 228–9.

59   In this sense, Tuđman's true counterpart in the Serbia of the 1990s was not Milošević but rather the nationalist writer Dobrica Ćosić.

60   Note that by contrast Mustač does not appear except in dramatization, and then as a tool of Belgrade.

61   Gaura Hodak, *Tuđman i Perković*, 125.

62   Dejan Jović, *Rat i mit: Politika identiteta u suvremenoj Hrvatskoj* (Zagreb: Fraktura, 2017); Ayşe Zarakol, 'States and Ontological Security: A Historical Rethinking,' *Cooperation and Conflict*, Vol. 52, No. 1 (2017), 48–68.

63   Christian Axboe Nielsen, 'Collective and Competitive Victimhood in the Former Yugoslavia,' in Nanci Adler, ed., *Understanding the Age of Transitional Justice: Crimes, Courts, Commissions, and Chronicling* (New Brunswick: Rutgers University Press, 2018), 175–93.

Bibliography

Akmadža, Miroslav. *Krunoslav Draganović, Iskazi komunističkim istražiteljima* (Zagreb: Hrvatski institut za povijest, 2010).

Batović, Ante. *The Croatian Spring: Nationalism, Repression and Foreign Policy under Tito* (London: I.B. Tauris, 2017).

Bergholz, Max. *Violence as a Generative Force: Identity, Nationalism, and Memory in a Balkan Community* (Ithaca: Cornell University Press, 2016).

Bergman, Ronen. *Rise and Kill First: The Secret History of Israel's Targeted Assassinations* (London: John Murray, 2018).

Biondich, Mark. 'Religion and Nation in Wartime Croatia: Reflections on the Ustaša Policy of Forced Religious Conversions,' *The Slavonic and East European Review*, Vol. 83, No. 1 (2005), 71–116.

Boljkovac, Josip. *Istina mora izaći van: sjećanja i zapisi prvog ministra unutarnjih poslova neovisne Hrvatske* (Zagreb: Golden Marketing, 2009).

Bušić, Bruno. *Jedino Hrvatska! Sabrani spisi* (Toronto: Ziral, 1983).

Clarkson, Alexander. *Fragmented Fatherland: Immigration and Cold War Conflict in the Federal Republic of Germany, 1945–80* (New York: Berghahn Books, 2013).

Clissold, Stephen. 'Croat Separatism: Nationalism, Dissidence and Terrorism,' *Conflict Studies*, No. 103 (January 1979).

Cvetković, Srđan. 'Kako je spaljeno pet kilometara dosijea UDB-e,' *Arhiv*, Vol. 9, No. 1-2 (2008), 71–84.

Cvetković, Srđan. *Između srpa i čekića 2: Politička represija u Srbiji, 1953–1985.* (Belgrade: Službeni glasnik, 2011).

Cvetković, Srđan. *Između srpa i čekića 3: Oblici otpora komunističkom režimu u Srbiji, 1944–1991.* (Belgrade: Službeni glasnik, 2013).

David, Steven R. 'Fatal Choices: Israel's Policy of Targeted Killings,' *Mideast Security and Policy Studies*, No. 51 (September 2002).

Dimitrijević, Bojan. 'Odjek Brionskog plenuma na službu unutrašnjih poslova,' *Istorija 20. veka*, No. 2 (2001), 75–88.

Đorđević, Obren Ž. *Osnovi državne bezbednosti: opšti deo* (Belgrade: VŠUP, 1980).

Dornik Šubelj, Ljuba. *Oddelek za zaščito naroda za Slovenijo* (Ljubljana: ARS, 1999).

Dornik Šubelj, Ljuba. *Ozna in prevzem oblasti 1944–46* (Ljubljana: Modrijan, 2013).

Dragišić, Petar. *Ko je pucao u Jugoslaviju? Jugoslovenska politička emigracija na zapadu 1968–1980.* (Belgrade: Institut za noviju istoriju Srbije, 2019).

Dulić, Tomislav. *Utopias of Nation: Local Mass Killing in Bosnia and Herzegovina, 1941–1942* (Stockholm: Elanders Gotab, 2005).

Đureković, Stjepan. *Ja: Josip Broz-Tito* (International Books, 1982).

Đureković, Stjepan. *Komunizam: velika prevara* (International Books, 1982).

Đureković, Stjepan. *Sinovi orla* (International Books, 1982).

Đureković, Stjepan. *Crveni manageri* (International Books, 1983).

Đureković, Stjepan. *Slom ideala (Izpovjed titovog ministra)* (International Books, 1983).

Elste, Alfred, Wilhelm Wadl, Hanzi Filipič und Josef Lausegger, *Titos langer Schatten: Bomben- und Geheimdienstterror im Kärntnen der 1970er Jahre, 2. korrigierte Auflage* (Klagenfurt: Kärntner Landesarchiv, 2015).

Feigin, Judy. 'The Office of Special Investigations: Striving for Accountability in the Aftermath of the Holocaust,' US Department of Justice, December 2006.

Ganović, Dragan. *Teroristi iz 'Šeste kolone': Dokumentarna hronika o terorističkoj aktivnosti protiv Jugoslavije* (Belgrade: Borba, 1979).

Gazit Nir and Robert J. Brym, 'State-directed Political Assassination in Israel: A Political Hypothesis,' *International Sociology*, Vol. 26, No. 6, 862–77.

Geiger, Vladimir, 'Human Losses of the Croats in World War II and the Immediate Post-War Period Caused by the Chetniks (Yugoslav Army in the Fatherland) and the Partisans (People's Liberation Army and the Partisan Detachments of Yugoslavia/ Yugoslav Army) and the Yugoslav Communist Authorities Numerical Indicators,' *Review of Croatian History*, Vol. 8, No. 1 (2012), 77–121.

Goldstein, Ivo. *Hrvatska, 1918.–2008.* (Zagreb: EPH Liber, 2008).

Goldstein, Ivo. *Jasenovac* (Zagreb: Fraktura, 2018).

Grahek Ravančić, Martina. *Bleiburg i križni put 1945. Historiografija, publicistika i memoarska literatura*, 2. izmijenjeno i dopunjeno izdanje (Zagreb: Hrvatski institut za povijest, 2015).

Greenberg, Robert D. *Language and Identity in the Balkans* (Oxford: Oxford University Press, 2008).

Hoare, Marko Attila. *Genocide and Resistance in Hitler's Bosnia: The Partisans and the Chetniks* (Oxford: Oxford University Press, 2006).

Hockenos, Paul. *Homeland Calling: Exile Patriotism and the Balkan Wars* (Ithaca: Cornell University Press, 2003).

Hodak, Orhidea Gaura. *Tuđman i Perković: Istina o tajnoj vezi koja je formirala Hrvatsku* (Zagreb: Profil, 2014).

Iqbal, Zaryab and Christopher Zorn. 'Sic Semper Tyrannis? Power, Repression, and Assassination since the Second World War,' *The Journal of Politics*, Vol. 68, No. 3 (August 2006), 489–501.

Ivanović, Vladimir. 'Obnavljanje diplomatskih odnosa između Socijalističke Federativne Republike Jugoslavije i Savezne Republike Nemačke,' *Istorija 20. veka*, Issue 2 (2005), 129–45.

Ivanović, Vladimir. *Geburtstag pišeš normalno: Jugoslavenski gastarbajteri u Austriji i SR Nemačkoj* (Belgrade: ISI, 2012).

Jakovina, Tvrtko. 'Hrvatski politički emigranti: Teroristi ili domoljubi?,' *Globus*, 25 July 2008, 42–8.

Jonjić, Tomislav. 'Organised Resistance to the Yugoslav Communist Regime in Croatia in 1945–1953,' *Review of Croatian History*, Vol. 3, No. 1 (February 2007), 109–45.

Jović, Dejan. *Rat i mit: Politika identiteta u suvremenoj Hrvatskoj* (Zagreb: Fraktura, 2017).

Katalinić, Kazimir. *Od poraza do pobjede: Povijest hrvatske političke emigracije, 1945.–1990.*, 3 Volumes (Zagreb: Naklada Trpimir, 2017–18).

Klasić, Hrvoje. *Mika Špiljak: revolucionar i državnik* (Zagreb: Ljevak, 2019).

Korb, Alexander. 'Understanding Ustaša Violence,' *Journal of Genocide Research*, Vol. 12, Nos. 1–2 (2010), 1–18.

Kostø, Pål. 'Bleiburg: The Creation of a National Martyrology,' *Europe-Asia Studies*, Vol. 62, No. 7 (September 2010), 1153–74.

Kovač, Svetko, Bojan Dimitrijević and Irena Popović Grigorov. *Slučaj Ranković* (Belgrade: Medija Centar Odbrana, 2014).

Kovačević, Sreten. *Hronologija antijugoslovenskog terorizma, 1960–1980* (Belgrade: IŠRO, 1981).

Lopušina, Marko. *Ubice u ime države* (Novi Sad: Prometej, 2012).

Lopušina, Marko. *Ubij bližnjeg svog: Jugoslovenska tajna policija 1945.–2002.* (Belgrade: Marso, 2014).

Lučić, Ivica. 'Hrvatska protukomunistička gerila u Bosni i Hercegovini od 1945. do 1951.,' *Časopis za suvremenu povijest*, Vol. 42, No. 3 (2010), 631–70.

Lukić, Vojin. *Brionski plenum: Obračun sa Aleksandrom Rankovićem* (Belgrade: Stručna knjiga, 1990).

Manolić, Josip. *Politika i domovina: Moja borba za suverenu i socijalnu Hrvatsku* (Zagreb, Golden Marketing, 2015).

Manolić, Josip. *Špijuni i domovina: Moja borba za suverenu i socijalnu Hrvatsku* (Zagreb, Golden Marketing, 2016).

Mertus, Julie A. *Kosovo: How Myths and Truths Started a War* (Berkeley: University of California Press, 1999).

Mihailović, Dragoslav et al. *Zatočenici Golog otoka: Registar lica osuđivanih zbog Informbiroa* (Belgrade: Arhiv Srbije, 2016).

Mijatović, Anđelko. *Bruno Bušić: Prilog istraživanju života i djelovanja* (Zagreb: Školska knjiga, 2010).

Miloradović, Goran and Aleksej Timofejev. *Između dve otadžbine: Jugoslovenski politički emigranti u Sovjetskom Savezu 1948–1956.* (Belgrade: Arhiv Srbije, 2016).

Molnar, Christopher A. 'Imagining Yugoslavs: Migration and the Cold War in Postwar West Germany,' *Central European History*, Vol. 47 (2014), 138–69.

Molnar, Christopher A. *Memory, Politics and Yugoslav Migrations to Postwar Germany* (Bloomington: Indiana University Press, 2018).

Nejašmić, Ivica. 'Iseljavanje iz Hrvatske. Brojčani aspekt stoljetnog procesa,' in Ivan Crkvenčić, ed., *Političko-geografska i demografska pitanja Hrvatske* (Zagreb: Savez geografskih društava Hrvatske, 1991), 61–82.

Nielsen, Christian Axboe. Review of Josip Manolić, *Politika i domovina: Moja borba za suverenu i socijalnu Hrvatsku, Southeastern Europe*, Vol. 41, No. 2 (2017), 231–3.

Nielsen, Christian Axboe. 'Collective and Competitive Victimhood in the Former Yugoslavia,' in Nanci Adler, ed., *Understanding the Age of Transitional Justice: Crimes, Courts, Commissions, and Chronicling* (New Brunswick: Rutgers University Press, 2018), 175–93.

Nielsen, Christian Axboe. 'Leadership Analysis in International Criminal Justice,' in Adejoké Babington-Ashaye, Aimée Comrie and Akingbolahan Adeniran, eds., *International Criminal Investigations: Law and Practice* (The Hague: Eleven International Publishing, 2018), 207–30.

Nielsen, Christian Axboe. 'Never-ending Vigilance: The Yugoslav State Security Service and Cominform Supporters after Goli Otok,' in Tvrtko Jakovina and Martin Previšić, eds., *The Tito-Stalin Split 70 Years After* (Zagreb and Ljubljana: Sveučilište u Zagreb, Univerza v Ljubljani, 2019), 109–20.

Nikolić, Kosta. *Mač revolucije, Ozna u Jugoslaviji* (Belgrade: Službeni glasnik, 2013).

Nobilo, Anto. *Obrana hrvatskog kontraobavještajca Josipa Perkovića na njemačkom sudu* (Zagreb: VBZ, 2018).

Omerza, Igor. *88 Stopnic do pekla* (Klagenfurt: Mohorjeva družba, 2013).

Omerza, Igor. *HRB, Fenix i Udba: Slučaj Stjepana Crnogorca* (Radenci: Društvo za raziskovanje polpretekle zgovodine, 2014).

Petrović, Goran. *Vesela Udba*, 2nd Edition (Valjevo: Topalović, 2016).

Previšić, Martin. *Povijest Golog otoka* (Zagreb: Fraktura, 2019).

Radelić, Zdenko. *Križari gerila u Hrvatskoj, 1945–1950* (Zagreb: Dom i Svijet, 2002).

Radelić, Zdenko. 'Ozna/Udba: Popisi neprijatelja i njihova kategorizacija (1940-ih i 1950-ih),' *Časopis za suvremenu povijest*, Vol. 49 (2017), 59–99.

Radelić, Zdenko. *Obavještajni centri, Ozna i Udba u Hrvatskoj (1942–1954.); Obavještajni centri, Ozna i Udba u Hrvatskoj: Kadrovi (1942–1954.)* (Zagreb: Hrvatski institut za povijest, 2019).

Ramet, Sabrina. 'The NDH–An Introduction,' *Totalitarian Movements and Political Religions*, Vol. 7, No. 4 (December 2006), 399–408.

Robionek Bernd. 'Gutachten zur Strafsache Prates,' Oberlandesgericht München, 20 March 2008.

Robionek Bernd. 'Geschichtswissenschaftliches Gutachten im Verfahren 7 St 5/14 (2) vor dem Oberlandesgericht München,' 2015.

Rullmann, Hans-Peter. *Mordauftrag aus Belgrad: Dokumentation über die Belgrader Mordmaschine* (Hamburg: Ost-Dienst, 1981).

Schweissguth, Edmund. 'Die Reorganisation des Staatssicherheitsdienstes in der SFR Jugoslawien,' *Jahrbuch für Ostrecht*, Vol. 10, No. 1 (1969), 45–68.

Spasić, Božidar. *Lasica koja govori: Osnovne pretpostavke borbe protiv terorizma*, 3rd Edition (Belgrade: Knjiga komerc, 2000).

Špegelj, Martin. *Sjećanja vojnika* (Zagreb: Znanje, 2001).

Tokić, Mate Nikola. 'Landscapes of Conflict: Unity and Disunity in Post-Second World War Croatian Émigré Separatism,' *European Review of History*, Vol. 16, No. 5 (2009), 739–53.

Tokić, Mate Nikola. 'Party Politics, National Security, and Émigré Political Violence in Australia, 1949–1973,' in Wilhelm Heitmeyer et al., eds., *Control of Violence: Historical and International Perspectives on Violence in Modern Societies* (New York: Springer, 2011), 395–414.

Tokić, Mate Nikola. *For the Homeland Ready! Croat Diaspora Terrorism during the Cold War* (West Lafayette: Purdue University Press, 2020).

Tomasevich, Jozo. *War and Revolution in Yugoslavia, 1941–1945: The Chetniks* (Stanford: Stanford University Press, 1975).

Verdery, Katherine. *Secrets and Truths: Ethnography in the Archive of Romania's Secret Police* (Budapest: Central European University Press, 2013).

Vojna bezbednost (Belgrade: Vojnoizdavački i novinski centar, 1986).

Vojnaobaveštajna služba (Belgrade: Vojnoizdavački i novinski centar, 1990).

Vojnović, Barbara. *Zapisnici politbiroa Centralnog komiteta Komunističke partije Hrvatske, 1945–1952.* (Zagreb: Hrvatski državni arhiv, 2005).

Vojtěchovský, Ondřej. *Iz Praga protiv Tita! Jugoslavenska informbiroovska emigracija u Čehoslovačkoj* (Zagreb: Srednja Europa, 2016).

Vukas, Branko. *Stjepan Đureković: Što ga je ubilo* (Zagreb: Naklada Pavičić, 2014).

Vukojević, Vice. *Vice Vukojević – Dosje 240271* (Zagreb: Hrvatski križni put, 2015).

Vukušić, Bože. *Tajni rat UDBE protiv hrvatskoga iseljeništva*, 3rd Expanded Edition (Zagreb: Klub hrvatskih povratnika iz iseljeništva, 2002).

Vukušić, Bože. *HRB – Hrvatsko revolucionarno bratstvo: Rat prije rata*, 2nd Edition (Zagreb: Klub hrvatskih povratnika iz iseljeništva, 2012).

Woodward, Susan. *Socialist Unemployment: The Political Economy of Yugoslavia, 1945–1990* (Princeton: Princeton University Press, 1969).

Yeomans, Rory. *Visions of Annihilation: The Ustaša Regime and the Cultural Politics of Fascism, 1941–1945* (Pittsburgh: University of Pittsburgh Press, 2013).

Zarakol, Ayşe, 'States and Ontological Security: A Historical Rethinking,' *Cooperation and Conflict*, Vol. 52, No. 1 (2017), 48–68.

Žerjavić, Vladimir. 'Kretanja stanovništva i demografski gubici Republike Hrvatske u razdoblju od 1900. do 1991.,' *ČSP*, Vol. 2–3, 1993, 65–85.

Žižić, Jakov, 'Što je hrvatska politička emigracija?,' *Političke analize* (December 2013), 61–4.

Zimmerman, William. *Open Borders, Nonalignment, and the Political Evolution of Yugoslavia* (Princeton: Princeton University Press, 1987).

Index

Note: Locators with letter 'n' refer to notes.

www.ingramcontent.com/pod-product-compliance
Lightning Source LLC
Chambersburg PA
CBHW071416290326
41932CB00046B/1887